A Shadow on Fallen Blossoms

Available from *tgl books*

Translated from the Chinese by Andrea Mary Falk
Jiang Rongjiao's Baguazhang
Li Tianji's The Skill of Xingyiquan
Yan Dehua's Bagua Applications
Di Guoyong on Xingyiquan: Volume I, Foundations
Di Guoyong on Xingyiquan: Volume II, Forms and Ideas
Di Guoyong on Xingyiquan: Volume III, Weapons
Zhang Wenguang's Chaquan

Researched and written by Andrea Mary Falk
A Shadow on Fallen Blossoms: The 36 and 48 Traditional Verses of Baguazhang
Falk's Dictionary of Chinese Martial Arts
Beijing Bittersweet
Shadowboxing in Shanghai

 www.thewushucentre.ca

A Shadow on Fallen Blossoms

The 36 and 48 Traditional Verses of Baguazhang

Compiled and translated, with commentary, by Andrea Mary Falk.
Copyright © Andrea Mary Falk, 2017.

Cover art © Marco Gagnon, 2017.

All rights reserved. This book or any portion thereof may not be reproduced or used in any manner whatsoever without the express written permission of the publisher except for the use of brief quotations in a book review or scholarly work.

First Printing: 2017.

Published by tgl books, Québec, Canada.

Library and Archives Canada Cataloguing in Publication

Falk, Andrea, 1954-, author, translator. A shadow on fallen blossoms : the 36 and 48 traditional verses of baguazhang / Andrea Mary Falk. Includes bibliographical references. Includes some text in Chinese.

ISBN 978-0-9879028-2-5 (softcover).--ISBN 978-0-9879028-3-2 (PDF)

1. Kung fu--China. 2. Hand-to-hand fighting, Oriental--China.
I. Title. II. Title: Baguazhang. III. Title: Ba gua zhang. IV. Title: 36 and 48 traditional verses of baguazhang. V. Title: Thirty-six and forty-eight traditional verses of baguazhang.

GV1114.7.F35 2017   796.815'9   C2016-906276-7   C2016-906277-5

ISBN soft cover print edition: 978-0-9879028-2-5
ISBN PDF edition: 978-0-9879028-3-2
ISBN EPUB edition: 978-0-9879028-4-9

The techniques described in this book are intended for experienced martial artists. The author, translator, and publishers are not responsible for any injury that may occur while trying out these techniques. Please do not apply theses techniques on anyone without their consent and cooperation.

tgl books is based in Canada. Its publications are available through www.thewushucentre.ca.

For my parents William Andre and Mary Elliott.

With me. Always.

"Tradition is not the worship of ashes,
but the preservation of fire."

Gustav Mahler

Dedicated to the memory of my Sifu,
Huan Dahai, 1924-2015.

Contents

Acknowledgments	xiii
Preface	xv
Introduction and Background	xix
Timeline	xxiv

PART ONE: THE THIRTY-SIX VERSES OF BAGUAZHANG
Full text in traditional Chinese characters 1
Full translation in English 4
Commentary and discussion
One: Foundational Structure 11
Two: Dragon Stretches its Talons 16
Three: Circle-walking 19
Four: Both Sides 22
Five: Connections in Spearing Strike 25
Six: Model for Spearing Strike 27
Seven: Internal Structure 29
Eight: Circle Walking Basins 31
Nine: Breathing 35
Ten: Palm Shape and Use 37
Eleven: *Koubu* and *Baibu* Stepping 40
Twelve: Special Footwork 43
Thirteen: Special Deep Power 45
Fourteen: Special Connections 47
Fifteen: Special Tactics 49
Sixteen: Triple Spearing Palm Strikes 51
Seventeen: Triangulation 54
Eighteen: Waist Power 56
Nineteen: Hard and Pliant 58
Twenty: Hardness and Pliancy in the Waist and Footwork 60
Twenty-one: Trade the Body for a Shadow 62
Twenty-two: Spirit Shown in the Neck 64

Twenty-three: Gaining Distance 67
Twenty-four: Tendons and Sinews 68
Twenty-five: Three Trues and Four Arrives 71
Twenty-six: Balance of Hardness and Pliancy..73
Twenty-seven: Hard and Pliant *Qian Kun* Hands...75
Twenty-eight: Hard and Pliant Waist and Footwork 77
Twenty-nine: Coordination of Stepping 79
Thirty: Short Steps 81
Thirty-one: *Heng* and *Ha* Sounds 82
Thirty-two: Disarming 85
Thirty-three: One Finger to Beat Ten Hundredweight..87
Thirty-four: Fighting in Darkness 89
Thirty-five: Slippery Ground 90
Thirty-six: Spirit 92
In Praise of the Thirty-six Verses 94

PART TWO: THE FORTY-EIGHT METHODS VERSES OF BAGUAZHANG
Full text in traditional Chinese characters 99
Full translation in English 104
Commentary and discussion
One: Method of Using the Body 113
Two: Method of Observing 114
Three: Method of Stepping 116
Four: Method of Walking 118
Five: Method of Continuous Steps 120
Six: Method of the Gathering Stance 123
Seven: Method of Using the Hands 125
Eight: Method of Using Power 128
Nine: Method of Reserving Power 130
Ten: Method of Continuing Power 132
Eleven: How to Subdue Opponents 133
Twelve: How to Ensure Victory 135
Thirteen: How to Apply Tactics 137
Fourteen: How to Seal Off 139
Fifteen: How to Meet an Attack 141
Sixteen: How to Release Grabs 143

Seventeen: How to Take a Single to Remedy a Double 145
Eighteen: The Tactic of Pointing at the Mountain to
    Make the Millstone 147
Nineteen: How to Trade your Body for a Shadow 149
Twenty: The Tactic of Turning and Getting Behind the Back
    151
Twenty-one: Tactics Against Hard Attacks 153
Twenty-two: How to Use Half-Circle Hands 156
Twenty-three: How to use Full-Circle Hands 158
Twenty-four: Method of using the Heart and Eyes 160
Twenty-five: The Tactic of Fixing the Regard 162
Twenty-six: How to Disarm 164
Twenty-seven: How to Protect the Body 166
Twenty-eight: How to Confuse your Adversary 167
Twenty-nine: Method of Opening and Closing 169
Thirty: The Tactic of Setting in the South 171
Thirty-one: The Tactic of Getting in Close 173
Thirty-two: Method of the Six Directions 175
Thirty-three: The Tactic of One and Only 177
Thirty-four: How to Prevent Slipping 178
Thirty-five: Method for Stable Footwork 180
Thirty-six: Method of Small Steps 182
Thirty-seven: Methods for the Palms 184
Thirty-eight: Avoid Slouching 187
Thirty-nine: Avoid Arching Back 189
Forty: Method of an Upright Body 191
Forty-one: Method of Supplementing the Body 193
Forty-two: Method of Twisting the Body 195
Forty-three: Tactic of Sidestepping and Turning Sideways
    197
Forty-four: Method of Shaking Off Side to Side 199
Forty-five: The Tactic of Hunkering Down 201
Forty-six: Avoid Grabbing 202
Forty-seven: Avoid Standing Still 207
Forty-eight: The Supreme Method 211
In Praise of the Forty-eight Methods Verses 212

NOTES 217
REFERENCES 225
ILLUSTRATIONS 229
GLOSSARY
  Chinese terms within the English text 231
  Chinese for the Stratagems and Tactics within the text
  233
PRONUNCIATION GUIDE FOR CHINESE IN PINYIN 235
ABOUT THE AUTHOR 237

ACKNOWLEDGMENTS

I have practiced kungfu since I was a teenager, and have learned baguazhang in Shanghai and Beijing off and on since 1980. I am now sixty years old, which is the age in the Chinese martial arts that you are expected to take more responsibility for passing on your style. Since the verses apply to all branches of baguazhang, and there are few translations, I thought I might be well placed to translate them. Although my skill and understanding is ordinary, I am lucky to have learned from masters of five main lineages – Cheng, Fan, Liang, Yin (Ma Gui), and Zhang (Jiang). I learn Cheng baguazhang with Xia Bohua and Lu Yan, Jiang baguazhang with Cai Yuhua, Huan Dahai, and Cheng Jiefeng (and briefly with Su Zifang, Zhao Yun, and Zou Shuxian), Ma Gui baguazhang with Li Baohua, Liang baguazhang with Di Guoyong, and lately Fan baguazhang with Philip Morrell.[1] They have taught or are teaching me this 'magical skill'.

Although this is a written translation, the learning is passed on from one person to another. This feeling is nicely encapsulated in this four-generational photo taken over brunch, of Jiang Rongqiao's adoptive daughter, great-grand-daughter, and I (lineage grand-daughter), enjoying my translation of Jiang Rongqiao's book.

I publish this book with love and gratitude for the people of baguazhang. I started out by wondering what were the linking factors between the branches and I found out – they are the people of baguazhang. From the teachers who answered my questions, to my friends who found mistakes and suggested improvements, to my students who insisted each verse made sense, to the people worldwide who contributed to the crowd funding – we all do our bit to continue the tradition.

I would like to thank my brilliant baguazhang teachers and friends. I have been lucky that my teachers unreservedly shared their knowledge and maintained high standards, and fully expected me to get it. I have also been very lucky that I have met and learned from fellow women. My continued lack of understanding and ability is entirely my fault.

I would like to thank Neil Bates, Michael Blackburn, and James Saper for their proof reading and suggestions. They took over the repetitive, finicky work that my parents did with great pride, and if I may say so, were more strict in questioning formatting and demanding explanations. A thanks to Marco Gagnon for the cover art. I particularly thank Jiang Xiaoying and Hans Järling for treating me as part of the family. Also Di Guoyong for taking the time to discuss the verses as I brought the book near completion. And thanks to Jarek Szymanski for suggesting the Shanghai library as a better use of my time in the afternoon, and helping with translation of some tricky older texts. The extra materials gave me the idea of using older texts to augment my commentary. The excellence of baguazhang is partly because of the founder's ability to incorporate the best in martial arts, so I felt that reference to older texts was relevant. I hope you enjoy the randomness of the old references and illustrations – and the evocative rather than instructional nature of the illustrations. And a thanks to the team at Plum Publications for making available a supply of Chinese books in the unilingual wilds of Québec. I also thank my brother Graham for his brilliant drawing of his take on the world of baguazhang. And a thank you to my husband Gilbert for continued support of my writing and teaching career and the occasional brainstorming session.

Without all these people the book would have been nowhere near what it has become. All remaining mistakes and misunderstandings and are my own.

Andrea Mary Falk

Morin-Heights, Québec, Canada,

June, 2017.

Preface

I have translated a number of books on baguazhang and xingyiquan, but this is my first book that includes my own extensive writing. I started out simply wanting to understand these verses for myself in more depth, and then realized that I should translate and comment on them for others. Further into the work, I spent a fair bit of time searching out old books on the martial arts and baguazhang. I realized that including more social and historical background would make the verses more interesting and relevant to the Western reader. Once I got going, I found that using the old books helped to place the verses in their context. I do not intend to deliberately re-interpret, over explain, or modernize the verses. Nor do I wish to slavishly reiterate what has been said before, either in Chinese commentary or English translation. Each of us comes from a different background and sees things from a different angle, just as baguazhang itself has developed through the personalities of the first generation disciples and on. My goal has been to 'preserve the fire' within the verses, and to take this into my training and teaching.

I first saw baguazhang at a competition in China in 1981, when a young girl flew magically around the carpet with an enormous sabre as long as she was tall. I turned to my teacher Xia Bohua, sitting beside me, "What is that?" Not noticing the 'mind-blown' nature of my question, he said "That's baguazhang, I know some. I can teach you, no problem." Thirty-five years later, one winter's day I got to wondering "what is really going on in baguazhang" and set out to re-read my pretty extensive library of baguazhang books in Chinese, looking for commonalities and differences in the branches. The verses were there in many of them, tucked in almost as filler pages. I had to buy some more books, some even in English (where I discovered that there is some good material in English now), and managed to get seventeen books that contained the verses. On examination, I found that the verses themselves differed in small ways, and the idea for this book was born. I found twelve non-identical versions of the thirty-six verses and nine of the forty-eight methods verses, within six major schools of Dong Haichuan's top disciples,[2] and finally determined on nine to use as sources. The degree of 'agreement but disagreement' in the sources indicates both that they come from a common root and that they have been transmitted separately, not copied from each other. The verses are now in published books, which opens up possibility of copy error and print error, so I took this into account when comparing them. When a version was exactly the same as another I assumed it had been copied directly and did not use it. As it is, for the sources that I used, each has its own version that they have handed down. It is amazing, considering all the oral instructions and hand copied texts, how close the versions are to each other. My favourite saying about copying is, "Copied three times, 鸟 and 焉 become 马."³

The verses are the main cross-lineage instructions on how to practice baguazhang. They have been told, written, chanted, and passed on because they are valuable to those of us who practise baguazhang. The work of copying them out and memorizing them is part of the training, part of the transmission. It was fun to compare my own hand written copy of my sifu Huan Dahai's hand written copy with the published texts. In a perfect world, the student copies out the verses, discusses them with her sifu, and asks about possible copy error. In my case, I was handed a huge notebook of an entire unpublished book by Jiang Rongqiao and other notes in my sifu's barely legible handwriting, and I had to copy it all out (by hand in those days) and get it back to him quickly before he regretted letting it out of his sight. The verses were in there, but passed almost unnoticed until years later.

The book is organized thusly: first, the entire original text in traditional characters, then my entire translation. The text mostly follows the majority of sources, but in some cases I have chosen what I feel is the best character in the variations. Following, the line-by-line original text for each verse (in modern characters) and my translation of the verse. Then my commentary on the meaning and background in indented paragraphs. This commentary may draw on other sources, in which case the translation is in full quotation marks, and the original Chinese is end noted. When leaving a term in Chinese within English text (words commonly used in English, such as *yin* and *yang*, and words best left alone such as *koubu* stepping), I have italicized it without tones. And finally the discussion of the texts, meanings of specific characters, and my choices as a translator. I present Chinese words by first the Chinese character, followed by the pinyin romanization with tones, then the translation in single quotation marks. I have underlined differences in the texts in the discussion. Comparing the different versions of the verses is not in any way intended to be an armchair discussion of fine distinctions between words. Often I say two words are 'the same thing' when there is actually a subtle difference between them. For readers who do not understand Chinese, you might still want to read the comparison discussion, as there are some interesting things aside from 'who wrote what'.

In explaining the verses, I used five distinct groups of references. One, the verses themselves, and so the commentaries in the books that include them. Two, my teachers' knowledge that is in my head and notes. Three, my forty-five years of martial arts experience, thirty-five in baguazhang. Four, Qing dynasty and earlier martial arts classics. Five, Republican era books about baguazhang. The books that include the verses are all modern books that were published after 1983, when the verses were first published (though I do have one hand-written copy dated 1980). I also read commentaries in modern books that did not have the full verses. I relied largely on body knowledge and what my teachers have taught me over the years, and I feel this is how the verses are meant to be understood. The other references are more to help place the verses in context for the readers. The classic books that I used the most – Chang Naizhou and the generals Qi Jiguang and Wang Minghe – are well known, especially to martial artists, because of their direct and practical writing. The brilliance of baguazhang is partly because it draws from the best of many sources, so classic military knowledge certainly had an influence. Those books were part of the martial social milieu, whether or not they were read. The Republican era books do not contain the verses. Most of those writers are of the next generation but living at the same time as the writer of the verses, so their vocabulary, and what they chose to write about, adds a facet to the interpretation of the verses. I in no way want to write the definitive book about baguazhang, I just want to present the verses as clearly as possible in their context.

After working on the book full time from January through September 2016, I went to China to consult with my teachers for a final polishing of the translation. I suffered from an overabundance of enthusiasm to help. Jarek Szymanski suggested that I should get a Shanghai library card, with the final result of changing my whole approach, calling for a massive rewrite. Di Guoyong's seventy-seven page analysis of the verses gave me yet another excellent commentary to examine. He popped that onto a USB key after we had discussed my questions – such a selfless and trusting sharing of material is a superb example of martial friendship. I do not think my analysis is better than his, far from it, but I feel my approach is better suited to Westerners. Different things need to be explained. I agree with him that the verses have not been given the attention they deserve. It was funny that we had both independently thought that the 36 verses needed names, and we had come up with pretty much the same names. While I was in final proof reading of a hard copy, Philip Morrell handed me a book that gave another version of the verses, leading to yet another rewrite and more delay, but again improving the book immensely.

I apologize that the translation cannot convey one brilliant aspect of Chinese martial arts chanted verses – the use of the seven beat line. Did they know that this is the number or words or numbers that people can remember? The last words of the first, second, and fourth phrases rhyme, while the third does not, which gives the whole verse a bit of a lilt. The seven beat line and the rhyming pattern are perfect for memorization and for chanting. Each line is a perfect length for *qigong* chanting with a full voice, drawing out the words to use up one breath. I cannot manage this perfection in English, so I've put *pinyin* with tones throughout, in case you want to do a *qigong* chant without knowing Chinese.

INTRODUCTION AND BACKGROUND

The thirty-six and forty-eight chanted mnemonic verses are transmitted within most baguazhang schools as the oral instructions of Dong Haichuan. Dong Haichuan and his original disciples did not write much down, and it is thought that these verses, or at least the knowledge in them, were orally transmitted. In the hand copied text that I have from my sifu Huan Dahai, the section on the 36 verses is titled *The 36 verses of Dong Haichuan's Bagua Turning Palms*.

It is generally thought that the person who wrote down the verses was Zeng Zengqi 曾增启 (1862-1951), original name Yuhui 毓慧, private name Shengsan 省三 (sometimes referred to with the surname Jin 金). He is said to have compiled the teachings of Dong Haichuan into the 36 and 48 verses, putting Dong's words into a more organized format to preserve them. Zeng was a Manchurian scholar, a blue banner imperial relative (or in the imperial household, not the same thing[4]). He was more educated than most baguazhang masters of his time, and passed the imperial examinations at the provincial level, before that examination system was abolished along with the dynasty in 1911. As is the story with many, he was sickly as a youth, and started baguazhang training to strengthen himself, gradually becoming a healthy and strong master in his own right, with an excellent understanding of the theories and principles of baguazhang. Zeng was Yin Fu's disciple, received pointers from Dong himself, and was popular with the other masters, who were willing to help him. He is also said to have had a wide knowledge and a good memory, which made him the perfect receptacle to compile the verses.

If we look at Zeng's dates of 1862-1951 we can see who he would have known among the masters of yesteryear – Dong Haichuan (1813-1884) taught in Beijing from 1856 to 1884, and the first generation masters included Liu Dekuan (1826-1911), Shi Jidong (1835-1908), Fan Zhiyong (1840-1922), Yin Fu (1842-1909), Li Cunyi (1847-1921), Cheng Tinghua (1848-1900), Song Changrong (1849-1920), Liu Fengchun (1853-1922), Zhang Zhaokui (1853-1940), Ma Gui (1853-1940), Liang Zhenpu (1863-1932), and others. All of these men could have helped Zeng, and indeed although he was second generation, he was not much younger than some of the youngest of the first generation. He would have also known his own generation of Zhou Xiang (b.1861), Sun Lutang (b.1861), Liu Qingfu (b.1862), Gao Yisheng (b.1866), and his long life put him in contact with the next generation of Yin Yuzhang (b.1880), Sun Xikun (b.1889), Yan Dehua, Jiang Rongqiao (b.1889), and Du Zhaotang (b. 1891) (listing only book authors). Zeng retired to private teaching after the palace work ended in with the collapse of the dynasty in 1911, and this is most likely when he wrote the verses.[5] He was close with Guo Gumin 郭古民 (1887-1968), and he wrote or compiled Dong's words in a book titled Survey of Bagua Turning Palms as a gift to Guo. Zeng did not need to teach for a living, but he did teach Guo Gumin as a younger friend. In an encyclopedic entry for Guo Gumin, it says "[Guo] was very close to Yin Fu's brilliant disciple [Zeng] Yuhui, and received the 36 and 48 verses from him."[6] I could find no information as to when Zeng gave the verses to Guo Gumin (their overlap dates would be about 1910-1951) but it is said that the verses were welcomed in the baguazhang world, and so passed on within practitioners.

This all sounds reasonable, as passing knowledge amongst friends is the norm in the world of baguazhang. Two things strike one when looking at the history of baguazhang in Beijing. One, that everyone learned from everyone – you learned not just from your sifu, but from your martial brothers, uncles, cousins, and friends. There is no pure one to one lineage, no 'family style'. Two, that things were not written down.

The absence of published material is part of the baguazhang tradition. Martial writing was well developed in China. Well before the 1600s, techniques, tactics, and theories were written down and illustrated in an intelligent and clear manner, with specialized vocabulary and a common theoretical base. But the first generation of bagua masters did not write anything that we have discovered. The tradition within the Zhang school is that Dong Haichuan was a member of the Bagua Sect[7], and that most of his disciples in the late 1800s were involved in the movement to overthrow the Qing dynasty and return the Ming, so they kept quiet. Aside from this, most were illiterate, and kept things in their heads.

Compared to many styles, including Shaolinquan, Taijiquan, and Xingyiquan, there was very little published on Baguazhang until post 1980. In an extremely unscientific survey I did of about 200 books from the Qing dynasty through to 1949, only eight were about baguazhang.[8] During the Republican period the central government encouraged publications on martial arts to help strengthen the country. During this time the 'classics' of baguazhang were written: Sun Lutang's *Bagua Sword* and *Bagua Fist* published in 1927 and 1928 respectively, Huang Bonian's *Dragon Baguazhang* in 1928, Yin Yuzhang's *Concise Baguazhang* in 1932, Sun Xikun's *Baguazhang Direct Transmissions* in 1934, Du Zhaotang's *Swimming Body Linking Baguazhang* in 1936, and Yan Dehua's *Shaolin Wall-Breaking Insights* (actually baguazhang) in 1936.[9] Not much was published at all during the ongoing war from 1937 to 1946, and through the civil war finally ending in 1949. In baguazhang, I only found Cao Zhongsheng's *Cao Clan*

Baguazhang Classics in 1942. A number of generalist books published in the 1930s mentioned baguazhang, and showed an overall lack of understanding about baguazhang that indicated it was still very much a mysterious art to most.[10]

I looked at these Republican era books first of all to see if they referred to the verses, and secondly, to look at the vocabulary, if not some reference to some lines of Dong Haichuan. The principles and names of the techniques were much the same, but not one of these published books quoted from the 36 or 48 verses. There are two possibilities here. One, the verses were not yet written or at least not yet passed around. Two, the authors knew of them, but were not giving anything away. Some authors attempted to be 'scientific', and to spread the idea of training the martial arts in a practical way. Huang Bonian's introduction went so far as to say that baguazhang was something that anyone could do, involving only walking, no jumping at all, and you didn't even need to change your long robes for a short and tight sports training outfit.[11] Some authors such as Sun Lutang brought scholarly theories to martial books, while others such as Yin Yuzhang recorded straight forward methods and theories as they had learned them. Du Zhaotang's book contains the organization and verses Gao Yisheng was working on as he developed his school (five introductory verses, 64 eight line verses specific to 64 applications, and seven verses for each of the seven star's techniques). The vocabulary of the books is certainly the techniques of baguazhang, but they do not describe the foundational basics, key methods, and the tactics and stratagem with the brevity and artistry of Zeng's verses.

The verses were not published openly until the early 1980s, in the next flourishing of government support of martial arts – the 'excavate and record' work. Li Ziming (1902-1993) published them in a magazine (1982 or 83, I could not find the exact magazine, even with quite a bit of help), and then again in his book of 1985. Perhaps because of this, or because Guo Gumin (who originally received the verses) was Liang Zhenpu's student, I have heard the verses referred to as 'the Liang lineage verses'. My hand copied version from my sifu in the Zhang lineage, did say 'copied from Pei Xirong, purported to be from Liang Zhenpu, 1980'. But to further muddy the waters, Zeng Zengqi was Yin Fu's student and Yin Yuzhang's senior, Pei Xirong was Yin Yuzhang's student and also studied with Jiang Rongqiao (Zhang Zhaokui's student), and Guo Gumin also learned with Liu Dekuan, Yin Fu, Yin Yuzhang, Liu Fengchun, and 'exchanged techniques' with Li Ziming. The published sources from which I have taken the verses are not exclusively from the Liang lineage, and it seems clear that most lineages passed them around as part of a common baguazhang heritage (though the Shi and Fan lineages do not).

Given these clues, the verses were based on notes written while listening to the oral tradition of Dong and the first generation of disciples through the

1880s – 1910s, by Zeng, a particularly bright and well educated young student. The verses were probably written up between 1910 to 1950, written in his retirement (with the 1911 collapse of the Qing he would no longer work at the palace). If he wrote them for Guo Gumin 郭古民 (1887-1968) this was likely done in the 1920s to 30s. His work was not published, and could have easily remained hidden from the world for quite a while, given the secretive nature of the baguazhang circles, but if they were written earlier you would think there would be at least some oblique reference to it in the books of the 1930s. A date in the 1930s would fit with the lack of reference in books of the 30s, the teaching and writing with Guo, and the long term silence as war and revolution disturbed publication until the early 1980s.

Are the verses legitimate words from Dong Haichuan and the first generation masters? I think so. The verses feel traditional. They are not particularly organized in a methodological way, from basic to advanced, simple to complex, or from structure to techniques to tactics. There are duplications in content between the 36 and 48 verses. The traditional learning is working things out for yourself, not having them presented in too orderly a fashion. There are 'note-takers' and 'not note-takers' (I have piles of notebooks), and Zeng sounds like a 'note-taker'. The verses often refer to fighting against weapons, as if the weapons involved were not firearms, which suggests they are based on early oral instructions. The verses give specific instructions for the structure, feeling, techniques, applications, tactics, use of power, and training methods of baguazhang. They do not contain any non-practical theory. They are specific enough to explain the unique flavour of baguazhang and general enough that most instructions apply to all its branches. The verses do not give away any secrets. They do not describe circle-walking in any detail. They remind you of the posture and movement details, and tell you some methods and tactics that work if you have done your circle-walking and achieved rooted footwork attached through your body. They do not describe specific techniques. They basically say 'do what I've taught you, keep to it, trust it, and it will work'. It is said that if you have done baguazhang for a while you will understand the thirty-six verses, and that you need more time before you will understand the forty-eight verses, because the thirty-six are more about structure and the forty-eight are more about tactics. No one could learn the real secret of baguazhang by reading these verses. They are unique in that they were not written to spread, or even teach, but to remind. They are meant as memory aids to those within the circle.

On the following pages is a timeline of some intersecting lives of baguazhang masters and authors. It is obviously not a complete list, I am just trying to place the baguazhang authors in their context. It is not organized by lineage, because right from the beginning people learned not just from their teacher, but from their martial uncles, brothers, and buddies.

xxiii

You can see that they naturally group into cohorts, or generational groupings.

The first cohort includes those born in the 1830s to 1850s, who lived when they could train directly with Dong Haichuan. They were mostly already skilled martial artists, and added skills to the base of training developed by Dong, working together with him to develop the style. This cohort includes (in alphabetical order) Cheng Dianhua, Cheng Tinghua, Fan Zhiyong, Li Cunyi, Liu Dekuan, Shi Jidong, Song Changrong, Yin Fu, and a younger group of Liu Fengchun, Ma Gui, and Zhang Zhaokui. This cohort grew up in the Qing dynasty and only the younger ones lived to see its end. Some were businessmen, but most were squarely in the *jianghu* world. They did not write.

The second cohort includes those born in the 1860s and 1870s, who lived when they could still have contact with Dong Haichuan, but mostly learned from the first cohort. This cohort includes Cao Zhongsheng, Cheng Youlong, Gao Yisheng, Gong Baotian, Liang Zhenpu, Liu Baozhen, Liu Bin, Liu Qingfu, Men Baozhen, Sun Lutang, Wu Lingshan, Zeng Zengqi, and Zhou Yixiang. They also grew up in the Qing dynasty, but lived to see the changes of the Republic and the war. They may have been influenced in their early years by the scholar-martial artist movement in the late Qing, and in their later years by the modern emphasis on health, and are more likely than the first cohort to have taken notes and thought about theories.

The third cohort includes those born in the 1880s to 1900s, who learned only from the previous cohorts, not Dong Haichuan. This cohort includes Di Zhaolong, Du Zhaotang, Fu Changrong, Guo Gumin, Huang Bonian, Jiang Rongqiao, Li Shao'an, Li Ziming, Liu Wanchuan, Sun Xikun, Yan Dehua, and Yin Yuzhang. They were born during the Qing dynasty, but most of their adult life was in modern China. This cohort includes the authors of many of the books published in the Republican period. Their attitude tend towards the balanced training for health and martial skill to strengthen the body and mind.

The fourth cohort includes those born in the 1910s to 1930s, and include Huan Dahai, Liu Xinghan, Pei Xirong, Sun Zhijun, Xie Peiqi, Yu Zhiming, Zang Xuefan, and Zou Shuxian. This cohort survived through war, revolution, and political movements as they struggled to preserve baguazhang.

Later generations of baguazhang practitioners have these men and women to thank for developing, preserving, and spreading baguazhang. Please forgive me if I left out an eminent person of your lineage, this is by no means a complete list.

1815	1820	1825	1830	1835	1840	1845	1850	1855	1860	1865	1870	1875	1880	1885	1890	1895	1900	1905	1910

Dong Haichuan 1813?-1884 teaching in Beijing

Gao Yunshen 1820-1901

Liu Dekuan 1826-1911

Shi Jidong 1835-1909

Fan Zhiyong 1840-1922

Yin Fu 1842-1909

Cheng Tinghua 1845-1900

Zhou Yuxiang 1845-1935

Liu Cunyi 1847-1921

Cheng Dianhua 1848-1935

Song Changrong 1849-1920

Liu Fengchun 1853-1922

Zhang Zhaokui 1853-1940

Ma Gui 1854-1941

Sun Lutang 1861-1932

Liu Qingfu 1862-1952

Zeng Zengqi 1862-1951

Liang Zhenpu 1863-1932

Gao Yisheng 1866-1951

Wu Lingshan 1868-1945

Men Baozhen 1870-1957

Cao Zhongsheng 1874-1949

Yin Yuzhang 1880-1950

Guo Gumin 1887-1968

Sun Xikun 1889-1952

Yan Dehua dates?

Du Zhaotang 1891-

Jiang Rongqiao 1891-

Li Ziming

Qing dynasty   dynasty ended 1911

Opium War 1839-1842. Treaty of Nanjing 1842.   Treaty of Tianjin 1858   Sino-Japanese war 1895

Tongzhi Restoration 1870s, Hundred Days Reform 1889

Nian Rebellion 1851-1868. Taiping Uprising 1851-1864   Boxer Rebellion 1900

DHC teaching 1856-1884

	1915	1920	1925	1930	1935	1940	1945	1950	1955	1960	1965	1970	1975	1980	1985	1990	1995	2000	2005	2010

(Fan Zhiyong)

Zhou Yuxiang
(Liu Cunyi)
Cheng Dianhua
(Song Changrong)
(Liu Fengchun)
Zhang Zhaokui
Ma Gui
books 26,28   (Sun Lutang)
Liu Qingfu
ZengZengqi verses written when?
notes?   (Liang Zhenpu)
Gao Yisheng
Wu Lingshan
Men Baozhen
Cao Zhongshan book 1940
Yin Yuzhang book 1932
Guo Gumin verses received when?
Sun Xikun book 1934
Yan Dehua book 1936
Du -1983 book 1936
Jiang -1974 books 1930   book 1963
Li Ziming 1902-1993   verses pub 1983, book 1985
Liu Xinghan 1909-2000 books   1986, 2010
Pei Xirong 1913-1999   notes 1980?
    Huan Dahai 1924-2015   notes 1980
        Zang Xuefan 1933- ?   book 2000
        Di Guoyong b. 1948   notes 2012

Warlord Period 1916-1928. Civil War 1926-1928.	Peoples Republic of China founded 1949		
Twenty-One Demands 1915	Invasion of Manchuria 1931. Sino-Japanese War 1937-1946	Hundred Flowers 1957. Great Leap Forward 1958-1963 Great Cultural Revolution 1966-1976		
May 4th Movement 1919			Tiananmen Incident, Democracy Wall 1976-1979	Tiananmen 1989 Massacre
Jing Wu Athletic Ass. founded 1907	Guoshuguan centralised martial academy 1928-1937			"dig out and record' traditional martial arts 1983 on

Part One

The Thirty-Six Verses of Baguazhang

Part One

The Thirty-Six Verses of Baguazhang

This is the version of the text that I have used in my translation. I compiled it by examining the differences and similarities between nine main sources.[12] In the discussion I will point out these differences and similarities and, among other things, explain why I chose this version as the standard to translate. For the text in modern characters see the discussions sections.

八卦掌三十六歌訣

一。　空胸拔頂下塌腰，扭步掰膝抓地牢。
　　　沈肩墜肘伸前掌，二目須從虎口瞧。
二。　後肘先疊肘掩心，手再翻塌向前跟。
　　　跟到前肘合抱力，前後兩手一團神。
三。　步彎腳直向前伸，行如推磨一般真。
　　　屈膝隨胯腰扭足，眼到三面不搖身。
四。　一勢單鞭不為奇，左右循環乃為宜。
　　　左換右兮右換左，抽身倒步自合機。
五。　步既轉兮手亦隨，後掌穿出前掌回。
　　　去來來去無二致，要如弩箭離弦飛。
六。　穿時直掌貼肘行，後肩改作前肩承。
　　　莫要距離莫猶疑，腳入襠兮是準繩。
七。　胸欲空兮氣欲沈，背緊肩垂意前伸。
　　　氣到丹田縮穀道，直拔顛頂貫精神。
八。　走時週身莫動搖，全憑膝下兩相交。
　　　低盤隨講平膝胯，中盤也要下腿腰。

1

九。　　　　抿唇閉口舌舔腭，呼吸全憑鼻孔過。
　　　　　　力用機處哼哈泄，混元一氣此為得。
十。　　　　掌形虎口要撐圓，中指無名縫開展。
　　　　　　先戳後打施腕骨，鬆膀長腰跟步鑽。
十一。　　　上步合膝倒步掰，換掌換步矮身骸。
　　　　　　進退退進隨機勢，祇須腰腿巧安排。
十二。　　　此掌與人大不同，進步抬前乃有功。
　　　　　　退步還先退後足，跨步盡外要離中。
十三。　　　此掌與人大不同，手未動兮膀先攻。
　　　　　　未從前伸先後縮，吸足再吐力獨豐。
十四。　　　此掌與人大不同，前掌後掌力相通。
　　　　　　欲使梢兮先動根，招招如是不得鬆。
十五。　　　此掌與人大不同，未擊西兮先聲東。
　　　　　　指上打下孰得知，捲珠倒流更神通。
十六。　　　天然精術怕三穿，不走外門是枉然。
　　　　　　他走外兮我走內，伸手而得不費難。
十七。　　　掌使一面不為功，至少仍須兩面通。
　　　　　　一橫一直三角手，使人如在我懷中。
十八。　　　高欲低兮矮欲揚，斜身繞步不須忙。
　　　　　　斜翻倒翻腰著力，翻到極處力要剛。
十九。　　　人道掌法勝在剛，郭老曾言柔內藏。
　　　　　　個中也有人知味，剛柔相濟是所長。
二十。　　　剛在先兮柔內藏，柔在先兮剛後張。
　　　　　　他人之柔腰與手，我則腰吸步穩揚。
二十一。　　用到極處須轉身，脫身化影不留痕。
　　　　　　如何變幻端在步，出入進退腰先伸。
二十二。　　轉身之神頸骨轉，轉項扭項手當先。
　　　　　　變時縮頸發時伸，要如神龍首尾連。
二十三。　　打人憑手膀為根，膀在肩端不會伸。
　　　　　　故欲進時進前步，若進後步枉勞神。
二十四。　　力足發自筋與骨，骨中出硬筋須隨。
　　　　　　足跟大筋通腦脊，發招跟步力能催。

二十五。	眼到手到腰腿到，心真伸真力又真。
	三真四到合一處，防己有餘能制人。
二十六。	力要剛兮更要柔，剛柔偏重功難收。
	過剛必折真物理，優柔太盛等於休。
二十七。	剛柔相濟是何言，剛柔相輔總無難。
	剛柔當用乾坤手，掀天揭地海波瀾。
二十八。	人剛我柔是正方，我剛人柔法亦良。
	剛柔相遇腰求勝，解此糾紛步法強。
二十九。	步法動時腰先提，收縮合宜顯神奇。
	足欲動兮腰不動，踉蹌邁去誤時機。
三十。	轉身變法步莫長，擦地而行莫要慌。
	看準來路方伸手，巧女穿針穩柔剛。
三十一。	人持利器我不忙，飛劍遙遙到身旁。
	看他來路哼哈避，邪不勝正语頗良。
三十二。	短兵相接似難防，哪怕鋒利似魚腸。
	伸手取來探囊物，指山打磨妙中藏。
三十三。	人眾我貧力難當，巧破千鈞莫要忙。
	一手不勞憑指力，犁牛猶怕反弓張。
三十四。	伸手不見掌前伸，又無油鬆照彼身。
	收縮眼皮努睛看，底盤掌使顯神奇。
三十五。	冰天雪地雨濘滑，前腳橫使且莫差。
	翻身切忌螺絲轉，高低緊避乃為佳。
三十六。	用時最要是精神，精神煥發耳目真。
	任憑他人飛燕手，蟻鳴我聽龍虎吟。
歌贊	掌法拳法與岳議，傳出日久或忘記。
	我歌我歌三十六，子子句句有真意。

Translation of the Thirty-Six Verses of Baguazhang
(The Original Verses Do Not Have Titles)

One: Foundational Structure

Leave the chest empty, pull up the crown of the head, settle down the waist,
Twist within the stance, brace the knees, and grasp the ground firmly.
Settle the shoulders, weigh down the elbows, extend the forward palm,
The eyes must look out through the tiger's mouth.

Two: Dragon Stretches its Talons

The rear elbow first folds in so the elbow covers the heart,
Then the hand rolls over to settle and press its heel forward.
It presses towards the forward elbow with a closing, wrapping power,
The front and rear hands are united in spirit.

Three: Circle-walking

The stance is flexed and each foot extends straight as it reaches forward,
Walk just like you were pushing a millstone.
The knees bend, the hips go along, and the waist twists fully,
The eyes see in three directions with no wavering of the body.

Four: Both Sides

It is not remarkable to strike a pose like Single Whip,
It is better to move freely side to side.
Changing from left to right and from right to left,
Withdraw and switch your stance to take what opportunity presents.

Five: Connections in Spearing Strike

As the footwork turns the hands follow,
As the rear hand spears out the lead hand returns.
(The hands) go and come, come and go, there is no difference (between them),
They should fly like bolts from a crossbow.

Six: Model for Spearing Strike

When doing a spearing strike, straighten the palm and slide alongside the elbow,
The rear shoulder takes on the role of the leading shoulder.
Don't leave any gaps and don't hesitate,
Gauge your strike to enter your foot between your opponent's legs.

Seven: Internal Structure

The more the chest is emptied the more the *qi* will sink down,
Tauten the upper back, drop the shoulders, and extend awareness forward.
Settle the *qi* in the *dantian* and draw in the 'grain path',
Draw the crown of the head straight upwards, and the vitality will pass throughout.

Eight: Circle Walking Basins

When walking, there must be no extraneous movement anywhere in the body,
All depends on the crisscrossing of the lower legs, from the knees down.
Although we talk of the low basin (walking), where the knee and hips are level with each other,
The middle basin (walking) should also lower the legs and back.

Nine: Breathing

Purse the lips lightly, close the mouth, lick the roof of the mouth with the tongue,
Breathe in and out entirely through the nostrils.
When using force to the fullest, give vent with a *heng* or *ha* sound,
This is how to obtain full original *qi*.

Ten: Palm Shape and Use

For the palm shape, brace the tiger's mouth so it is rounded,
Spread the space between the middle and ring fingers.
First poke then hit using the wrist bone,
Release the shoulder girdle and lengthen the waist, use a follow-up step to drill in.

Eleven: *Koubu* and *Baibu* Stepping

Gather the knees when stepping forward, brace them when reversing,
Lower the entire body to change palms and change stance.
To advance and retreat, retreat and advance, and take what opportunity presents,
You just need to skillfully arrange your waist and legs.

Twelve: Special Footwork

This palm differs greatly from the others,
Our advancing step picks up the front foot, and so gets results.
Our retreating step first retreats the rear foot,
Our sidestep gets to the (opponent's) outside, away from the centre.

Thirteen: Special Deep Power

This palm differs greatly from the others,
The shoulder girdle takes the offensive before the hand has moved.
Before extending forward, first gather back,
When you breathe in fully then 'spit' it out you have our unique and plentiful power.

Fourteen: Special Connections

This palm differs greatly from the others,
The power connects between the front and rear palms.
To use the tip, first move its root,
All techniques must be thus – do not neglect any.

Fifteen: Special Tactics

This palm differs greatly from the others,
Before hitting to the West we first make noise in the East.
Pointing high and hitting low – who can figure us out,
Rolling up (a hanging curtain of) pearls and flowing in reverse is even more remarkable.

Sixteen: Triple Spearing Palm Strikes

Even skilled martial artists fear the triple spearing palms,
It is more effective if I move to his outside doorway.
But if he moves to my outside I move to his inside,
Extending my hand I easily get what I want.

The Thirty-Six Verses

Seventeen: Triangulation

Being only able to use one side of the hand is incompetent,
You need to be thoroughly proficient on at least two sides.
With one across and one straight, the hands triangulate,
It is as if I embrace my adversary to my breast.

Eighteen: Waist Power

When high prepare to lower, when low prepare to rise,
If you angle the body and step around, you don't need to rush.
Use the power of the waist to roll at angles and wheel back,
When you turn to the furthest reach (of your waist), then use hard power.

Nineteen: Hard and Pliant

People say that our palm wins by its hard strikes,
Guo the elder used to say that pliancy is hidden inside.
There are some who understand this flavour (secret),
That our real forte is hardness and pliancy working together.

Twenty: Hardness and Pliancy in the Waist and Footwork

When hardness is foremost, pliancy is hiding within,
When pliancy is foremost, hardness is drawing back.
The pliancy of others is in their waist and hands,
But we suck in the waist and our footwork is stable and agile.

Twenty-one: Trade the Body for a Shadow

When you have gone to the fullest you must turn the body,
Shed the body and trade it for a shadow without leaving a trace.
How we change unpredictably is all in the footwork,
Going in and out, back and forth – the waist first extends.

Twenty-two: Spirit Shown in the Neck

The spirit of our turning palms is transmitted in the bones of the neck,
Turn the nape of the neck, twist the nape of the neck, the hands take the lead.
Retract the neck when changing, extend when emitting power,
You should be connected like the mystical dragon is connected from head to tail.

Twenty-three: Gaining Distance

> Striking someone depends on the shoulder girdle acting as the root of the hand,
>
> The arm is attached to the distal end of the shoulder and cannot extend any further.
>
> So when you want to enter, take an advancing step with the front foot,
>
> If you step through with the rear foot your effort will be in vain.

Twenty-four: Tendons and Sinews

> Abundant strength is emitted from the sinews/tendons and bones,
>
> Hard power comes from within the bones and the sinews must follow.
>
> The Achilles tendon connects through up the spine to the brain,
>
> When making a move, using a follow-up step will allow you to release full power.

Twenty-five: Three Trues and Four Arrives

> When the eyes arrive, the hands arrive, and the waist and legs arrive,
>
> The heart is true, the spirit is true, and the strength is also true.
>
> When the 'three trues' and the 'four arrives' unite as one,
>
> There is enough and to spare to defend oneself and control the adversary.

Twenty-six: Balance of Hardness and Pliancy

> Power should be hard but even more so should be pliant,
>
> Emphasizing hardness or pliancy at the expense of one another makes it difficult to develop skill.
>
> It is a law of nature that things that are too hard will break,
>
> And that taking pliancy too far is tantamount to stopping.

Twenty-seven: Hard and Pliant *Qian Kun* hands

> What does it mean to combine hardness and pliancy?
>
> Coordinating hardness and pliancy isn't difficult.
>
> (When you) use hardness and pliancy properly with *qian kun* (heaven and earth) hands,
>
> You can shake heaven, expose the earth, and surge like waves in the ocean.

Twenty-eight: Hard and Pliant Waist and Footwork

> If my adversary is hard and I am pliant, this is the conventional way,
> If I am hard when my adversary is pliant, then this works too.
> When both can use hardness and pliancy, use the waist to seek victory,
> Strong footwork will resolve this issue.

Twenty-nine: Coordination of Stepping

> When stepping, first lift the waist,
> Gather in just the right amount for the magical skill to be apparent.
> If, just before the foot moves, the waist does not move,
> Charging forward with huge steps, your timing will be off.

Thirty: Short Steps

> When turning and changing techniques the steps should not be long,
> Rub the ground while walking, there is no need to get flustered.
> Observe the attack and then extend the hand,
> (Be like) a skillful woman threading a needle: steady, gentle, and firm.

Thirty-one: *Heng* and *Ha* Sounds

> If an assailant is holding a sharp weapon I'm not bothered,
> Even as his sword flies towards me from afar.
> I watch his approach and avoid with a *heng* or *ha* sound,
> It is an apt saying that the evil cannot beat the righteous.

Thirty-two: Disarming

> It seems difficult to deal with a short weapon,
> But what is there to be afraid of in a sharp blade like the 'fish gut sword'?
> Extend your hand to fetch it, like reaching in to take something out of a pouch,
> The secret is hidden in 'pointing at the mountain to get the millstone'.

Thirty-three: One Finger to Beat Ten Hundredweight

> It is difficult to defend against the combined force of a mob on your own,
> With skill you can defeat ten hundredweight if you do not panic.
> One hand is not needed, just the strength of one finger,
> Even a plough ox is afraid when you draw the 'reverse bow'.

Thirty-four: Fighting in Darkness

> When you can't see your hand extended in front of you,
> And you don't have a torch to illuminate your assailants.
> Narrow your eyes and concentrate on seeing,
> Go to a low stance and all will become clear.

Thirty-five: Slippery Ground

> When it is icy, snowy, or muddy from rain so the ground is slippery,
> Employ the front foot crossways and you can't go wrong.
> When doing a full turn, by all means avoid pivoting,
> Strictly avoid going high or low, and then you should be fine.

Thirty-six: Spirit

> In fighting, the most vital factor is spirit,
> When the spirit shines the eyes and ears are true.
> Even if an assailant flies at me as fast as a swallow,
> The scurrying of ants sounds to me as the roar of dragons and tigers.

In Praise of the Thirty-six Verses

> The palm methods and fighting methods are discussions from the mountains,
> They have been transmitted for many years, and with the passing of time may have been forgotten.
> There are thirty-six of our verses,
> Each and every word and phrase has true meaning.

The Thirty-Six Verses

One

空胸拔顶下塌腰，
扭步掰膝抓地牢。
沉肩坠肘伸前掌，
二目须从虎口瞧。

Leave the chest empty, pull up the crown of the head, settle down the waist,
Twist within the stance, brace the knees, and grasp the ground firmly.
Settle the shoulders, weigh down the elbows, extend the forward palm,
The eyes must look out through the tiger's mouth.

The thirty-six verses do not have titles as do the forty-eight methods verses, so I took to giving them my own, just for ease of reference. I call this one Foundational Structure. The verse describes the fundamental posture of the body. In this first verse you can see the importance of the foundational posture as the sources differ, as if searching for just the right word to express the posture and feelings. Because each segment is dealt with very specifically in this verse, I have gone through the postures in great detail in the line by line discussion below. As with all things baguazhang, the words themselves are not set in stone. Using the knees as an example, the variation of words chosen to describe the knees depends on how the person copying interpreted what is being described – the reaching out of the leg or the landing. Reaching out, the knees are held together, thus closing or hugging. Landing, the knees are firm, thus bracing or engaging. Done properly, gripping with the feet firms the knees – the knees are together yet each is set separately. Gripping very firmly with the feet and ankles without engaging the knees can cause a collapse through the lower legs. The engaging, or bracing with the knees ensures that they stay aligned with the feet during any movement. There is a phrase that describes this connection nicely: 'to turn around with the folding step, you must first move the foot, then brace the knees, and then twist the hip joints'.[13]

Looking at the upper body, 'the shoulders' and 'the elbows' mean the entire structure around the joints. Discussion of any joint includes the bones, muscles, tendons and ligaments of the fairly large area that is involved in the movement of that joint, both distally and proximally.

The extension and height of the forward hand describes the most standard position of baguazhang. No other circle-walking posture is described in the verses.

Does this mean that different postures were not done at the time the verses were created? Not necessarily, though since the early books also did not mention any other positions, it is possible the other positions were latecomers. The structure of the body and movement of the legs is the same for all postures in any case, only the positioning and power/energy flow through the body changes.

The last line shows that right from the start, baguazhang treats the body and spirit as one. The basic structure of baguazhang is all there – nothing is left out. The focus of the eyes is not something we can leave until later, when we 'get the moves'. There is no separation of external and internal. Everything we need to do is in this verse. If we follow the instructions while we circle-walk, our body will naturally balance and centre erect, *qi* will sink to the *dantian*, the tendons of our lower legs will be strengthened, the tendons of our shoulders and arms will open up, and our spirit will rise and focus. If we train just this it is enough to give us a long healthy life.

36.01.1   Leave the chest empty, pull up the crown of the head, settle down the waist,

空	胸	拔	頂	下	塌	腰,
kòng	xiōng	bá	dǐng	xià	tà	yāo,

The exact wording for the verbs describing the chest and head is agreed on by almost all sources (Huan, Li, Lin, Luo, Tu, Wang, and Wu). The use of 空胸 kòng xiōng means to 'leave the chest empty', neither puffed up with air nor collapsed inward. The character 空 kòng is a verb, as this line consists of verb/noun phrases, and means 'to leave empty', i.e. let the breath settle down to the belly. It does not mean to collapse the chest, which triggers a sunken chest and hunched back.

The use of 拔頂 bá dǐng: 'pull up the crown of the head' is quite standard in internal martial arts, and describes a lengthening of the neck through its middle, like pulling up weeds. This is best thought of as pulling up a bit, then settling the waist while maintaining the lift. It is definitely not holding the neck stiffly.

For the verb describing the waist, six sources (Huan, Li, Lin Luo, Tu, Wang) use 塌腰 tà yāo: 'settle the waist', which is an action of settling and expanding until the lower back is straight. Liu uses 拓腰 tuò yāo: 'to open up, expand the waist', as does another Cheng lineage source (Xiang).[14] This is very close to the more common 'settle the waist', but with more of a feeling of expansion than a settling. This character 拓 tuò is also pronounced tà with the meaning 'to make rubbings'. So perhaps a little used character, pronounced wrongly, became written as the more commonly used 塌 tà? Sometimes one dissenting version gives a new outlook on a common phrase, and as such should not be immediately discarded or seen as a mistake in copying or typesetting. The phrase 塌腰 tà yāo has come to be the standard way to say 'release and settle the waist and sit into the hips'. The Cheng lineage, however, tucks in more on the push while walking, because of the longer step. Wu and Zang have 单腰 dān yāo: 'make the waist single', which is a phrase that usually refers to the action of settling one side of the back firmly into each leg, keeping the whole back erect, as you set onto the leg.

The character 腰 yāo: 'waist', is always difficult to translate, as it encompasses so much – the entire area between the hips and the costal region, both front and back, through the middle. In the past I have sometimes translated this as 'lower back' and 'lumbar sacral area' but this suggests it is the back alone. I have returned to 'waist' because this includes the front and middle of the trunk and is easier to think of moving. Power comes from 'the waist', but this is not as simple as turning the waist.

36.01.2   Twist within the stance, brace the knees, and grasp the ground firmly.

| 扭(拗) | 步 (胯) | 掰 | 膝 | 抓 | 地 | 牢。 |
| niǔ (ǎo) | bù (kuà) | bāi | xī | zhuā | dì | láo. |

Throughout the verses, 扭 niǔ and 拗 ǎo are both used to refer to a stance where the hips and shoulders are turned, or reversed, in relation to each other (opposite hand and foot forward) rather than 顺 shùn: 'smooth' or 'aligned' (same hand and foot forward). This is often translated as a cross stance, reverse stance, or twisted stance. The character 拗 ǎo is also pronounced niù, with the meaning of stubborn or obstinate, which may be why it came to be written 扭 niǔ from an oral tradition. After going through all the thirty-six and forty-eight verses, I came to count the use of 扭 niǔ or 拗 ǎo as an agreement in this context, as the sources consistently used one or the other in the same place (Huan, Li, Lin, Luo, Tu, Wang, and Wu tend to use 扭 niǔ, Liu and Zang tend to use 拗 ǎo). The meaning is that, to walk in a circle looking into the circle, the body is 'twisted' or 'crossed' in relation to the feet, which follow the circle. The 'front' is the centre of the circle, so when the feet and hips are following the circle and the upper body is facing the circle, the stance is 'reverse'. The outside shoulder pulls around toward the centre of the circle, twisting the body so the feeling is of crossing. Even when the outside leg is forward, its hip joint has a feeling of cutting, not of releasing smoothly into a *shunbu*, or smooth stance.

As well as being split between the use of 扭 niǔ: 'twisted' and 拗 ǎo: 'crossed', to describe the stance, the sources are split between the use of 步 bù: 'stance' and 胯 kuà: 'hip joints'. Four sources (Lin, Liu, Luo, and Wang) have 步 bù: 'stance'. Five sources (Huan, Li, Tu, Wu, and Zang) have 胯 kuà: 'the hip joints'. Instead of twisting the 'stance', the emphasis is on twisting in the hip joints, which makes sense in the feeling. The 胯 kuà: 'hip', refers to the entire area around the deep hip joint, including the thigh bones, muscles, tendons and ligaments – it does not mean the pelvis. When the pelvis is the intended meaning, the word is 髋 kuān. When looking for the feeling, it is often found in a cut at the inguinal crease[15], so the hip joint is often translated as 'inguinal crease'.

There is again a searching among the sources for a word to describe the feeling of the knees. Two sources (Wang and Liu Jingru) use 掰 bāi: 'brace', or 'pry'. The dictionary meaning of 掰 bāi: 'brace', is the action of pulling something apart with the hands, which calls for a bracing on both sides, thus a connection of power. Huan has 摆膝 bǎi xī, 'open the knees'. The word 摆 bǎi is usually used in baguazhang to mean the opening out step, with 步 bù, step, not 膝 xī, knee, so it would seem the wrong verb to use here, except that this source uses the same word again in the same context. The two words 掰 bāi: 'brace' and 摆 bǎi: 'open' normally refer to distinctly different actions with different joints. I mention this because in verse 36.11 Huan uses the term 摆 bǎi instead of 掰 bāi, so it is intentional. Wu and Liang Shouyu use 拿膝 ná xī: 'to have a firm grasp at the knees', which is a good descriptive verb for engaging the knees. (In verse 36.11, Liang uses this term again instead of 掰 bāi., while Wu uses 合 hé.) Two sources (re-edited Li and Liu) have 合膝 hé xī: 'join the knees'. Wu comments that 拿膝 ná xī: 'grasp' and 合膝 hé xī: 'join' differ in that 'grasp' has the connotation of lifting, while 'join' does not. Five sources (Li, Lin, Luo, Tu, and Zang) have 掰膝 gé xī: 'hug the knees'. The knees are not referred to as 'joined' or 'hugging' elsewhere in the verses, except in verse 36.11 in reference to moving forward with a *koubu* step. In verse 36.08 they are referred to as 'intersecting', which implies that they are close.

In what I see as a very informative case, Gao(2) quotes this line as 合 hé: 'join' when discussing moving the foot forward, but quotes it as 掰 bāi: 'brace' when discussing grabbing the ground.[16] I think this is what is going on in this line – those who think the description is of the knees landing have used a more 'setting' meaning, and those who think the description is of the knees moving have used a more 'joining' meaning. The action of 'prying' involves both an opening and a closing, and is relevant to both the reaching and the gripping phase, like when you pry apart an apple, your fingers are first pushed together then open out. This is why I chose to use 掰 bāi:

'brace', or 'pry' as the best word. You can see that when an experienced person copies the lines, they think about them and sometimes change them.

All sources agree on the phrase for grasping the ground firmly. Combined with the extended leg of verse 36.03, a flat foot landing may be inferred.

36.01.3   Settle the shoulders, weigh down the elbows, extend the forward palm,

沉　　肩　　坠　　肘　　伸　　前　　掌，
chén　jiān　zhuì　zhǒu　shēn　qián　zhǎng,

All sources have the identical wording of the shoulder placement and the hand placement. The shoulders always remain settled within the body, never shrugging up. The hand placement is further described in verse 36.02.

Seven sources (Li, Lin, Luo, Tu, Wang, Wu, and Zang) agree on the wording on the elbow structure. Huan uses 裹肘 guǒ zhǒu: 'wrap the elbows'. This wrapping power is an emphasis of the Zhang style, so this may have been deliberately changed to describe the wrapping feeling at the elbows in his style. Liu uses 堕肘 duò zhǒu: 'sink the elbows'. The character 坠 zhuì is the simplification of 墜, not 堕 duò, so I suspect this may be a misprint, using the wrong character. The placement of the elbows is caused by a rotation within the shoulder joint, so that the elbow crease is always settled as much as possible in any position, and there is always a twisting power in the arms.

Although all the sources have the same phrase for the extension of the front palm, Li Ziming comments that there are two understandings of this phrase. One – to extend the arm to almost full straightness. Two – to extend the shoulder joint, the root of the arm, forward, but to leave the arm slightly bent. Settling of the elbow usually infers that the arm remains slightly bent. Different styles interpret this either way.

36.01.4   The eyes must look out through the tiger's mouth.

二　　目　　须　　从　　虎　　口　　瞧。
èr　　mù　　xū　　cóng　　hǔ　　kǒu　　qiáo.

The exact wording of this line is agreed on by seven sources (Li, Lin, Liu, Luo, Wu, and Zang) while three differ in a minor descriptive way on the exact action of the eyes without changing the meaning. The re-edited Li and Wang use 二目须冲 èr mù xū chòng: 'the eyes must look with vigour'. Tu has 二目须向 èr mù xū xiàng: 'the eyes must look in the direction of'. The meaning may be interpreted as looking towards the hand but context makes it clear that it means in the same direction that the hand is reaching. Huan has 两目随从 liǎng mù xū suí: 'both eyes must follow'. The phrase keeps the same meaning, with the emphasis on the movement as the eyes follow the hand in looking through the tiger's mouth.

The tiger's mouth is the thumb/ forefinger web. We are so used to this term that we tend not to think of it, but once someone has come into your 'tiger's mouth', they are under your control. In one old text, the front hand is referred to as the 'tiger's mouth', and the rear hand is referred to as the 'ox tongue'.

None of the differences change the meaning of looking past, following the movement of the hand. In addition to the gaze, it gives the placement of the hand at eye height, so that the head can remain upright in all movement. Verses 36.03 and 48.32 clarify that the gaze takes in the entire surroundings.

Two

后肘先叠肘掩心，
手再翻塌向前跟。
跟到前肘合抱力，
前后两手一团神。

The rear elbow first folds in so the elbow covers the heart,
Then the hand rolls over to settle and press its heel forward.
It presses towards the forward elbow with a closing, wrapping power,
The front and rear hands are united in spirit.

I call this verse Dragon Stretches its Talons. It adds the details to the circle-walking position described in verse 36.01. Nowadays the hand positioning of different schools varies a bit, as does the name. It is variously called 青龙探爪 qīng lóng tàn zhuā: 'dragon stretches its talons', 推转掌 tuī zhuàn zhǎng: 'pushing turning palm', 推磨掌 tuī mò zhǎng: 'millstone pushing palm', 推磨式 tuī mò shì 'millstone pushing posture', 转身掌 zhuàn shēn zhǎng: 'turning body palm', 推掌 tuī zhǎng: 'pushing palms', 鸿雁出群 hóng yàn chū qún: 'swan leaves the flock', 搭掌势 dā zhǎng shì: 'contacting palms stance', 穿掌 chuān zhǎng 'spearing palm', and 龙形 lóng xíng: 'dragon structure'.

To the details of the body described in verse 36.01, this verse adds how to use the rear elbow and hand to connect through to the front hand and give power to the posture and prepare for a potential strike. There is more agreement on the words in this verse, perhaps because the posture of the arms is easier to describe. With very slight differences, the sources agree on the meaning that the rear elbow tucks in to protect the

THE THIRTY-SIX VERSES   17

solar plexus and ribs. It is more important that the posture joins the arms together through the back than that the elbow actually tucks onto the solar plexus. This stance connects the power and feeling through the body, and is also a practical defensive position.

In the first two verses, the position and power lines of the body are established. Other authors have described this, but no one so succinctly.

Yin Yuzhang, for example, describes the walking posture as "Standing with the feet pointing in the *xun* direction, facing to the *li* direction… place the right hand to the *qian* direction with the elbow slightly bent and the palm at eyebrow height. Take the sight line of the index finger. Place the left hand under the right elbow, with its elbow at the solar plexus. Bend both legs, press up the neck, empty the chest, stretch the upper back, tuck in the buttocks, and tuck the jaw in towards the hollow of the right shoulder. Close the mouth and breathe through the nose, settling the *qi* to the *dantian*." In the further notes at the back of the book, it says, "The point in the middle of the circle is very important, it is the key because as soon as you start to walk, the positioning of your elbows, hands, and jaw is very easily lost. This first position is the template. If the template is lost then you might as well not bother to train."[17]

Throughout the verses, the 'external' and 'internal' intertwine and flow together. The wording of the last line is important, as it shows that there is no dichotomy between body and soul in baguazhang.

The sounds of *xin*, *gen*, and *shen* are close, but not exact rhymes. There are so many words that sound exactly the same in Chinese that, to avoid the triteness of 'the moon in June', the pattern of rhyming is to have words almost the same. The verses come from the words of Dong Haichuan but were put into rhyme later, so the pronunciation is much as spoken in Beijing today.

36.02.1   The rear elbow first folds in so the elbow covers the heart,

后   肘   先   叠   肘   掩   心,
hòu   zhǒu   xiān   dié   zhǒu   yán   xīn,

Seven sources (Li, Lin, Luo, Tu, Wang, Wu, and Zang) have this exact line. Huan and Luo use 迭肘 dié zhǒu, which, although not the official simplified character for 叠 dié, can be assumed to be the normal shorthand, as it occurs consistently throughout the verses. The 'heart' refers to the solar plexus.

Two versions differ slightly in the elbow action. In Huan, the hand is referenced instead of the elbow 后手 hòu shǒu: 'the rear hand', perhaps just to not repeat the word 'elbow' in the same line, perhaps describing a slightly different hand position, and perhaps as a copy error. Liu and another Cheng source, Xiang, have 后肘前叠 hòu zhǒu qián dié: 'the rear elbow folds forward'. This puts a bit more emphasis on the fact that the rear elbow folds towards the front in order to cover the heart. I think 先 xiān: 'first', fits better with the following line, which says 再 zài: 'then'.

36.02.2   Then the hand rolls over to settle and press its heel forward.

手	再	翻	塌	向	前	跟。
shǒu	zài	fān	tà	xiàng	qián	gēn.

Seven sources (Huan, Li, Lin, Luo, Wang, Wu, and Zang) have this line exactly. Of interest here is the use of 跟 gēn: 'follow-up', as a verb applying to the hand. Tu has 向前伸 xiàng qián shēn: 'reach forward', instead of 'press into the heel of the hand', and his branch, the Ma Gui school, does tend to reach the rear hand forward quite a lot, leaving it fairly flat, so this may be a deliberate change.

The Cheng sources again (Liu and Xiang) have an interesting variation in one character in the four character phrase 手再翻拓 shǒu zài fān tuò: 'the hand then rolls and expands'. The character 拓 tuò: 'expand', is an excellent word to use. This is the same character they used for the waist in verse 36.01. The character 拓 tuò has a secondary pronunciation of tà, so it may actually have been the original word, and the other 塌 tà a substitute, as a character more commonly seen in the martial arts and very commonly used with this meaning. The use of 翻塌 fān tà: 'roll and set', is common in Baguazhang, Xingyiquan, and Chen Taijiquan. It is an internal rotation of the forearm coupled with a settling action of the wrist, turning the fingers upwards while settling the wrist downwards, putting power forward.

36.02.3   It (the hand) presses towards the forward elbow with a closing, wrapping power,

跟	到	前	肘	合	抱	力,
gēn	dào	qián	zhǒu	hé	bào	lì,

This phrase is agreed on word for word by all sources.

The Thirty-Six Verses

36.02.4 The front and rear hands are united in spirit.

前	后	两	手	一	团	神。
qián	hòu	liǎng	shǒu	yī	tuán	shēn.

This phrase is agreed on word for word by most sources. Wu has 两掌 liǎng zhǎng: 'two palms', in the first phrase, meaning the same thing. The hands are united by power through the back, and are united in the sense that they can easily change from being the front or the rear hand when reversing the circle walking direction, defending, or attacking.

Three

步弯脚直向前伸，
行如推磨一般真。
屈膝随胯腰扭足，
眼到三面不摇身。

The stance is flexed and each foot extends straight as it reaches forward,
Walk just like you were pushing a millstone.
The knees bend, the hips go along, and the waist twists fully,
The eyes see in three directions with no wavering of the body.

I call this verse Circle-walking. It describes walking in a posture that twists to face towards the centre of the circle, but not any specific arm position. The first line emphasizes three things, that the stance must be lowered, that the feet must remain aligned with the legs, and that the leg stepping to the front must be fully extended out to the foot. Baguazhang trains circle-walking with the feet always aligned straight with the legs and the heels kept down, so that the connection of the heel tendon through the tendons of the body is formed and strengthened. This is further explained in verse 36.24. In the context of the first line – the stance is bent – the action is referring to the extension and flexion of the leg rather than the direction of the stepping. This extension sends *qi* to the end of the leg. The extended foot ensures the flat foot land. If the ankle remains flexed like in the stance, the heel will land, the power will dissipate, and the grab will be late. This is the key – not reaching to put the foot flat – but extending the whole leg to the natural end of the leg (where you put the cleats on your bike shoes to apply force with the most direct line to the pedals. This is also why you must train with absolutely flat shoes. In addition to ruining your knees, any raised heel in a shoe will destroy the power connection.). One explanation, from Chang Naizhou, which predates baguazhang, is, "The foot can extend or dorsi-flex. If the toes reach forward, the power and *qi* settle down and plant. If the ankle is dorsi-flexed to raise the toes, the power and *qi* rise and float."[18] Some branches train this reaching part of the step as a short kick power – thousands of repetitions of this one inch kick. Taking the first line to mean that one foot lines up straight and one turns, as some do, is both adding to and taking away from what it actually says.

The reference to 'pushing a millstone' operates on quite a few levels. Firstly, and most obviously, you are walking in a circle. When operating a millstone you walk in a natural circle with no need to overthink it, the feet and knees stay aligned. Secondly, to grind fine grain you walk around and around and around for a very long time. Thirdly, a degree of force from the centre of the body and rooting in the feet is needed to push the heavy central stone. This suggests that the branches that emphasize the steady and firm walk are closer to the original sense than those that emphasize speed, though fast walking, done conscientiously, can maintain the rooting and force.

The position of the arms is not described in this verse. Real millstone pushing is done with the arms down on the lever. The posture described in 36.01 and 36.02 with the hands up and extended towards the centre of the circle, is sometimes referred to as 'millstone pushing', but it seems clear to me that here 'millstone pushing' refers to the stepping, not the upper body posture. The foundational posture that some schools start out with – the one that warms up the body and gets the *qi* circulating within the torso – is more like this real millstone walking. The posture is variously called 按掌 àn zhǎng: 'pressing down palms', 按球掌 àn qiú zhǎng: 'press down the ball', 猛虎下山 měng hǔ xià shān:'fierce tiger comes down from the mountian', 双塌掌 shuāng tā zhǎng: 'double settling palms', 下沉掌 xià chén zhǎng: 'downward sinking palm', and 熊形 xióng xíng: 'bear structure'.

GEF

This makes me think of a classic martial couplet: 宝剑锋从磨礪出, 梅花香自苦寒来. 'The sharpness of a precious sword is honed on the whetstone, The fragrance of a plum blossom is grown during the winter's bitter cold'. To this verse about the cause and effect of gongfu training, baguazhang could add 'The sweetness of refined flour comes from walking around the millstone'. In fact, one author joked that in the old days they used to say that if you wanted some flour ground, you should call in some of Eyeglasses Cheng's fellows.[19]

When the body is turned and the circle is walked, the full turn through the waist develops the special power of baguazhang that comes from a full and powerful *dantian*. The well turned waist differs from real millstone pushing, and is a distinguishing feature of baguazhang. The hips following, or tracking, can be taken to mean that the pelvis may be allowed to slightly turn into the circle in a natural way. It can also be taken to mean that the hips go along without driving the move. The turn does not come from the pelvis, but the waist.

The eyes can see all around without having to adjust the body in any way. When performing fast circle-walking, if the eyes are fixed just at the middle of the circle or on a tree, one can become dizzy. If the eyes make slight movements back and forth without moving the head, taking in the surroundings to the edge of peripheral vision, the dizziness does not occur. The usefulness of this is explained in verse 48.32. This again reiterates the unity of body and spirit. The body moves and the eyes are alert to changes in direction.

36.03.1   The stance is flexed and each foot extends straight as it reaches forward,

步	弯	脚	直	向	前	伸，
bù	wān	jiǎo	zhī	xiàng	qián	shēn,

All but one source have this exact line. Only Huan differs in a couple of characters 步弓脚直往前伸 bù <u>gōng</u> jiǎo zhī <u>wǎng</u> qián shēn: 'the stance is <u>arced</u> and the feet are straight, extending forward'. Huan again uses this same term 'arced like a bow' when the others used 'bent' in verse 48.04. The phrase 往前伸 wǎng qián shēn is just another way of saying the same thing as 向前伸 xiàng qián shēn: 'reach forward'.

36.03.2   Walk just like you were pushing a millstone.

行	如	推	磨	一	般	真。
xíng	rú	tuī	mò	yī	bān	zhēn.

Four sources (Huan, Li, Liu, and Zang) have this exact line. Six (re-edited Li, Lin, Luo, Tu, Wang, and Wu) have 形如推磨 <u>xíng</u> rú tuī mò: '<u>have the structure</u> like pushing a millstone'.

36.03.3   The knees bend, the hips go along, and the waist twists fully,

屈	膝	随	胯	腰	扭	足，
qū	xī	suí	kuà	yāo	niǔ	zǔ,

This line is agreed on by five sources (re-edited Li, Lin, Liu, Wang, and Zang). Wu has 屈肘 qū zhǒu: 'bend the elbows', instead of bend the knees, which doesn't seem to fit the line. Two sources (Huan, Li) use 曲膝 qū xī: 'bend the knees', instead of 屈膝 qū xī. With the same pronunciation and meaning, both 曲 qū and 屈 qū are essentially the same thing. You can start to see how some of the differences come from hearing a phrase and writing down what you think it is. Other differences seem to come from copying a phrase and getting a character wrong. Copying hand written texts is difficult, as each person jots down what they understand perfectly well, not thinking of their poor students who will copy it later when they become the teacher.

36.03.4   The eyes see in three directions with no wavering of the body.

眼　　到　　三　　面　　不　　摇　　身。
yǎn　dào　sān　miàn　bù　yáo　shēn.

This is agreed on word for word by almost all sources. Liu has one differing word：眼前三面 yǎn qián sān miàn: 'in front of the eyes in three directions'. Since only three directions are covered, this is essentially the same, they may have changed it just to clarify that you are viewing in front and to the sides, not behind. This brings up another way the text is sometimes different – the person copying it thinks to improve upon it. That is a slippery slope!

Four

一势单鞭不为奇，
左右循环乃为宜。
左换右兮右换左，
抽身倒步自合机。

It is not remarkable to strike a pose like Single Whip,
It is better to be move freely side to side.
Changing from left to right and from right to left,
Withdraw and switch your stance to take what opportunity presents.

I call this verse Both Sides. It speaks of the necessity of practising many moves equally on both sides, advancing and retreating, and switching and reversing. This type of practice is typical of Baguazhang and Xingyiquan, which tend to have shorter routines, combinations like the changes, and straight line drills, all of which are easily done on both sides. When you can use either side equally you are developing your body and skill in a balanced way and, together with stepping, you are able to get to the most effective side of your opponent without worrying about which side you are on.

This verse may be aimed at other practitioners, also in Beijing in the late 1800s, with their routines done mostly on one side – suggested by the use of 单鞭 dān biān: 'Single Whip', which is also occasionally called 单边 dān biān: 'Single Side'. Single Whip is a common move, named in books by the 1500s,[20] but not used in Baguazhang. Certainly Single Whip was a stance known to Dong Haichuan. Watching some Taijiquan players trying to do 'the other side' of a routine, one sees that they understand the movements differently from Baguazhang players, puzzling over whether the last move was on the right or the left. In Baguazhang, we refer always to the compass or trigram directions, our placement on the circle, inside and outside, and *koubu* or *baibu* turning, so changing from left to right isn't really an issue.

This illustration shows the Single Whip posture of various styles, through the years, in *aobu* and *shunbu*, and called both Single Whip and Single Side.

36.04.1   It is not remarkable to strike a pose like Single Whip,

一	势 (式)	单	鞭 (边)	不	为	奇,
yī	shì (shì)	dān	biān (biān)	bù	wéi	qí,

Six sources (Huan, Li, Liu, Luo, Wu, and Zang) use 单鞭 dān biān: 'single whip'. Four sources (re-edited Li, Lin, Tu, and Wang use 单边 dān biān: 'a single side'. Commentaries say that the meaning is 'a move on one side' and not a specific move 'single whip', but both terms can refer to the same move. The pronunciation is the same. Single Whip is an old stance, common to many styles, but not to Baguazhang. It could be saying that it is not enough just to look good and pose, you need to move around. It could also be saying that knowing only one move, or that doing a move only on one side, is not good enough.

Some sources (Huan, Liu, Wu, and Zang) use 式 shì instead of 势 shì, which is common throughout the verses, so can be considered as the same thing. Properly, 式 shì is 'a pattern or model', while 势 shì is 'the outward appearance of an object' (it also refers to the 'momentum' of an army, but not here). Both often refer simply to stances, placement, postures, or moves.

Slight differences in 不为奇 bù wéi qí: 'not remarkable', are grammatical linking words, not changing the meaning. Five sources (re-edited Li, Lin, Luo, Tu, and Wang) have 不为奇 bù wéi qí, while five (Huan, Li, Liu, Wu, and Zang) have 不足奇 bù zú qí: 'not <u>sufficiently</u> remarkable'.

36.04.2 It is better to be able to move freely side to side.

左　　右　　循　　环　　乃　　为　　宜。
zuǒ　yòu　xuán　huán　nǎi　wéi　yí.

All sources have this exact line.

36.04.3 Changing from left to right and from right to left,

左　　换　　右　　兮　　右　　换　　左，
zuǒ　huàn　yòu　xī　yòu　huàn　zuǒ,

All sources have this exact line.

36.04.4 Withdraw and switch your stance to take what opportunity presents.

抽　　身　　倒　　步　　自　　合　　机。
chōu　shēn　dǎo　bù　zì　hé　jī.

The sources differ on just the last two characters of the line, without changing the meaning. Seven sources (Huan, Li, Lin, Liu, Tu, Wu, and Zang) have the entire line. The phrase 抽身 chōu shēn means 'to draw the body back', by sitting back, sucking in the body, or both. The phrase 倒步 dǎo bù often means 'to step back continuously, but also means 'to pull in the foot and quickly step out the other to switch sides'.

For the final phrase, Luo has 自如机 zì <u>rú</u> jī: '<u>freely</u> take any opportunity'. This is also quite nice. The Wang book looks to have a typographical error 自兮机 zì <u>xī</u> jī. The character 兮 xī is a filler word that doesn't make this into a complete phrase. Typographical error is one more source of differences in the sources, once they started being printed up as books. The people setting up the print, or now typing in by computer, do not always understand the source and do not notice errors that creep in. Proof reading for modern books is often slack.

Five

步既转兮手亦随，
后掌穿出前掌回。
去来来去无二致，
要如弩箭离弦飞。

As the footwork turns the hands follow,
As the rear hand spears out the lead hand returns.
(The hands) go and come, come and go, there is no difference (between them),
They should fly like bolts from a crossbow.

I call this verse Connections in Spearing Strike. It introduces the importance baguazhang places on the feet and hands working together. Although the hands are not moving during circle walking, the power is flowing and coiling around the circle with the stepping. The second line emphasizes how the hands always work together, joined as one, and this is the first mention of the spearing palm (*chuanzhang*, piercing palm, threading palm, penetrating palm) specifically. The spearing palm technique threads along or through something, like putting on a shirt, intending to pierce through your opponent. It is accomplished by turning the upper body, as further described in verse 36.06, so the rear hand returns, giving power to the striking hand. The third line emphasizes that the hands not only work together, but have equal and opposite power. They are integrally connected through the back, and cannot work independently.

The last line emphasizes the speed at which the hands can move when they are well coordinated with the footwork and each other. Also, because the arms are connected and already coiling, pre-loaded, as it were, the strike is cold and immediate, not needing any preparatory movement. The cross-bow is an ancient weapon in China, and one difference between it and a long bow is that it is pre-loaded with a chain, with more strength than you could pull a bow, so that the shot itself is immediate and penetrating. This is a drawing from the Ming dynasty, from a manual that showed many methods of loading the crossbow.

36.05.1　　As the footwork turns the hands follow,

步	既	转	兮	手	亦	随，
bù	jì	zhuàn	xī	shǒu	yì	suí,

Seven sources have this exact wording (Li, Lin, Luo, Tu, Wang, Wu, and Zang). Huan and Liu use 步即转 bù jí zhuàn. Use of 即 jí might be taken to mean that 'just before' the footwork turns, the hands follow, but is also could be a lazy way to write 既 jì, as this shows up throughout the verses. 即 jí is usually used in the verses with its meaning of 'that is', or 'even if'. 既 jì often means 'since', or 'as well as'. One source has 手也随 shǒu yě suí: 'the hands also follow', which is essentially the same meaning.

36.05.2　　As the rear hand spears out the lead hand returns.

后	掌	穿	出	前	掌	回。
hòu	zhǎng	chuān	chū	qián	zhǎng	huí.

All but one source have this line. Only Huan differs, with the phrase 后掌抽出 hòu zhǎng chōu chū: 'as the rear hands draws out'. I would suspect that this is a copy error, except that Huan Dahai does Zhang style, which uses the spearing palm less than other branches. The word 抽出 chōu chū: 'to send out', is a technique less specific than 穿出 chuān chū: 'to thread out'. The characters 抽 chōu and 穿 chuān look nothing alike, so I don't see how I could have copied it wrong, and they do not sound alike, so it would be a strange oral transmission error.

36.05.3　　(The hands) go and come, come and go, there is no difference (between them),

去	来	来	去	无	二	致，
qù	lái	lái	qù	wú	èr	zhì,

Almost all sources have this line exactly. Liu and Wu (backed up by Liang Shouyu) reverse the first phrase, with 来去 去来 lái qù qù lái: 'come and go, go and come', not changing the meaning at all.

36.05.4　　They should fly like bolts from a crossbow.

要	如	弩	箭	离	弦	飞。
yào	rú	nǔ	jiàn	lí	xián	fēi.

Six sources (Li, Lin, Liu, Tu, Wu, and Zang) have exactly this line, and the others have just slightly different ways of saying the same thing. Huan and Luo have 犹如弩箭 yóu rú nǔ jiàn: 'just like bolts from a crossbow'. Wang has 要如弓箭 yào rú gōng jiàn: 'they should be like arrows from a bow'. The cold power of baguazhang is more like a crossbow. Bow is a more standard description of using the body, used in other styles. The word in Chinese for 'bolts' is the same as for 'arrows', but crossbows fire bolts.

The Thirty-Six Verses

Six

穿时直掌贴肘行，
后肩改作前肩承。
莫要距离莫犹疑，
脚入裆兮是准绳。

When doing a spearing strike, straighten the palm and slide alongside the elbow,
The rear shoulder takes on the role of the leading shoulder.
Don't leave any gaps and don't hesitate,
Gauge your strike to enter your foot between your opponent's legs.

I call this verse Model for Spearing Strike. It continues to explain that a strike depends on the footwork working in coordination with the hands and whole body to make an effective strike. The meaning is clear, that the movement, power and reach of the hand strike come from the movement, power and reach of the shoulder girdle section of the body. The strike does not come from the extension of the elbows, but from the movement of the body and the concomitant extension through the shoulders. The power of the lower back pushes the shoulders into the strike. If shooting from the position described in verses 36.01 and 36.02 the rear hand's starting point is already at the front elbow. And the entire strike is dependent on the feet getting you to the right place for it to be effective.

36.06.1   When doing a spearing strike, straighten the palm and slide alongside the elbow,

穿	时	直	掌	贴	肘	行，
chuān	shí	zhí	zhǎng	tiē	zhǒu	xíng,

Four sources have this line (Li, Liu, Wu, and Zang). Six sources (Huan, re-edited Li, Lin, Luo, Tu, and Wang) have 穿时指掌 chuān shí zhǐ zhǎng: 'the fingers and palm must stick to and align with the elbow'. This gives the same result, but the version I chose reminds you to keep the hand straight. It also reminds people to extend the strike out past the front hand, not to pull the front hand back.

For the verse, the line I chose keeps the line as a four character plus three character beat – 'when doing a spearing strike straighten the hand', and 'keep close to and aligned with the front elbow'. The overall meaning of the phrase is the same in all counts – it is referring to the spearing strike.

36.06.2   The rear shoulder takes on the role of the leading shoulder.

后	肩	改	作	前	肩	承。
hòu	jiān	gǎi	zuò	qián	jiān	chéng.

Three sources (Li, Luo, and Zang) have this line (counting 作 zuò: 'do' as the same as 做 zuò: 'do'). Three sources (Huan, Liu, Wang) have 前肩成 qián jiān <u>chéng</u>: '<u>becomes</u> the leading shoulder'. With the two characters pronounced chéng, this is perhaps a case where sometimes the easier and more common 成 chéng: 'become', was used. I prefer the character 承 chéng: 'take on the role' as having a bit more depth of meaning. Lin and Tu use 前肩行 qián jiān <u>xíng</u>: 'as the shoulder <u>moves</u>', but this repeats the 行 xíng: 'move' of the first line. Wu has 前肘成 qián zhǒu chéng: '<u>becomes</u> the leading <u>elbow</u>, changing the meaning of the line. Wu comments that the shoulder urges the elbow, the elbow urges the wrist, an the wrist urges the hand.

36.06.3   Don't leave any gaps and don't hesitate,

莫	要	距	离	莫	犹	疑,
mò	yào	jù	lí	mò	yóu	yí,

Four sources (Li, Liu, Luo, and Zang) have this exact wording while four (Huan, Lin, Wang, and Wu) have 莫犹豫 mò yóu <u>yù</u>: for 'don't hesitate'. The re-edited Li was changed to be unlike the others, 看准距离 kàn zhǔn jù lí: '<u>judge</u> the spacing <u>correctly</u>'. Tu had this line but also had an alternate version 动手须用看距离 dòng shǒu xū yòng kàn jù lí: 'moving the hands you must judge the spacing correctly'.

36.06.4   Gauge your strike to enter your foot between your opponent's legs.

脚	入	裆	兮	是	准	绳。
jiǎo	rù	dāng	xī	shì	zhǔn	shéng.

Six sources (Huan, Lin, Luo, Tu, Wang, and Wu) have this exact line. The word used is 裆 dāng: 'crotch of the trousers', which I chose to translate as 'between the legs'. Li uses 步入裆兮 <u>bù</u> rù dāng xī: 'the <u>steps</u> enter between the legs', which emphasizes that it is the stepping that enters, so that you do not confuse this with a kick. The re-edited Li was changed to agree with the others. Liu has 脚入裆<u>中</u> jiǎo rù dāng <u>zhōng</u>: 'the foot enters <u>in between</u> the legs' – entering <u>into the middle</u>, rather than using the meaningless spacing word 兮 xī. Zang uses 脚入?兮 <u>bù</u> rù <u>dāng</u> xī: with the same meaning, but with a character that my Chinese entry keyboard can't do. It has the flesh radical in the character for 'crotch' instead of the cloth radical, and should exist as a word, since it makes perfect sense. I don't know how it was printed in a book.

Seven

胸欲空兮气欲沉，
背紧肩垂意前伸。
气到丹田缩谷道，
直拔颠顶贯精神。

The more the chest is emptied the more the *qi* will sink down,
Tauten the upper back, drop the shoulders, and extend awareness forward.
Settle the *qi* in the *dantian* and draw in the 'grain path',
Draw the crown of the head straight upwards, and the vitality will pass throughout.

  I call this verse Internal Structure. It gives a more in depth explanation of the posture described in verse 36.01, or any circle walking posture, or indeed the goal of the trained body at any time. This verse has returned to the basics after a couple of verses on *chuanzhang*, this time emphasizing the internal workings. The first line refers not only to the structure and posture of the chest, but to diaphragmatic breathing, keeping the chest empty, settling the shoulder girdle down, and pulling the breath down to the belly, even when the arms are raised.

  The feeling in the upper back is a difficult one to describe. The upper back sometimes refers to the area through the shoulder blades, and often includes the entire costal region. The use of 紧 jǐn: 'tauten' with 背 bèi: 'upper back' is non-standard. The word 拔 bá: 'pull out', 'draw out', is more common in other styles. Yin Yuzhang uses the word 弝 bà: which means '(use the upper back as) the part of a bow grasped while shooting'. The word for the lower costal region in Chinese is 肋弓 lèi gōng: 'bow of the ribs'. This 弝 bà is such a good word that I wonder if, way back, it was the intended word in the oral transmission of many styles. This description of the opening and connection of the upper back through the shoulder joints is repeated in verses 36.13, 36.14, 36.22, 36.24, and others. This upper part of the body is connected to the arms like an empty room with connecting doors, or a soaring bird strong from the keel.

  Dong Haichuan was said to have 'a square back with aligned ribs'[21] – meaning a full torso with a fused rib cage. In cases such as Dong Haichuan this refers not just to a thickening of the torso but a concomitant thickening of the surrounding tissue so that you can't feel separate muscles or bones of the back, which is possible, as I have felt it on a master. This feeling of having an impenetrable shell on your back is the meaning of the 'turtle back', whether or not the tissues are actually fused.

The lower *dantian* 'point' is three finger widths below the navel and two finger widths in (on a lean person) but in our understanding we talk of the *dantian* as the area that includes the entire belly. Settling *qi* does not mean to strain the belly to put strength there, but to allow the breath to sink. It is standard for internal styles to draw up the 'grain path' lightly so that the *qi* flow will continue around the torso and the *qi* can be stored in the *dantian*. The term 'grain path' is often used for the anal sphincter, but it more properly names the *Huiyin* point, slightly in front of that. If you tighten up the anal sphincter too much then the pelvis rolls under too much. If you draw up the *Huiyin* or lightly close the sphincter, like closing your eyes, then the lower back remains open and released, and ready to store the *qi*. Combined with the spread back, this can develop a very solid torso. I like that the structure is described before the breathing, because this is how one learns. The tongue touching the roof of the mouth is not described until verse 36.09, and this is needed for the *qi* to settle properly, completing the circle of the *Ren* ('Conception') and *Du* ('Governing') vessels.[22] But first the habit must be set of settling down but not leaving the bottom of the container loose. Breathing deeply and pressing the tongue to connect the flow won't do much good if you have not set the rest of the structure.

The last line reminds us again to pull up through the crown of the head, to not let the settling into the *dantian* pull us down to a scrunched position, which will lead to stagnation of the *qi*, blood, and spirit. This allows the spirit to remain lively, not sunken and depressed. Again, the 'external' structure is aiding the 'internal' movement, and visa versa. The connection between the two is explained again in verse 48.38.

36.07.1 The more the chest is emptied the more the *qi* will sink down,

胸 欲 空 兮 气 欲 沉，
xiōng yù kōng xī qì yù chén,

Most sources use these exact words. Huan has a more colloquial connecting word 胸越空兮气越沉 xiōng yuè kōng xī qì yuè chén: 'the more the chest is able to be empty, the more the *qi* is able to settle to the *dantian*'.

36.07.2 Tauten the upper back, drop the shoulders, and extend awareness forward.

背 紧 肩 垂 意 前 伸。
bèi jǐn jiān chuí yì qián shēn.

Most sources have the initial phrase, while Wu has 背紧肩松 bèi jǐn jiān sòng: 'tauten the upper back and release the shoulders'. For the final phrase, five sources (Huan, Li, Liu, Wu, and Zang) have 意前伸 yì qián shēn: 'extend the awareness forward'. Four sources (Lin, Luo, Tu, and Wang) have 臂前伸 bì qián shēn: 'the arm extends forward'. The re-edited Li and Li Ziming's student Zhang Quanliang both have 臂前伸 bì qián shēn: 'the arm extends forward. I much prefer the majority because firstly, the arm extending forward has just been described in verses 36.01 and 36.02, and secondly, this verse is talking about the internal workings of this positioning, so I feel the 'intent' fits the context better. Of course, the arms are extended forward, so that is right, too.

36.07.3   Settle the *qi* in the *dantian* and draw in the 'grain path',

气	到	丹	田	缩	谷	道,
qì	dào	dān	tián	suō	gǔ	dào,

Most sources have this exact wording. Wu has 气入丹田 qì rù dān tián: 'the *qi* enters the *dantian*'.

36.07.4   Draw the crown of the head straight upwards, and the vitality will pass throughout.

直	拔	颠	顶	贯	精	神。
zhí	bá	diān	dǐng	guàn	jīng	shén.

All but one source have this wording. Liu has 头顶 tóu dǐng: 'press the head up'. When everyone else has 颠 diān: 'the crown of the head', why change it to 头 tóu: 'head'? If you think of lifting the head instead of pushing up the crown on the head, you may end up with the tilting error explained in verse 48.39.

Eight

走时周身莫动摇，
全凭膝下两相交。
低盘虽讲平膝胯，
中盘也要下腿腰。

When walking, there must be no extraneous movement anywhere in the body,
All depends on the crisscrossing of the lower legs, from the knees down.
Although we talk of the low basin (walking), where the knee and hips are level with each other,
The middle basin (walking) should also lower the legs and back.

I call this verse Circle Walking Basins. It very clearly states the requirements of circle-walking, while remaining general enough to apply to both the short firm stepping walk and the long stepping mud walk. Circle-walking is essentially a standing training, but walking, which develops a moving root. The upper body does not move at all during circle-walking – if the body moves randomly then *gongfu* will not be honed. Some martial styles start with standing and develop the connection to the movement later. Some styles emphasize the strength of the thighs with deep stable stances. Baguazhang does use deep horse stance training, but emphasizes walking over stance work. Baguazhang circle-walking is very distinctly from the lower legs, walking from the knees down. The legs work like scissors. This is simple to understand, but many people make the errors of dipping the supporting knee when circle-walking, and even more wobble about. This may be partly because they are trying to go lower than their present strength and connections allow.

The character 盘 pán has richer associations in Chinese than any translation can manage, which is why it has been translated as 'basin' for years. The character 盘 pán includes all its meanings, which is why classical Chinese is so concise yet rich in meaning. 1) As a noun it means 'a basin', 'a plate', or 'a flat receptacle', or things that are like flat receptacles, thus can refer to the pelvis and shoulder girdle. 2) As a measure word it applies to things that are or are like flat receptacles, like a plate, basin, millstone or a coil of wire, thus can be a measure word for the posture of circle-walking, which maintains a flatness. 3) As a verb it means 'to twine' like the roots twine around a tree, 'to coil' like coiling up a rope, thus applies to circle-walking that twines around a tree and coils within the body. 'Carriage' or 'bearing' are the closest I can come to as a translation, which are pretty weak, so I have left it as 'basin'.

A measure word is like a 'pair' of shoes in English. In Chinese, every noun needs one when counting. Grammar is fluid in Chinese – words can be used as a noun or a measure word depending on the context. For example 一张纸 yī zhāng <u>zhǐ</u>: 'a piece of <u>paper</u>' and 一纸公文 yī <u>zhǐ</u> gōng wén: 'a (<u>paper of</u>) document'. This verse uses the word 盘 pán: 'basin' almost as a measure word for circle-walking, as in 低盘, 中盘 dī pán, zhōng pán: 'low basin' (circle-walking), 'middle basin' (circle-walking). The term for the height of a moving stance must of necessity differ from that of a static stance, so the term 桩 zhuāng: 'stance' cannot be used for circle-walking. The word 步 bù also means 'stance', as in 马步 mǎ bù: 'horse stance', but is used for stepping, as in 扣步 kòu bù: '*koubu* step', so it would be confusing to use it for a circle-walking height as well.

In this verse, the 'basins' refer to the height of circle-walking. Lower basin walking is with the hips and knees level, as described in line three. It refers to the well known training of baguazhang to walk in very low posture, which develops deep skill. It is not hard to hold this in a stance but to walk continuously like this might do more damage than good. In high basin walking the knees are only slightly bent, so there is less training effect. It is practical for fast walking once the connections to the feet have been trained. This is why most people train the middle basin height. This verse emphasizes that in the middle basin, which is the height normally used in training, one should not be lazy, but should sit well into the stance, and the power should settle down. The 'middle height' is never really defined. I feel that a comfortable middle basin training is if the body feels settled and the foot reaches a foot length away, keeping the knees together and not moving the body. If the foot is any closer you are in a high stance. A push will then take the mud stepping step further out. Middle basin height, properly done, develops deep skill in a natural, gradual way. The basins are explained again in verse 48.37, which again emphasizes the use of the middle basin.

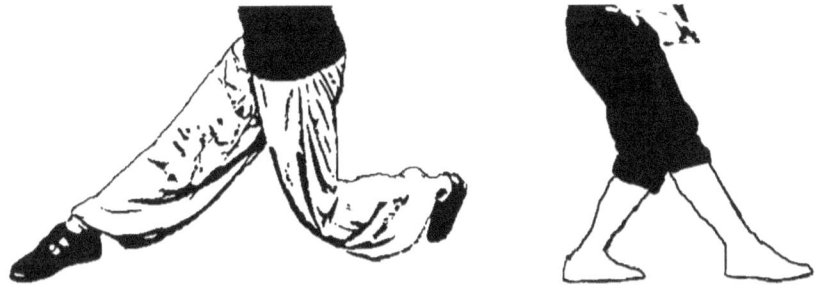

The illustration shows the middle basin as it refers to the height of the stance, whether walking in the long *tangnibu* step or the short step.

While this verse refers directly to the height of the stance while circle-walking, the term 'basin' is also used to define body segments and the placement of power within the body while walking. One such definition is: the upper basin is the upper body and arms, the middle basin is the torso and *dantian* area, and the lower basin is the legs including below the knees, much as we say the 'shoulder girdle' and 'pelvic girdle' in English when we want to include the entire structure. This leads to one way of referring to the basins by power: high basin circle-walking is centered in the chest and arms, middle basin is centered in the torso, and low basin is centered in the legs.

Another definition that applies basins to body segments is: the upper is in the *dantian*, the middle is in the thighs, and the lower is in the shin/calves and feet. With this definition, the height of the stance is not important, but rather how we apply power. Low basin training sends power deep into the ankles and lower legs. The stance does not need to be low to apply the power and work low in the body. With this definition the stance can be long or short, low or high, as the focus is on the power within the body. The basins in the body are also called heaven (upper), man (middle), and earth (lower).

The origin of the word 盘 pán: 'basin' to refer to height or power placement of circle-walking comes maybe from the circle-walking around trees, maybe from the idea of the millstone. Tree roots are said to 盘 pán: 'coil', and circle-walking coils around the tree like its roots. The word 盘 pán is the measure word for pair of millstones, and again, circle-walking is walking the millstone. When you think of it, 'basin' is a perfect measure word for circle-walking and noun for the levelly held body segments during circle-walking. The pleasure of writing in Chinese characters is that you can hold all of these meanings and associated thoughts in your head without any problem.

Whichever interpretation you are taking, the term 'basin' in baguazhang refers specifically to circle-walking, and circle-walking emphasizes the low and middle basin training, not the upper. With any interpretation, the middle basin enables you to change easily from high to low both within the stance and within the body. The mid-height stance should be low enough to be hard work and build deep skill. The power should feel like it is reaching forward to the end of the extended leg.

36.08.1   When walking, there must be no extraneous movement anywhere in the body,

走 时 周 身 莫 动 摇,
zǒu shí zhōu shēn mò dòng yáo,

All sources have this line. The phrase 摇动 yáo dòng: 'an abrupt movement', is the normal order of the characters 动摇 dòng yáo, but switching the order makes it rhyme. Chinese grammar is fun that way – word order often doesn't really make a difference.

36.08.2   All depends on the crisscrossing of the lower legs, from the knees down.

全 凭 膝 下 两 相 交。
quán píng xī xià liǎng xiāng jiāo.

All sources have the exact wording.

36.08.3   Although we talk of the low basin (walking), where the knee and hips are level with each other,

低 盘 虽 讲 平 膝 胯,
dī pán suī jiǎng píng xī kuà,

Five sources (Huan, Lin, Luo, Tu, and Zang) have this exact wording. Li, Liu, and Wu have the character 底 dǐ: 'bottom', instead of 低 dī: 'low'. Wang has 低垂 dī chuí: 'the lower hangs down', probably an error.

36.08.4	The middle basin (walking) should also lower the legs and back.
中	盘　　也　　要　　下　　腿　　腰。
zhōng	pán　　yé　　yào　　xià　　tuǐ　　yāo.

All sources have this line, except that Li, Wu, and Zang use the more formal 亦 yì instead of 也 yé for 'also'. The re-edited Li has been changed back to 也 yé.

Nine

抿唇闭口舌舔腭，
呼吸全凭鼻孔过。
力用极处哼哈泄，
混元一气此为得。

Purse the lips lightly, close the mouth, lick the roof of the mouth with the tongue,
Breathe in and out entirely through the nostrils.
When using force to the fullest, give vent with a *heng* or *ha* sound,
This is how to obtain full original *qi*.

I call this verse Breathing. The closed mouth and tongue placement is standard for internal styles. Keeping the mouth shut and the tongue lightly up connects the *Ren Mai* ('Conception') and *Du Mai* ('Governing') vessels up and down the torso so that the *qi* can flow, creates saliva so we can train without thirst, and develops good habits so we don't bite our tongues in a fight. Opening the mouth, on the contrary, dries it, allows the *qi* to rise into the chest, and risks biting the tongue. There is no actual acupoint inside the mouth, just an understanding that the tongue will connect the flow, so I think that placing the tongue in a natural position – like on the ridge just behind the teeth, as in zazen – allows the mouth to be closed and relaxed. Rolling the tongue up and back 'like a lion holding a ball' isn't natural or practical for fighting.

Breathing through the nose seems clear and simple, but difficult to do when you're training hard. This verse points out that is more important to remain settled down than to train so hard that you pant. Breathing deeply, and being able to do so through the nose, is vital to the basic structure and later to the ability to remain calm in a fight. Breathing through the nose makes you breathe steadily, making each breath and heart beat count, which serves to train the cardiovascular system. If you want to maintain the requirements of the previous verses, you have to breathe through the nose.

The *heng* and *ha* sounds are used by other martial arts styles, as well as in *qigong* health exercises. They are a natural sound that is issued when doing a power strike, and serve to solidify the body to strike or throw, or take a punch or fall. They protect the body by firming it at the proper instant. The sound *heng* comes naturally with a slight restriction of the throat, and a relatively closed mouth, almost a grunt. The sound *ha* comes naturally with a more relaxed throat and a more open mouth. The use of the breath expulsion is an expression of full *qi* being applied to a power issue. One should not make the sounds just for the sake of making the sounds. This power is key to baguazhang, and the sounds are further discussed in verse 36.31.

36.09.1   Purse the lips lightly, close the mouth, lick (press) the roof of the mouth with the tongue,

抿　　唇　　闭　　口　　舌　　舔(顶)　　腭，
mǐn　　chún　　bì　　kǒu　　shé　　tiǎn (dǐng)　　è,

Huan, Liu, and Wu use the phrase 舌舔腭 shé tiǎn è: 'lick the roof of the mouth with the tongue'. I like 'licking' as a verb, it gives a much clearer image of what the tongue is doing, and has a lightness to it. There is largely agreement in the other sources with the more commonly seen verb 顶 dǐng: 'press'. 'Press' is a strong word, and tends to make people push too hard with the tongue.

36.09.2   Breathe in and out entirely through the nostrils.

呼　　吸　　全　　凭　　鼻　　孔　　过。
hū　　xī　　quán　　píng　　bí　　kǒng　　guò.

There are a few different ways of saying this. The phrase used by most sources is 'breathing in and out depends entirely on going through the nostrils'. Li uses 鼻口 bí kǒu for 'nostrils' instead of 鼻孔 bí kǒng, which is a relatively standard variation. Huan is a bit more emphatic 呼吸须从 hū xī xū cóng: 'breathing must go'. Wu and Zang have 呼吸全从 hū xī quán cóng: 'breathing goes through'.

36.09.3   When using force to the fullest, give vent with a *heng* or *ha* sound.

力　　用　　极　　处　　哼　　哈　　泄，
lì　　yòng　　jí　　chǔ　　hēng　　hā　　xiè,

Most sources use the character 泄 xiè: 'give vent', 'release'. Huan uses 洩 xiè, which is the traditional character, and 泄 xiè is its simplification. The sources were printed in the modern era, so the source editors may have put 泄 xiè.

For the power output, Liu has 力到极处 lì <u>dào</u> jí chǔ: 'when power <u>reaches</u> the fullest'. This agrees with the main meaning, which suggests that breath normally goes in and out through the nose, but with a strong, voiced, exhalation on use of full power.

36.09.4 This is how to obtain full original *qi*.

混	元	一	气	此	为	得。
hùn	yuán	yī	qì	cǐ	wéi	dé.

All sources have this line, except Li wrote 浑元 <u>hún</u> yuán instead of 混元 hùn yuán. They are often used interchangeably in martial arts writings, but 混元 hùn yuán is more standard. This line sums up that in order to have complete internal power you must follow these rules. It also means that this breathing and breath expulsion is an expression of your fully connected *qi*.

Ten

掌形虎口要撑圆，
中指无名缝开展。
先戳后打施腕骨，
松膀长腰跟步钻。

For the palm shape, brace the tiger's mouth so it is rounded,
Spread the space between the middle and ring fingers.
First poke then hit using the wrist bone,
Release the shoulder girdle and lengthen the waist, use a follow-up step to drill in.

  I call this verse Palm Shape and Use. It describes the naturally open hand used by most schools of baguazhang. Within this definition of hand shape there is a large range of possibilities. There are various names for the different hand shapes, including: 龙爪掌 lóng zhǎo zhǎng 'dragon talons palm', 柳叶掌 liǔ yè zhǎng 'willow leaf palm', 瓦拢掌 wǎ lǒng zhǎng 'tiled palm', 八字掌 bā zì zhǎng 'character eight palm', and 牛舌掌 niú shé zhǎng 'ox tongue palm'.[23] The verse suggests that the open palm shape was more standard in early time, and Yin Fu's ox tongue palm developed within Yin's school. In the Shi lineage verses, verses 48.12 and 48.16 say that in the standard position the forward hand reaches out with an open tiger's mouth and the rear hand lies in ambush with an ox tongue palm.

Because the hands shapes differ does not mean they are unimportant, or that they can be done casually. Each branch of baguazhang has a hand shape that reflects the type of power that that branch uses. The wrapping power of Jiang style is completed with a willow leaf palm. The smooth power of Liang style is completed with an open palm. From that base, the hand shape changes constantly as it takes on the power flow of each different technique. A spiral hand completes a drilling up deflection. Whichever palm shape is the standard one for the branch, and the best one for the technique, it is important to get its particular power correct. Here are some of the hand shapes of various schools of baguazhang, each one gracefully expressing the power of its school.

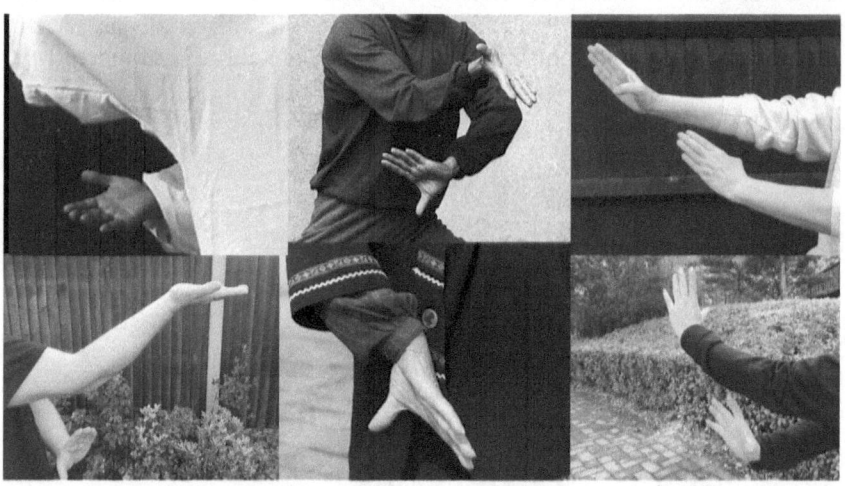

The separation of the middle and ring finger described in line two may be taken to mean that the index and middle fingers are together, and the ring and little fingers are together, which makes it a little like a Vulcan greeting, which doesn't make sense. All the fingers are spread, but we need to pay a bit of attention to keeping those two fingers separate. Li Ziming comments that the index and middle finger are more extended than the ring and little fingers, so the fingers naturally separate a bit, and the overall palm shape remains rounded. He also comments that the *Zhongchong* point (PC9) on the middle finger should not touch the *Guanchong* point (SJ1) on the ring finger, as this would block *qi* flow. This is because the PC9 point of middle finger, as the end of the pericardium meridian, is the final place of *qi* flowing out, and the SJ1 point of ring finger is the beginning of the Yang Triple Burner meridian, where the *qi* begins to flow in. This is just one commentary, though, and may be reading too much into a natural hand shape. It is a practical shape that sends power into the palm and palm edge and switches easily between striking and grabbing.

The wrist striking of baguazhang, which is one of its characteristic hits, comes quite early here in the verses. The equally characteristic use of the base of the palm, which is the end of the arm bone at the wrist, which makes the 'palm strike' so strong, is also described. A spearing palm, followed immediately by dropping into the base of the palm, requires baguazhang's cold power (see verse 48.08) and the ability to change techniques on the fly. This verse does not mention any change in the palm shape for those strikes, possibly assuming that people know.

This is the first mention of advancing and retreating with use of the half follow-up step (see also verses 36.24 and 48.03). Baguazhang practises long steps in straight line drills, using the follow-up step as a stealing step. The follow-up step of baguazhang is light, without sound, touching down and sending the body forward. All power is sent through the body to the striking segments, which have landed with the front foot. The final line describes how to add power and distance to the cold strike of the wrist or end of arm, charging in with full power coming from the waist and shoulder joints. It does not suggest leaning forward, but expanding through the waist and spine to lengthen and balance the power. Lengthen the waist means to expand up and out through the spine. The follow-up step gains any extra distance that is needed.

36.10.1   For the palm shape, brace the tiger's mouth so it is rounded,
掌　　形　　虎　　口　　要　　撑　　圆，
zhǎng xíng　hǔ　kǒu　yào　chēng yuán,

All but three sources have 撑圆 chēng yuán: 'brace in a rounded way'. Li, Wang, and Wu use 挣圆 zhèng yuán: '<u>open out</u> in a rounded way', the re-edited Li went back to 撑圆 chēng yuán: 'brace'. A specific use of 挣 zhèng is 'a power that opens to opposing sides to give a balanced power'. Both verbs describe a braced open thumb/forefinger web to give power to the palm. This line does not say 'spread the fingers open', only the tiger's mouth.

36.10.2   Spread the space between the middle and ring fingers.
中　　指　　无　　名　　缝　　开　　展。
zhōng zhǐ　wú　míng　fèng　kāi　zhǎn.

Most sources have this line, with slight variations. six (Huan, Li, Liu, Luo, Wu, and Zang) have 缝开展 fèng kāi zhǎn. Wang has 裂缝开 <u>liè</u> fèng kāi: and three (re-edited Li, Lin, Tu) have 缝裂开 fèng <u>liè</u> kāi, both meaning 'splitting open'. The meanings are the same, but kāi doesn't rhyme with yuán and zuān in the other lines, and the 'splitting' phrase doesn't say 'spreading' as specificially as it should.

36.10.3　　First poke then hit using the wrist bone,
先　　戳　　后　　打　　施　　腕　　骨，
xiān　chuō　hòu　dǎ　shī　wǎn　gǔ,

Four sources (Huan, Li, Liu, Luo) have 施腕骨 shī wǎn gǔ: 'use the wrist bone'. Six sources (re-edited Li, Lin, Tu, Wang, Wu, and Zang) have 使腕骨 shǐ wǎn gǔ: '<u>use</u> the wrist bone'. Both mean 'to use or employ', but 施 shī is a bit more definite. The only alternate version of the first phrase is Huan, 前戳后打 <u>qián</u> chōu hòu dǎ: 'poke <u>to the front</u> and hit to the rear'.

36.10.4　　Release the shoulder girdle and lengthen the waist, use a follow-up step to drill in.
松　　膀　　长　　腰　　跟　　步　　钻。
sōng　bǎng　cháng　yāo　gēn　bù　zuān.

Six sources have this line (Lin, Luo, Tu, Wang, Wu, and Zang). Most sources have 松膀 sōng bǎng: 'release the shoulder girdle', but Liu has 松胯 sōng kuà: 'release the <u>hips</u>'. In the final phrase, three sources (Huan, Li, and Liu) use 跟步躜, gēn bù <u>zuān</u>: '<u>dash</u> forward with a follow-up step', though the re-edited Li was made to agree with the others. The character 躜 zuān: 'rush', is less specific about what technique is being done, and describes the power well. The characters 躜 zuān and 钻 zuān are pronounced the same, so it is fun to speculate on which it was originally. To add to the confusion, the original character for 钻 zuān is 鑽, which looks a lot like 躜 except for the metal radical 金 instead of foot radical 足.

Eleven

上步合膝倒步掰，
换掌换步矮身骸。
进退退进随机势，
只须腰腿巧安排。

Gather the knees when stepping forward, brace them when reversing,
　　Lower the entire body to change palms and change stance.
To advance and retreat, retreat and advance, and take what opportunity presents,
　　You just need to skillfully arrange your waist and legs.

The Thirty-Six Verses 41

I call this verse *Koubu* and *Baibu* Stepping. It can be taken to explain the overall process of stepping to turn and move, and of the specific stepping in the first palm change. The term 換掌 huàn zhǎng: 'changing palms', is the term we use for the palm changes, which suggests this is referring to the specific first palm change, not just moving about. The footwork and lowering is exactly that of the first palm change in most schools – that is, basically a *koubu*, a *baibu*, and done. Stepping forward with the knees turned in with a *koubu* step, the reversing step is to what was the rear but is now the side, with a *baibu* step. In the palm change, the body is set down, and all movement to front or back is done this way. The waist and legs determine the size and direction of the turning, as the waist continues to turn with the *koubu* step, so that although the step is small (as described in other verses) the turn itself can be quite large. In either case, the body must lower to take the steps, otherwise it disconnects at the hips.

The last line serves to emphasize that all movement of the feet must be closely coordinated with the waist. The size and direction of the steps, how you turn the waist with them, and the power put into each, determine how you can put this stepping to use. In order to use the stepping pattern stated in lines one and two, to move freely, as stated in line three, you need to have practiced it diligently so that it works, as stated in line four. The turn, initiated by the rotation in the hip joint, which turns the thighs and feet, is taken further by the waist, and allows for even more turning in the second step. The turning and moving is accomplished not just by turning the feet – the waist initiates and completes the turn.

36.11.1 Gather the knees when stepping forward, brace them when reversing,

上	步	合	膝 (胯)	倒	步	掰,
shàng	bù	hé	xī (kuà)	dào	bù	bāi,

Five sources (Lin, Luo, Tu, Wang, and Wu) agree that the 膝 xī: 'knees' gather in. Four (Huan, Li, Liu, and Zang) put the gathering at the 胯 kuà: 'hip joints'. Any action in the knees comes from the hip joints, so this is more a case of emphasis rather than difference. This is the stepping pattern of *koubu* and *baibu* to turn around. The use of 上步 shàng bù: 'step forward', not 进步 jìn bù:'advance', describes a step through from the rear foot with a *koubu* step. The use also of 倒步 dào bù: 'reverse step', not 退步 tuì bù: 'retreat', indicates that the line is about turning around and going back, as in the first palm change. The use in the next line of 换掌换步 huàn zhǎng huàn bù: 'changing palms and changing steps', also suggests that this is about the use of *koubu* then *baibu* as in the first palm change.

Stepping back, the same word 掰 bāi: 'brace', or 'pry', as some used in verse 36.02, implies more of a strong setting than a turning opening. The power comes from the hips when pressing into the thighs as if trying to pry the knees apart. Huan says 倒步摆 dào bù *bǎi*: 'stepping back, open them'. Nowadays the word 摆 bǎi is commonly used for the opening out step, but Huan is the only one to have the term 摆 bǎi anywhere in the verses. Liang Shouyu has 倒步拿 dào bù *ná*: 'stepping back, set them', which is a firming up of the knees without the outwards connotation. Both these sources used their particular word in verse 36.01 instead of 掰 bāi, so it is intentional and the meaning is doubtless intended to be the same as in that verse. Both these sources say they are copied from Pei Xirong, so this is an interesting example of how copying is never quite just copied.

36.11.2   Lower the entire body to change palms and change stance.

换　　　掌　　　换　　　步　　　矮　　　身　　　骸。
huàn　zhǎng　huàn　bù　ǎi　shēn　hái.

Five sources (Lin, Luo, Tu, Wang, Zang) use 换步 huàn *bù*: 'change the footwork' or 'stance'. Four (Huan, Li, Liu, and Wu) use 换式 huàn *shì*: 'change the posture' or 'technique', which suggests it refers to a palm change.

36.11.3   To advance and retreat, retreat and advance, and take what opportunity presents,

进　　　退　　　退　　　进　　　随　　　机　　　势，
jìn　tuì　tuì　jìn　suí　jī　shì,

All sources have this exact wording. Here, the terms 进步 jìn bù: 'advance', and 退步 tuì bù: 'retreat' are used, so this is a further stepping skill that comes from the careful training.

36.11.4   You just need to skillfully arrange your waist and legs.

只　　　须　　　腰　　　腿　　　巧　　　安　　　排。
zhǐ　xū　yāo　tuǐ　qiǎo　ān　pái.

Most sources have 腰腿 yāo tuǐ: 'waist and legs'. Two differ slightly, Liu with 两腿 liǎng tuǐ: 'both legs', and Wu with reversed order 腿腰 tuǐ yāo: 'legs and waist'. In some branches 'waist and legs' means the hip joints, or what is between the waist and the legs, what connects them. Small adjustments need to be made through the hips to 1) keep the pelvis level when stepping, 2) lighten the legs to enable free movement, and 3) settle the *dantian* to keep mobility. That the 'arrangement' of the waist and legs refers to lifting in the waist, *dantian*, or hips, is indicated as it is specifically explained in 36.20, 36.21, and 36.29.

Three sources (Li, Liu, Zang) use 只要 zhǐ yào instead of 只须 zhǐ xū for 'you just need to'. This doesn't make any difference to the meaning, both mean 'must'. It may be trying to sort out 只须腰腿 zhǐ xū yāo tuǐ, which, if you didn't see the characters or perhaps missed the tone, you might think was 只须要腿 zhǐ xū yào tuǐ: 'you just need your legs to', instead of 'waist and legs'. Wu has 只凭 zhǐ píng: 'just count on', which solves this pronunciation difficulty.

Twelve

此掌与人大不同，
进步抬前乃有功。
退步还先退后足，
跨步尽外要离中。

This palm differs greatly from the others,
Our advancing step picks up the front foot, and so gets results.
Our retreating step first retreats the rear foot,
Our sidestep gets to the (opponent's) outside, away from the centre.

I call this verse Special Footwork. This verse starts a series of four verses that explain how baguazhang is 'not like the others'. The verses are not simply setting out methods and tactics, but setting out how these differ from other styles. In the late 1800s, when baguazhang flourished in Beijing, Xingyiquan, Taijiquan, Shaolinquan, Mizongquan, and other styles were well known in the area. These four verses point out the footwork, deep body work, body connection, and elusive tactics of 'this palm', or 'our style'. Nowadays, we recognize the similarities and differences between Xingyiquan, Taijiquan, and Baguazhang in particular, but in the late 1800s the body structure, power applications, techniques, tactics, routines – in fact, everything – were still being worked out. It is easy to take this for granted and forget how brilliant the men of the first generation were. Our palm does indeed differ greatly from the others, and there is good reason for the pride that sometimes shows itself in the verses.

This verse speaks of the skill of baguazhang in advancing, to always advance with the front foot first, then follow in with the rear foot, and in retreating, to step the rear foot back. This stepping gives speed, reach, agility, and power, and keeps the body stable and moving with the footwork. It says here that this is unique, but Xingyiquan for one does much the same thing. The point is not so much that the stepping is unique, but that a lot of thought and practice has been put into it. This footwork has been chosen as the most effective. Again and again in the verses, it is reiterated how all advancing, retreating, and dodging start from the footwork. Verse 48.35 adds some detail on how to step.

The term 跨步 kuà bù means to 'sidestep'. The exact step differs according to the situation. This verse describes how to do this step when one needs to step to the side. The usual dictionary meaning is 'to straddle something'. Stepping to the side is a sidestep with either the front or rear foot. In the verses it usually refers to a step around your opponent with a flanking step. This term is used in verses 48.20, 48.22, 48.28, and 48.43 with a clear meaning of stepping around to flank your adversary. It is often a longer step than the *koubu* step, which is used more for turning than charging in.

36.12.1 This palm (our style) differs greatly from the others,

此　　掌　　与　　人　　大　　不　　同，
cǐ　　zhǎng　yǔ　　rén　　dà　　bù　　tóng,

This line is agreed on by all but Liu, who uses the plural for people 此掌与众 cǐ zhǎng yǔ zhòng: 'the multitude', with the same meaning. 'This palm' refers to baguazhang as a style, not to any specific palm technique.

36.12.2 Our advancing step picks up the front foot, and so gets results.

进　　步　　抬　　前　　乃　　有　　功。
jìn　　bù　　tái　　qián　　nǎi　　yǒu　　gōng.

Again, all sources have this line except Liu, whose first phrase is 进步招前 jìn bù zhāo qián: 'advance to a move forward'.

36.12.3 Our retreating step first retreats the rear foot,

退　　步　　还　　先　　退　　后　　足，
tuì　　bù　　hái　　xiān　　tuì　　hòu　　zǔ,

Most sources have this exact wording. Liu and Luo use the word 'must' (退步还须 tuì bù hái xū, 退步需先 tuì bù xū xiān respectively), but this does not fit so well here, as this verse is descriptive of what the style does, it is not telling you what to do.

36.12.4 Our sidestep gets to the (opponent's) outside, away from the centre.

跨　　步　　尽　　外　　要　　离　　中。
kuà　　bù　　jǐn　　wài　　yào　　lí　　zhōng.

All sources have this exact line. Verse 48.20 corrects a misunderstanding perhaps caused by the use of 尽 jǐn: 'as much as possible' in this line, of going too far away with the sidestep. Grammatically, 'as much as possible' here means 'as much as you can, get to the outside', and not 'get as much to the outside as you can'.

Thirteen

此掌与人大不同，
手未动兮膀先攻。
未从前伸先后缩，
吸足再吐力独丰。

This palm differs greatly from the others,
The shoulder girdle takes the offensive before the hand has moved.
Before extending forward, first gather back,
When you breathe in fully then 'spit' it out you have our unique and plentiful power.

I call this verse Special Deep Power. It is again explaining that the arms do not work alone. The hands are sent out by the breath, body, and shoulders, they move by being pushed forward from the lower body and the shoulder girdle – the root of the hands – as described in verse 36.06. Sometimes people act as if the shoulders are where the collarbone connects to the scapula, or as if the deltoids did the main work of striking and throwing. Baguazhang operates the shoulder as a large unit that includes the entire structure through the chest, upper back, and upper arm, connected down to the lower back. The settling and opening of the shoulders described in verses 36.01, 36.07, and 36.10 are key to this power.

The power is gathered naturally deep inside the body, not with a large sucking action that telegraphs your intentions. The last line clarifies that it does not mean to telegraph a movement by drawing back. It means to draw power in, storing kinetic energy for a release of power, 'breathing' power (not air) into the *dantian* area.

36.13.1   This palm (our style) differs greatly from the others.

此	掌	与	人	大	不	同,
cǐ	zhǎng	yǔ	rén	dà	bù	tóng

Most sources have this line, except Luo, who was a bit less repetitive, with 又不同 yòu bù tóng: '<u>also</u> not the same', and Liu, who again has the plural for 人 rén: person – 众 zhòng: '<u>the multitude</u>'.

36.13.2　　The shoulder girdle /upper arm takes the offensive before the hand has moved.

手	未	动	兮	膀	先	攻。
shǒu	wèi	dòng	xī	bǎng	xiān	gōng.

Most sources have this wording, except Liu, who has 腰先功 yāo xiān gōng: 'the waist first works', perhaps meaning 'gets to work', or 'needs to have skill', but perhaps a typo.

36.13.3　　Before extending forward, first gather back,

未	从	前	伸	先	后	缩，
wèi	cóng	qián	shēn	xiān	hòu	suō,

Five sources (Li, Liu, Luo, Wu, and Zang) have this line. Wang (and Liu Jingru) have a reversed order of a couple of words 未从伸前 wèi cóng shēn qián, without changing the meaning. Lin and Tu have the phrase 未曾前伸 wèi céng qián shēn: 'before extending forward'. Huan has a more specific term for the gathering back 先宛蓄 wǎn xù: 'wind up and store up', also meaning a gathering movement before a strike. The power, to be delivered from the roots to the tips, must first be gathered in the roots.

36.13.4　　When you breathe in fully then 'spit' it out you have our unique and plentiful power.

吸	足	再	吐	力	独	丰。
xī	zú	zài	tǔ	lì	dú	fēng.

Most sources have this line. For the final phrase, Wu has 力足丰 lì zú fēng: 'power is fully plentiful'. Liu has 力能半 lì néng bàn: 'the strength is halved'. This doesn't rhyme, and really mean the opposite, but could be taken to mean 'the power effort is halved for the same result'. Liu also uses the more common 发力 fā lì, but this doesn't fit the four/three beat of the line. The line is 吸足再吐: 'first gather in and then spit out' followed by the result of 力独丰 lì dú fēng: 'the power is plentiful'.

Fourteen

此掌与人大不同，
前掌后掌力相通。
欲使梢兮先动根，
招招如是不得松。

This palm differs greatly from the others,
The power connects between the front and rear palms.
To use the tip, first move its root,
All techniques must be thus – do not neglect any.

I call this verse Special Connections. It explains whole body power, with the connection through from the body to the hands, and between the hands. It refers to the connection between the hands through the body, and especially the upper back and shoulder girdle, explained in earlier verses. It adds the concept, held in common with Xingyiquan in particular, of dividing the body into segments made up of roots, trunk, and branches/tips. In the whole body, the feet are the roots, the torso is the trunk, and the arms are the branches. Each of these three segments can also be divided into three. In the torso, the *dantian* is the root, the heart area is the trunk, and the head is the tip. In the upper limbs, the shoulders are the roots, the elbow the trunk, and the hands the tip. In the lower limbs, the hips are the root, the knees the trunk, and the feet the tips. In baguazhang, the root, or proximal end, of a segment gives power to move the tip, or distal end, of the segment. Our focus cannot relax, or forget, to keep this connection from the ground, through the body, and out to the hands, in training all techniques.

On a general level, this power connection is applied in other martial arts. The rear palm should always be doing something that aids the power output and direction of the front hand. For instance, a teacher or judge always looks at the left hand during a sword routine to see if the line of power is correct through the sword. The feeling here is a bit more than that. The phrase 相通 xiāng tōng: 'connect' literally means connected like two rooms are connected by a

mutual doorway. The figurative sense is thus connected as if there were a communicating doorway – the upper back. This, combined with the dragon-body connection described in verses 36.22 and 36.24, connects the feet through to the hands.

36.14.1   This palm (our style) differs greatly from the others,

此　　掌　　与　　人　　大　　不　　同，
cǐ　　zhǎng　　yǔ　　rén　　dà　　bù　　tóng,

Most sources have this line, except those who were more literary. Luo, less repetitive, has 还不同 hái bù tóng: 'as well'. And Liu again had the plural, repeating 此掌与众: cǐ zhǎng yǔ zhòng: 'the multitude'.

36.14.2   The power connects between the front and rear palms.

前　　掌　　后　　掌　　力　　相　　通。
qián　zhǎng　hòu　zhǎng　lì　xiāng　tōng.

Six sources (Huan, Lin, Liu, Luo, Tu, Wang) have this line. Wu and Zang have 前掌后手 qián zhǎng hòu shǒu: 'the front palm and the rear hand'. Li has 前手后手 qián shǒu hòu shǒu: 'the front hand and the rear hand' (and both were changed to 'palm' in the re-edited Li). These don't change the meaning at all.

36.14.3   To use the tip, first move its root,

欲　　使　　梢　　兮　　先　　动　　根，
yù　　shǐ　　shāo　　xī　　xiān　　dòng　　gēn,

Five sources (Huan, Li, Lin, Luo, and Wang) have this line. Liu and Luo use 先动跟: xiān dòng gēn: 'first move the heel'. This puts the root more specifically at the heel of the foot, which is the root of the whole body. Both are correct (though I suspect accidentally, in a convenient typo), as the use of the roots includes both the connection through of the whole body and the connections through the segments. Liu, Tu, Wu, and Zang have 欲使稍兮 yù shǐ shāo xī: 'to use a trifle', which I suspect is a typo.

36.14.4   All techniques must be thus – do not neglect any.

招　　招　　如　　是　　不　　得　　松。
zhāo　zhāo　rú　shí　bù　dé　sòng.

Seven sources (Huan, Li, Lin, Luo, Tu, Wu, and Zang) have these exact words. Wang has 不能松 bù néng sòng: 'cannot slacken', to give the same meaning. Liu has an odd version, 粘黏如是: zhān nián rú shì: 'adhere and stick like this', which doesn't seem to fit the context here, and is not as inclusive.

Fifteen

此掌与人大不同，
未击西兮先声东。
指上打下孰得知，
卷珠倒流更神通。

This palm differs greatly from the others,
Before hitting to the West we first make noise in the East.
Pointing high and hitting low – who can figure us out,
Rolling up (a hanging curtain of) pearls and flowing in reverse is even more remarkable.

I call this verse Special Tactics. Other styles may make use of some of these tactics, as indeed they are not unknown or new. The special tactic of baguazhang is to be unpredictable – if anything can be predicted, it is that baguazhang will borrow and take advantage of any difficult situation. A old novel referred to baguazhang as a school "of dark deeds", with descriptions such as "others will have held off well before the extreme to which bagua fighters will go", and "bagua fighters win by all means fair or foul, martial artists see them and hang back in alarm."[24]

Attack and defense are not as distinct as they may be in other styles. The tactic of making noise in the East and striking to the West is to throw a feint or a real hit to one area to draw attention there, followed closely by an attack to another area. It could be a number of real (not necessarily fake) kicks to the thigh to make your opponent wary of his leg, and then an attack to the head. This tactic is not unique to baguazhang, indeed it is one of the thirty-six stratagems, known as Make Noise in the East and Attack the West or Threaten the East and Strike to the West. The word 聲 shēng: 'sound' is often used interchangeably with the word 響 xiǎng: 'make noise' in this case. When you appear to attack in one area, the enemy focuses his defenses there, leaving you free to pick and chose your target, which may well be the same place. Verse 48.29 gives a warning to watch out for this. In his book on applications, Yan Dehua often used the word 'sounding' for hitting, not faking. In his book on sword and spear methods, Ming dynasty general Wang Minghe also used 'make noise' for both, writing "only the very skilled can make the distinction between making noise and then entering, and entering and then making noise."[25] Feinting is such an well known tactic that it is important to use the feint as a real attack if the opportunity presents.

The tactic of 'pointing high and hitting low' may be a normal feint and attack, or a fake telegraphing, which is common to many styles, but particularly effective in baguazhang because of the elusive footwork. The feint does not need to continue as a feint if it gets in. Because of the ability of baguazhang to change instantly, it can turn into the real attack, or a double attack. If the opponent assumes it to be a feint and ignores it, they are in trouble. Because it is used here linked with other tactics, and this phrase uses the same verbs 指 zhǐ: 'point' and 打 dǎ: 'hit', this may be the tactic of Pointing to the Mountain to Get the Millstone, referred to later in verses 36.32 and 48.18. If so, it does suggest that this tactic is going high then low.

The tactic of 'rolling up' and 'flowing in reverse' refers to a shaking power that comes up from below, or a counter attack that responds by partially absorbing, then coming back strongly. A rolled hanging curtain drops down naturally, but needs effort to be rolled up, so the name of this skill/tactic implies that it is a trained skill that does not come easily. The phrase 卷珠 juǎn zhū: 'roll up pearls' is the standard shorthand reference for 珍珠倒卷帘 zhēn zhū dào juǎn lián: 'furl the precious pearl curtain'. The 'pearls' can be thought of as balls of *qi*. The ability to absorb and shoot back, returning the power of an attack, is needed to use this tactic effectively. In any method that uses elasticity and sensitivity, it is common to think of it more as a '*qi*' method than a 'strength' or 'skill' method.

It helps to think of the suck of the tide and the crash of breakers on the shore – it is hard to resist either. In this verse the tactic refers to a deflection or absorption and a reversal of direction instantaneously and coming back with an attack. In baguazhang, this reversal can involve stepping, or just a reversal through the body.

36.15.1   This palm (our style) differs greatly from the others,
此　　掌　　与　　人　　大　　不　　同，
cǐ　　zhǎng　　yǔ　　rén　　dà　　bù　　tóng,

All sources have this line, except again those who are more literary. Luo, less repetitive, uses 也不同 yě bù tóng: '<u>also</u> not the same'. And Liu, once again with the plural 此掌与众: cǐ zhǎng yǔ <u>zhòng</u>: '<u>the multitude</u>'.

36.15.2   Before hitting to the West first make noise in the East.
未　　击　　西　　兮　　先　　声　　东。
wèi　　jī　　xī　　xī　　xiān　　shēng　　dōng.

All sources have this line. As the sixth of the thirty-six stratagems, 声东击西 shēng dōng jī xī: Make Noise in the East and Attack on the West, is a well known phrase to any martial artist in China.

36.15.3 Pointing high and hitting low, who can figure us out,
指　　　上　　　打　　　下　　　孰　　　得　　　知，
zhǐ　　shàng　　dǎ　　　xià　　shú　　　dé　　　zhī,

Five sources (Li, Lin, Liu, Tu, and Zang) have with this line. Huan and Wu use more simple language, with 谁得知 shéi dé zhī: 'who can figure us out'. Luo seems to have a slightly different take (or typo), with 指上打击就得知 zhǐ shàng dǎ jī jiù dé zhī: 'point high and hit, we simply know how'. Wang also has the final phrase 就得知 jiù dé zhī: 'we simply know how'.

36.15.4 Rolling up (a hanging curtain of) pearls and flowing in reverse is even more remarkable.
卷　　　珠　　　倒　　　流　　　更　　　神　　　通。
juǎn　　zhū　　dào　　liú　　gèng　　shén　　tōng.

Four sources have this line (Huan, Li, Luo, Zang). The others have a slightly different version of the 'rolling up pearls'. Wang has 卷廉 juǎn lián: 'roll up the side walls in a traditional courtyard house'. The re-edited Li, Lin, Tu, and Wu have 卷帘 juǎn lián: 'roll up a hanging curtain'. Liu has used the traditional character for the verb 捲 juǎn, instead of the character 卷 juǎn, but the sources printed in traditional characters just have 卷 juǎn, as that is the usual reference to this technique. All of these are the old style hanging blinds, like what we still have in rolled bamboo hangings. All of these variants are descriptive of the feeling and tactic. As I mentioned above, the phrase 卷珠 juǎn zhū: 'roll up pearls' is a shorthand.

Sixteen

天然精术怕三穿，
不走外门是枉然。
他走外兮我走内，
伸手而得不费难。

Even skilled martial artists fear the triple spearing palms,
It is more effective if I move to his outside doorway.
But if he moves to my outside I move to his inside,
Extending my hand I easily get what I want.

I call this verse Triple Spearing Palm Strikes, which is easier to say in Chinese – *san chuan*. Baguazhang places particular emphasis on the spearing palm, and practises this skill to become quite fearsome. A spearing palm has a longer reach than a punch, can get through a smaller space, and can change more easily to a different strike. The triple spearing palm is, of course, even nastier than just one. Because of the connection through the hands and the placement, one comes after the other with no pause at all. Triple strikes do not need to be alternating hands – there is no set pattern. The triple spearing palm can be alternate hands or the same hand charging in, and the spearing palm does not need to be a finger strike – the entire arm can make contact.

This verse emphasizes that the footwork is vital to effective spearing strikes, and especially trying to step a bit to the outside to slide the technique in along your opponent's off side. The body, shoulder, and arm technique of the spearing palm has been explained in verses 36.05, 36.06, 36.10, 36.13, and 36.14. Doorways are further described in verse 48.31.

As Cao explains triple spearing palms in his 1942 book, "Advance your body to his inside door, inside his oncoming arm, to hit his chest. If you get into his outside door then you can push his back or armpit with one or both arms."[26]

The 'outside doorway' or 'outer door' is the offside of the outstretched arm (i.e. if his left arm is forward you would move to your right side, his left side, to be on the outside of his left arm), outside his legs. This puts the strike into the ribs or armpit, or over the arm to the neck and face. The 'inside doorway' or 'inner door' is inside his outstretched arm or in between his legs.

Yan Dehua's drawings show the entrances to the opponent. The first is through the outer door and the second is the inner door. As you can see, it is the footwork that is key – the hands might go to the outside or inside as opportunity presents.

OUTSIDE

INSIDE

The Thirty-Six Verses

The third line is important in emphasizing that tactics need to change according to the situation, and to be not quite so predictable. Even if we prefer to go to the outside, sometimes we have to go inside. Because of the triangulation of the hands, while continuing to alternate spearing palms, even on the inside one arm will deflect so the other arm can still get in. If the footwork and technique are both effective, there should be no problem. This is further explained in verse 36.17.

The fourth line uses the phrase 'just extend the hand', which comes up fairly often – 'just reach out', 'just go straight' – indicating the ease with which one hits the desired target when one's footwork is effective.

36.16.1 Even skilled martial artists fear the triple spearing palms,

天　　然　　精　　术　　怕　　三　　穿，
tiān　rán　jīng　shù　pà　sān　chuān,

All main sources have this wording. Liu Jingru has 天下精术 tiān xià jīng shù: 'all (all under heaven) skilled martial artists'.

36.16.2 It is more effective if I move to his outside door.

不　　走　　外　　门　　是　　柱　　然。
bù　zǒu　wài　mén　shì　wǎng　rán.

Almost all sources have this line, which is stated in the negative 'If I don't move to his outside door it is ineffective'. This could also be translated as 'if I don't get to his outside door I am less effective'. Chinese grammar has no problems with the double negative. Liu has 不是穿外 bù shì chuān wài: 'if you don't spear to the outside'.

36.16.3 But if he moves to my outside I move to his inside,

他　　走　　外　　兮　　我　　走　　内，
tā　zǒu　wài　xī　wǒ　zǒu　nèi,

Six sources (Huan, Li, Lin, Luo, Tu, Wang) have this line. Wu and Zang have 我穿内 wǒ chuān nèi : 'I spear to his inside'. Liu has 彼走外兮我穿内 bǐ zǒu wài xī wǒ chuān nèi: 'if he moves to the outside I spear to the inside'. The line is discussing footwork, and the spearing technique is understood, so the change does not improve on the more standard line.

36.16.4 Extending my hand I easily get what I want.

伸　　手　　而　　得　　不　　费　　难。
shēn　shǒu　ér　dé　bù　fèi　nán.

All sources have this line this except Wang, who has 伸有而得 shēn yǒu ér dé: 'extend and have and get', and I suspect a typo.

Seventeen

掌使一面不为功，
至少仍须两面通。
一横一直三角手，
使人如在我怀中。

Being only able to use one side of the hand is incompetent,
You need to be thoroughly proficient on at least two sides.
With one across and one straight, the hands triangulate,
    It is as if I embrace my adversary to my breast.

I call this verse Triangulation. The use of arcing stepping is important in baguazhang, and people often mistake the circle-walking to mean that all techniques are done in circles. Most techniques can go straight out easily from the triangulated position described in the first two lines, the footwork determining whether you arc around, wedge in, move off, or change sides. Your adversary is under your control without over extending yourself.

Each body part can be divided into four sides, and should be able to take care of four directions – front, back, left, and right – with coordination and balance between them. Only using the palm edge to cut out or only using the spearing palm to stab forward isn't using the hands to their full abilities. Baguazhang has many more techniques than that. The hands, and by assumption other body parts, must be able to strike with at least two of their sides, which means with different techniques and power flow. The idea that we need to be able to switch back and forth equally on both sides has already been dealt with in verse 36.04, so this verse is most likely specifically with using the arms and hands differently, with fingers, palms, heels, edges, wrists, etc.

Triangulation places the hands in the *qian kun,* or heaven and earth, position further explained in verse 36.27: one forward one back, one hard one pliant, one high one low, one straight one slightly crossing, and always ready to reverse that placement and power. The power between the hands is also balanced between the crossing and straight, wrapping through the back. The position Old Monk Begs for Alms is an on guard position that uses this triangulation and segues easily into other techniques (as do Dragon Stretches its Talons and Ask the Way Leaning on a Horse, though slightly less so). The arm position is both like embracing and gives you the control and opportunity as if your opponent is already in your arms. This position sets up the hands for a variety of counters and attacks, one of which is the spearing strike. The use of the shoulders to send the hands forward ensures that the hands often just switch places and remain in triangulation, ready for the next strike. This image shows a version of the triangulation.

36.17.1   Being only able to use one side of the hand is incompetent,

掌	使	一	面	不	为	功,
zhǎng	shǐ	yī	miàn	bù	wéi	gōng,

All sources have this line.

36.17.2   You need to be thoroughly proficient on at least two sides.

至	少	仍	须	两	面	通。
zhì	shǎo	réng	xū	liǎng	miàn	tōng.

Five sources (Huan, re-edited Li, Lin, Luo, Tu) have this line. Four sources (Li, Liu, Wu, and Zang) differ with 两面攻 liǎng miàn gōng: 'you must attack with two sides'. Wang has 四面通 sì miàn tōng: '<u>four</u> sides'.

There are also minor differences in the grammar of how to say 'you must at least'. Wang has 致少仍需 zhì shǎo réng xū, and Huan has 至少应该 zhì shǎo <u>yīng gāi</u>.

36.17.3   With one across and one straight, the hands triangulate,

一	横	一	直	三	角	手,
yī	héng	yī	zhí	sān	jiǎo	shǒu,

Most sources have this line. Only Liu differs, with 三穿手 sān <u>chuān</u> shǒu: 'triple <u>spearing</u> hands', which is not, I think, what was intended. The previous verse just dealt with the spearing hands, which can shoot out from this position.

36.17.4   It is as if I embrace my adversary to my breast.

使	人	如	在	我	怀	中。
shǐ	rén	rú	zài	wǒ	huái	zhōng.

Seven sources (Li, Lin, Luo, Tu, Wang, Wu, and Zang) have these exact words. Huan has 自怀中 zì huái zhōng: 'in my breast' (自 zì is less colloquial than 我 wǒ, but both mean 'oneself'). Liu 使人必在 shǐ rén bì zài: 'my adversary must be, instead of 'it is as if my adversary is'.

Eighteen

高欲低兮矮欲扬，
斜身绕步不须忙。
斜翻倒翻腰着力，
翻到极处力要刚。

When high prepare to lower, when low prepare to rise,
If you angle the body and step around, you don't need to rush.
Use the power of the waist to roll at angles and wheel back,
When you turn to the furthest reach (of your waist), then use hard power.

I call this verse Waist Power. It speaks of always being ready to go in any direction, and being prepared to apply full power in extremity. The waist must be trained in many dimensions – it does not simply turn with the footwork. Once you can't turn any more, or once you are put in extremis, it is time to go in hard, so the waist must be strong. Your power is the greater from having turned to the fullest, if this is well trained. Combined with the stepping, the power all comes from the waist. Baguazhang uses a pliant turning power while moving to control, and a hard power to finish the job. This verse gives a good reason for the deep training of the waist of baguazhang, as this tactic only works with a strong waist. In the next verses the use of hardness and pliancy, which enables this variability in the waist, is explained.

It may also be understood as 'when the opponent is tall, go low, and when the opponent is short, go high' – the tactic of going for a tall person under their guard and going for a short person over it, instead of adjusting to their height to square up properly. The necessity and ability to move like this is not a new concept – the Book of the Chang Clan Martial Skills, from the late 1700s, describes it clearly, using similar wording. "If they attack with *yin* I counter with *yang*. If they attack with *yang* I counter with *yin*. A high attack I return low. A low attack I return high. An attack from the side I return straight on. A straight on attack I return at the side. Like this I and twist and turn, rotating back and forth. I invariably win this way."[27] This tactic is also explained in verse 48.13.

The phrase 斜翻 xié shēn: 'roll at angles' means to turn the body at an angle to the opponent, neither square on nor completely sideways. Cao Zhongsheng, in 1942, defined *xieshen* as "the front door of your body is presented at an angle to your opponent."[28] In addition, baguazhang uses agile footwork to get where we want to be and more easily control our opponent before they figure out quite what we are doing.

36.18.1   When high prepare to lower, when low prepare to rise,

高	欲	低	兮	矮	欲	扬，
gāo	yù	dī	xī	ǎi	yù	yáng,

All sources agree on the general structure of this line. Six sources (Li, Lin, Luo, Tu, Wu, and Zang) have these exact words. Two sources (Huan, Wang) have the more common and easier to write 与 yǔ: 'give, offer' instead of 欲 yù: 'about to, on the point of', or 'want to'. Huan repeats the 低 dī: 低与扬 dī yù yáng: 'low offer rising'. Liu has 短与扬 duǎn yù yáng: 'short offer rising' instead of 'short in stature'.

Because Chinese does not need a subject in the sentence, this line could refer to you or to your opponent, which allows the alternate translation mentioned above.

36.18.2   If you angle the body and step around, you don't need to rush.

斜	身	绕	步	不	须	忙。
xié	shēn	rào	bù	bù	xū	máng.

All but one source have these exact words. Huan has 抽手绕步 chōu shǒu rào bù: 'gather the hand and step around', instead of 斜身 xié shēn, 'take the body to the angle'. The stepping around is key, and the overall effect and meaning doesn't really change. Huan has 不用忙 bù yòng máng, which means the same thing as 不须忙 bù xū máng, and is just the way people usually say 'no need to fuss' rather than write it.

36.18.3   Use the power of the waist to roll at angles and wheel back,

斜	翻	倒	翻	腰	着(著)	力，
xié	fān	dǎo	fān	yāo	zhuó	lì,

All sources have this line. The character 著 zhuó is the traditional character of 着 zhuó, which some writers, even those using modern characters, prefer.

The use of 翻 fān: 'roll' or 'wheel', for turning implies a rolling turn – a turn that uses more than one plane – not a simple rotation. This roll is commonly used in baguazhang, and much less commonly used in other styles.

36.18.4   When you turn to the furthest reach (of your waist), then use hard power.

翻　　到　　极　　处　　力　　要　　刚。
fān　　dào　　jí　　chù　　lì　　yào　　gāng.

All sources have this line. The characters 力 lì: 'strength' and 劲 jìn: 'power' are often used interchangeably in Chinese texts for 'trained power'. The character 力 lì: 'strength' does not refer to brute or untrained strength in this context.

Nineteen

人道掌法胜在刚，
郭老曾言柔内藏。
个中也有人知味，
刚柔相济是所长。

People say that our palm wins by its hard strikes,
Guo the elder used to say that pliancy is hidden inside.
There are some who understand this flavour (secret),
That our real forte is hardness and pliancy working together.

    I call this verse Hard and Pliant. The previous verse suggested that a hard strike often wins the fight. This verse acknowledges that, and presents something a bit more subtle. The amount of agreement on the exact wording of this verse shows the importance in the system of combining hard and pliant power. One of the special ways of baguazhang is to move with pliancy but to hit hard. This verse is the first of a series of verses that reflect on the blending of hardness and pliancy by which baguazhang operates. In general, the verses recommend pliant defense seguing smoothly into hard offense.

    There is a difference of opinion among commentators over who exactly 'Guo the elder' was. Li, Wu, and Zang note that 'Guo the elder' was Guo Jiyuan 郭济元, from Zhaoyuan in Shandong province. Huan notes that this Guo was the third martial uncle of Dong Haichuan, but Wu and Zang note that he was a contemporary of Dong Haichuan. Zang also quoted Dong Haichuan as saying 'Guo the elder' said "Everyone who is good at this palm understands the principles of hardness and pliancy. When you get to the stage of combining and coordinating the two, that is the most enjoyable level."[29] This uncle would not have done baguazhang, as Dong created it, but

Dong could have learned this principle from him. Looking at the language of the verse, Dong Haichuan could refer to a martial uncle as 郭老 guō lǎo: 'Guo the elder'. A contemporary he would have more likely call 老郭 lǎo guō: 'old Guo', a term of friendship. Against these identifications – normally one quotes famous people, or at least someone that the intended audience would know.

Liu and Tu think 'Guo the elder' refers to Guo Yunshen 郭云深 (1820-1901), also called Yusheng 峪生, the famous Xingyi master from Hebei province. When he moved to Beijing he became friends with Dong Haichuan, and they exchanged ideas that further developed both their styles. Jiang Rongqiao, in his book on Taijiquan, suggested that Guo Yunshen had a great deal of influence on Baguazhang, more than what is normally thought.[30] On the side of this identification, who better to quote on hardness and pliancy than a master of Xingyiquan, famous for his hard half-step driving punch? It would be saying, even the hardest of the hard men, the great Guo Yunshen, says that pliancy is hidden inside. Against it, this goes against the traditional knowledge. Also is the reference to 郭老 guō lǎo: 'Guo the elder'. This is a term used for at least one generation up from you, and Dong Haichuan (1813-1882) would not refer to a friend in this way. But the person who wrote down the verses, Zeng Zengqi, would refer to Guo Yunshen with this term, even if it meant changing what exactly Dong had said. Overall, this is maybe who the quote should be from, but wishing doesn't make it so.

36.19.1   People say that our palm wins by its hard strikes,
人　　道　　掌　　法　　胜　　在　　刚,
rén　　dào　　zhǎng　　fǎ　　shèng　　zài　　gāng,

All sources have this line. In verses 36.12, 36.13, 36.14, and 36.15, baguazhang is referred to as 此掌 cǐ zhǎng: 'this palm'. Here it is simply 掌法 zhǎng fǎ: 'palm methods'.

36.19.2   Guo the elder used to say that pliancy is hidden inside.
郭　　老　　曾　　言　　柔　　内　　藏。
guō　　lǎo　　céng　　yán　　róu　　nèi　　cáng.

Most sources have this line. Two minor differences are Lin, who has 柔内存 róu nèi cún: 'pliancy is <u>accumulated</u> within', and Liang Shouyu, who has 拳经曾言 quán jīng céng yán: '<u>the classics</u> say' instead 'Guo the elder says'.

36.19.3   There are some who know this flavour (secret),
个　　中　　也　　有　　人　　知　　味,
gè　　zhōng　　yě　　yǒu　　rén　　zhī　　wèi,

All sources have this line.

36.19.4　　That our real forte is hardness and pliancy working together.

刚　　柔　　相　　济　　是　　所　　长。
gāng　róu　xiāng　jì　shì　suǒ　cháng.

Most sources have this line. Only Huan differs slightly in the final phrase, with 是拳长 shì quán cháng: 'is the forte of this style' (if I copied it correctly).

Twenty

刚在先兮柔内藏,
柔在先兮刚后张。
他人之柔腰与手,
我则腰吸步稳扬。

When hardness is foremost, pliancy is hiding within,
When pliancy is foremost, hardness is drawing back.
The pliancy of others is in their waist and hands,
But we suck in the waist and our footwork is stable and agile.

  I call this verse Hardness and Pliancy in the Waist and Footwork. It refers to general principles and mechanics. It can also refer literally to the on guard posture of *qian kun* hands – the forward hand appearing hard and the rear hand appearing pliant, but the power actually the reverse, both ready to switch places at any time (described in verses 36.05, 36.06, 36.13, and 36.17). The preparation for the hard hit comes from within the pliancy, and the ability to be softly effective relies on the firmness behind, as explained in the previous verse. The two first lines explain the principle of *yin* and *yang* that permeates the whole body – each is within the other and each supports the other.

  The general meaning is that other styles may understand a bit about using pliancy or hardness, but baguazhang differs in two aspects. One, baguazhang connects pliant power through to the feet, and maintains firm stepping while alternating between hardness and pliancy. Two, baguazhang does not simply relax the waist, keeping the whole body pliant, but gathers power into the waist. In this way, a soft circling deflection can becomes a hard direct strike with no apparent preparation. This is referred to as a key power in verses 48.42 and 48.43. Sucking in the waist in further explained in verses 36.11, 36.21, and 36.29. It is understood variously as drawing in the hip joints, raising inside the *dantian*, or drawing back the body, depending on the circumstances.

36.20.1   When hardness is foremost, pliancy is hiding within,

刚	在	先	兮	柔	内(后)	藏,
gāng	zài	xiān	xī	róu	nèi (hòu)	cáng,

There is a split between the sources on whether pliancy is hidden 'inside' or 'behind'. Four sources (Lin, Tu, Wang, and Wu) use 内 nèi : 'inside' and five (Huan, Li, Liu, Luo, Zang) use 后 hòu: 'behind'. Lin also has 柔内存 róu nèi cún: 'pliancy is <u>contained</u> inside', which is in the same vein. Some think of pliant power gathering in, and some think of it as gathering back, but in any case, power gathers to be able to shoot out hard.

36.20.2   When pliancy is foremost, hardness is drawing back.

柔	在	先	兮	刚	后	张。
róu	zài	xiān	xī	gāng	hòu	zhāng.

All sources have this line.

36.20.3   The pliancy of others is in their waist and hands,

他	人	之	柔	腰	与	手,
tā	rén	zhī	róu	yāo	yù	shǒu,

All but one source have this exact line. Huan has 他人只有腰与手 tā rén <u>zhǐ yǒu</u> yāo yù shǒu: 'he <u>only has</u> his waist and hands'.

36.20.4   But we suck in the waist and our footwork is stable and agile.

我	则	腰	吸	步	稳	扬。
wǒ	zé	yāo	xī	bù	wěn	yáng.

Six sources (Huan, Lin, Liu, Tu, Wu, and Zang, but plus two more if one counts the re-edited Li and Zhang Quanliang) have the order 我则腰吸 wǒ zé yāo xī: 'we then, at the waist, suck in'. This order balances the line with its following noun-verb phrase – 步稳扬 bù wěn yáng: 'footwork is stable and agile'. Three sources (Li, Luo, and Wang) have the order 我则吸腰 wǒ zé <u>xī yāo</u>: 'we then <u>suck in the waist</u>', which is the more normal order one would say this phrase. This is a grammatical rather than an informational difference.

Twenty-one

用到极处须转身，
脱身化影不留痕。
如何变幻端在步，
出入进退腰先伸。

When you have gone to the fullest you must turn the body,
Shed the body and trade it for a shadow without leaving a trace.
How we change unpredictably is all in the footwork,
Going in and out, back and forth – the waist first extends.

I call this verse Trade the Body for a Shadow. It emphasizes once again that effectiveness calls for the combined skill and power of the waist and the footwork. The first line refers to your technique or application reaching as far as it can usefully go, when you must change it. The changeability is one of the characteristics of baguazhang. When you take a step, the body does not go along passively, but 'first extends' – that is, it leads the step, though without leaning or losing stability. This is more apparent with weapons play, as the weapon extends before the final foot push off, so that the body follows it. To be able to step well and with power, the waist needs to remain level and under control, but still lively. In verse 36.29 the term 提腰 tí yāo: 'lift the waist' is used. Here, 伸腰 shēn yāo: 'extend the waist' is used. Specifically, 'lift' usually refers to a slight lightening for agile stepping or kicking, and 'extend' usually refers to a slight expansion to transfer power on stepping. This is how you can suddenly disappear and appear beside someone like their shadow.

The phrase 脱身化影 tuō shēn huà yǐng: 'shed the body and trade it for a shadow', is commonly used in baguazhang, both in movement names and as a descriptor of the stepping and techniques. It is a wonderfully descriptive phrase, worthy of the speed and elusiveness of baguazhang stepping, and is further explained in verse 48.19. It should be one of the thirty-six stratagems, but it is not. It is to complete an attack and disappear, not to run away, but rather to appear instantaneously nearby for the next attack. The image includes both the elusiveness and the stickiness of a shadow. No matter how hard you try, you cannot escape your shadow, nor can you hit it.

The Thirty-Six Verses

36.21.1 When you have gone to the fullest you must turn the body,

用	到	极	处	须	转	身，
yòng	dào	jí	chù	xū	zhuàn	shēn,

Most sources have this exact line. For the action Luo has 撤转身 <u>chè</u> zhuàn shēn: '<u>withdraw</u> and turn the body', an interesting detail.

36.21.2 Shed the body and trade it for a shadow without leaving a trace.

脱	身	化	影	不	留	痕。
tuō	shēn	huà	yǐng	bù	liú	hén.

Almost all sources have this line. An outlier, Liu Jialin, has 脱身幻影 tuō shēn <u>huàn</u> yǐng: 'shed the body for an <u>unreal</u> image', which is also evocative. The phrase 脱身 tuō shēn: 'shed the body' implies the speed and elusiveness of the escape. The phrase 化影 huà yǐng: 'become a shadow' implies the continued attachment to the opponent. Wang has probably a typo, with 不面痕 bù <u>miàn</u> hén: 'with no <u>face</u> trace'.

36.21.3 How we change unpredictably is all in the footwork,

如	何	变	幻	端	在	步，
rú	hé	biàn	huàn	duān	zài	bù,

Most sources have these exact words. Li differs only in having a slightly different word for 变幻 biàn huàn: 'change unpredictably', with 如何变换 rú hé biàn <u>huàn</u>: 'how we <u>change</u>'. I prefer 变幻 biàn huàn because the unpredictableness of the change is inherent in the word 幻 huàn.

36.21.4 Going in and out, back and forth – the waist first extends.

出	入	进	退	腰	先	伸。
chū	rù	jìn	tuì	yāo	xiān	shēn.

Almost all sources have this exact wording. For the final phrase, Wu has 腰要伸 yāo <u>yào</u> shēn: 'the waist <u>must</u> extend'.

Twenty-two

转掌之神颈骨传，
转项扭项手当先。
变时缩颈发时伸，
要如神龙首尾连。

The spirit of our turning palms is transmitted in the bones of the neck,
Turn the nape of the neck, twist the nape of the neck, the hands take the lead.
Retract the neck when changing, extend when emitting power,
You should be connected like the mystical dragon is connected from head to tail.

  I call this verse Spirit Shown in the Neck. It re-emphasizes that the neck must be upright, and move from within the spine, through the centre of the neck. This verse reiterates the connection of the neck with the entire body, how it controls and balances movement and power. The neck needs to stay relaxed and lively, not held stiffly, so that it can move easily to aid power. Weakness of the spirit and the health is first shown in a hanging neck, as is described in verse 48.38. It is commonly said in baguazhang that the eyes move after the hands, and then the hands follow the movement of the eyes. The spirit, shown in the eyes and transmitted through the neck, is one with the movements. Also, if we practise always watching what we are doing, with the neck in a comfortable position, we develop the habit of watching, which transfers to when we face an opponent.

  Li Ziming's commentary says not to overdo the retraction and extension of the neck. He says this concept is to keep the neck relaxed and natural when preparing a technique, and to straighten the neck when striking, to balance the power. Di Guoyong's commentary says that this verse is more about the spirit than the movement of the neck. Holding the head and neck straight and keeping focus on the movements connects the spirit through the body. With different explanations, both agree that this verse doesn't mean to stick the neck in and out like a turtle. I have been told to 缩颈 suō jǐng: 'retract the neck' when I needed to tuck in the jaw slightly (repeatedly, and for about an hour, since I had been travelling with a heavy rucksack). This is often called 下頜收回 xià hàn shōu huí: 'tuck the jaw in'. The slight settling and expansion of the neck is reflected in the settling and expansion of all the segments of the body. It is more an emphasis than a movement. The neck is always held straight and balanced. In movement, the feeling is of tucking in the jaw. In striking or throwing, the feeling is of pressing to the base of the head, at the hairline at the back of the neck, to balance the power.

The dragon's body is often used to describe a litheness of the body similar to that of a snake. It is said that if you attack the head of a snake the tail reacts, if you attack the tail the head strikes you, and if you grab the centre then both ends coil around your arm. I feel the meaning of a snake or dragon body speaks more of the fusion of the entire body so that it moves freely, going along with the neck. By this I mean the linkage of all tendons, ligaments, muscles, and bones through the lines of pull all the way from the feet to the neck. Western science has caught up with this idea of fascial links that connect from the heel of the foot up through to the nape of the neck. These links are further explained in verse 36.24. The body of a snake or dragon flows as one from head through to the tip of the tail – the musculature and tissues are indistinguishable from the bones. As one of my teachers said, in all seriousness, 'the lion is a poor analogy for us, because there are no lions in China, but everyone knows what a dragon looks like'. A body developed by baguazhang can either be slim and lithe like a snake or thick and solid, as long as it can move with the grace becoming of a dragon.

Dragon dances in the street are one reason why 'everyone knows what a dragon looks like', and a good dragon dance team shows the perfect connection from head to tip of the tail.

36.22.1   The spirit of our turning palms is transmitted in the bones of the neck,

转　　掌　　之　　神　　颈　　骨　　传，

zhuàn zhǎng　zhī　shén　jǐng　gǔ　chuán,

All sources but Huan have this exact wording, which once again makes me doubt my hand copied version. I have copied 转掌精神动骨传 zhuàn zhǎng jīng shén <u>dòng</u> gǔ chuán: 'the spirit of the turning palms is in the <u>movement</u>

of the bones'. The difference is 动 dòng: 'move' instead of 颈 jǐng: 'neck', which is unlikely to be a copy error, so this may be the intended character. Since the neck and head are in the following line, perhaps this is intended to say that movement goes through all the bones.

Here, as usual, the term 转掌 zhuàn zhǎng: 'turning palms' refers to the style of baguazhang itself, not to a specific technique.

36.22.2　　Turn the nape of the neck, twist the nape of the neck, the hands take the lead.

转　　　项　　　扭　　　项　　　手　　　当　　　先。
zhuàn　xiàng　　niǔ　　xiàng　　shǒu　　dāng　　xiān.

Seven sources (Li, Lin, Luo, Tu, Wang, Wu, and Zang) have this exact line. Two sources took out the repetition while maintaining the same meaning. Huan has 转项扭头 zhuàn xiàng niǔ tóu: 'turn the nape of the neck, twist the <u>head</u>'. Liu has 转头扭项 zhuàn <u>tóu</u> niǔ xiàng: 'turn the <u>head</u>, twist the nape of the neck'. The nape of the neck is the back of the neck, particularly at the hairline, where the tendons attach to the skull.

36.22.3　　Retract the neck when changing, extend when emitting power,

变　　　时　　　缩　　　颈　　　发　　　时　　　伸，
biàn　　shí　　suō　　jǐng　　fā　　shí　　shēn,

Six sources (Li, Lin, Liu, Tu, Wang, and Wu) have this exact line. The differences are slight, and do not change the meaning. Luo has 蓄时缩颈 <u>xù</u> shí suō jǐng: 'when <u>preparing</u> to move'. Huan has 变式缩颈 biàn <u>shì</u> suō jǐng: 'when changing <u>techniques</u>'. Zang has 变时缩项 biàn shí suō <u>xiàng</u>: 'when changing, retract the <u>nape of the neck</u>'.

36.22.4　　You should be connected like the mystical dragon is connected from head to tail.

要　　　如　　　神　　　龙　　　首　　　尾　　　连。
yào　　rú　　shén　　lóng　　shǒu　　wěi　　lián.

All sources have this line.

Twenty-three

打人凭手膀为根，
膀在肩端不会伸。
故欲进时进前步，
若进后步枉劳神。

Striking someone depends on the shoulder girdle acting as the root of the hand,
The arm is attached to the distal end of the shoulder and cannot extend any further.
So when you want to enter, take an advancing step with the front foot,
If you step through with the rear foot your effort will be in vain.

    I call this verse Gaining Distance. The importance of the use of the full shoulder girdle connecting through to the hands is seen in how many times this point is emphasized – in verses 36.3, 36.6, 36.10, 36.13, and 36.14. A well trained and released shoulder joint and the use of the open hand instead of the fist allows for a great deal of extension, but still, the arm can only extend so far. Footwork is needed to get the necessary distance. The third line repeats what has been said before in verse 36.12 – step the front foot first for speed, distance, and control. This verse gives one main reason for the stepping – to get more distance while maintaining power and speed – and emphasizes how the footwork and handwork act as a unit. Moving the rear foot through is slower, less powerful, less effective, and gains less distance.

    Ming dynasty general Wang Minghe, in 1599, in a short analysis of how his spear technique is better than the famous Yang family spear, wrote, "We use the same theory of *yin* and *yang*, of empty and solid, and their ability to attack from both sides is excellent. But where they are deficient is when they strike with their hands they do not enter with their feet."[31] Baguazhang has taken the best of martial theory and applications. I am not saying someone consciously read and copied the ideas of classic texts, but that these ideas were around and available as part of the martial background.

36.23.1   Striking someone depends on the shoulder girdle acting as the root of the hand.

打	人	凭	手	膀	为	根，
dǎ	rén	píng	shǒu	bǎng	wéi	gēn,

Seven sources (Huan, Li, Lin, Liu, Luo, Wang, and Wu) have this exact wording. Tu has 膀为先 bǎng wéi xiān: 'the shoulder girdle acts first'. Zang has 打人全凭膀为根 dǎ rén quán píng bǎng wéi gēn: 'striking someone all depends on the shoulder girdle acting as the root', leaving out 'the hand' to allow for the extra character 'all', without losing the meaning.

36.23.2   The arm is attached to the distal end of the shoulder and cannot extend any further.

膀 在 肩 端 不 会 伸。
bǎng zài jiān duān bù huì shēn.

All main sources have exactly this line. Extra sources Liang Shouyu and Xiang have 不全伸 bù quán shēn: 'does not fully extend'. This indicates that the unit of the shoulder girdle and arm should not fully extend, not simply that it cannot.

36.23.3   So when you want to enter, take an advancing step with the front foot.

故 欲 进 时 进 前 步,
gù yù jìn shí jìn qián bù,

Five sources (Huan, Li, Liu, Luo, and Wang) have this wording. Zang has 故于进时 gù yú jìn shí, with the same meaning. The re-edited Li, Lin, Tu, and Wu have 欲要进时 yù yào jìn shí: 'when you want to enter'. The slight differences do not change the meaning.

36.23.4   If you step through with the rear foot your effort will be in vain.

若 进 后 步 枉 劳 神。
ruò jìn hòu bù wǎng láo shén.

All main sources have exactly this line. This means to step through with the rear foot without first stepping the front foot.

Twenty-four

力足发自筋与骨,
骨中出硬筋须随。
足跟大筋通脑脊,
发招跟步力能催。

Abundant strength is emitted from the sinews/tendons and bones,
Hard power comes from within the bones and the sinews must follow.
The Achilles tendon connects through up the spine to the brain,
When making a move, a follow-up step will enable you to release full power.

I call this verse Tendons and Sinews. The Chinese word 筋 jīn: 'sinews / tendons', means more than the Western word. The Western anatomical definition is that tendons connect muscle to bone, and ligaments connect bone to bone. In Chinese martial arts, 筋 jīn: 'tendons', mean a range of soft connective tissue that includes the tendons, ligaments, fascia, and the muscles enclosed in the fascial tissue, although most particularly the tendons themselves. Baguazhang moves by the tendons and develops the tendons. Circle-walking strengthens weak tendons, tightens loose tendons, thickens thin tendons, smoothens lumpy tendons, and elasticizes tight tendons throughout the body.

This verse repeats verse 36.22, that the body is linked like that of a dragon, fully connected from heel to head, but explains it is a bit more detail. Power comes from the tendons, ligaments, and fascia and their connections through the bones. Baguazhang, as most internal styles, emphasizes the use of the tendons, ligaments, and sinews over that of independent muscular exertion. In Western myofascial terms this can be seen as the combination of the lateral line, spiral line, and superficial back line, though it is nowhere near as simple as that. The lateral line connects from each side of the foot and up the sides of the legs and body to connect to the head. The spiral line connects from the arch of the foot, spiraling around and across to the opposite shoulder and back to its side of the head. The superficial back line is the most obvious direct line of the 'dragon body', connecting from the Achilles tendon and up the back of the legs and body to the top of the head. It is the more structural link of an erect body, while the other are more involved with movement. What is referred to as fascial lines are lines of tendons, ligaments, and bones that connect to each other with the muscles tucked around them like sausage links. When moving any segment of the body, the movement goes through its centre, through the bones, by involving all the soft tissue that surrounds the bones.

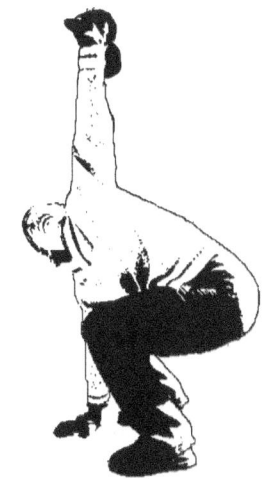

This image with the kettlebell, similar to the traditional stone lock, helps show how when the bones, sinews, and fascia are aligned and connected, the body can apply power in many odd directions and positions.

Baguazhang does not use overt muscularity, though of course muscles play a part in movement. The muscles and all the enveloped segments of the body pull just enough to take up the slack and cause movement. Moving from the entire segments instead of tensing individual muscles saves energy and allows for more speed because the body is full of potential energy. Uncoordinated or improperly timed use of body segments and muscles working out of synch lead to jerky movement that lacks focus. Also, a hard 'palm' strike is actually done with the end of the arm bone, facilitated by the movement always through the centre of the bones. When the bones are aligned, the power of the entire body can be used with without excessive tension.

The follow-up step is the rear foot stepping up after the front foot has advanced. It is further explained in verses 36.10 and 48.03. This step, when well connected through the body, drives the body forward with full power.

36.24.1 Abundant strength is emitted from the sinews/tendons and bones,

力 足 发 自 筋 与 骨,
lì zú fā zì jīn yǔ gǔ,

Six sources (Li, Lin, Luo, Tu, Wang, and Zang) have this line. Huan and Wu reverse the order to 骨与筋 gǔ yǔ jīn: 'bones and sinews'. Perhaps on purpose to fit better with the following line, which uses the order bones, then sinews. With either order, this line does not rhyme very well with suí and cuī anyway. Liu seems to have gone to typo land, with 力足发身筋具骨 lì zú fā shēn jīn jù gǔ: 'abundant strength is emitted body, sinews tools bones'.

36.24.2 Hardness comes from within the bones and the sinews/tendons must follow.

骨 中 出 硬 筋 须 随。
gǔ zhōng chū yìng jīn xū suí.

Almost all sources have this wording. Huan has 筋相连 jīn xiāng lián: 'the sinews are joined together', rather than 'must follow'. The copier of this line might have given up on the rhyming due to the importance of the concept – the sinews and tendons are joined not just to each other, but to the bones. They do not so much follow the bones, but work all together.

36.24.3 The Achilles tendon connects through up the spine to the brain,

足 跟 大 筋 通 脑 脊,
zú gēn dà jīn tōng nǎo jǐ,

Six sources (Lin, Liu, Luo, Tu, Wu, and Zang) have this line. Two (Li and Wang) use 足根 zú gēn: 'root of the foot', although the re-edited Li is changed back to 足跟 zú gēn: 'heel of the foot'. Huan reverses the character order without changing the meaning 大筋 足跟 dà jīn zú gēn: 'the Achilles tendon', because in Chinese, 'the Achilles tendon' is simply 'the big tendon of the foot/heel'.

36.24.4　　When making a move, a follow-up step will enable you to release full power.

发	招	跟	步	力	能	催。
fā	zhāo	gēn	bù	lì	néng	cuī.

All sources have this exact wording.

Twenty-five

眼到手到腰腿到，
心真神真力又真。
三真四到合一处，
防己有余能制人。

When the eyes arrive, the hands arrive, and the waist and legs arrive,
　The heart is true, the spirit is true, and the strength is also true.
　　When the 'three trues' and the 'four arrives' unite as one,
There is enough and to spare to defend oneself and control the adversary.

I call this verse Three Trues and Four Arrives. This verse emphasizes once again that baguazhang relies on not just full coordination, but the total melding of mind, body, and spirit into one. The goal of baguazhang is to realize this whole body power with the full integration of body and mind. This verse further internalizes the realization of the goal of whole body power, but also points out that we cannot have just the mental without the physical – the 'trueness' does not happen in the imagination, but in conjunction with the eyes, hands, waist, and legs.

It is tempting to see the 'true' mind, spirit, and strength as the 'right mind' of Ch'an (*Chan*, Zen) Buddhism. We see throughout the verses a Zen-like insistence on not fixating or stopping in mind or body, and there are remarkably similar requirements for the body position and mental focus of both circle-walking and zazen. Takuan Soho wrote in The Unfettered Mind, "The Right Mind is the mind that does not remain in one place. It is the mind that stretches throughout the entire body and self. The Confused Mind is the mind that, thinking something over, congeals in one place."[32] This concept is brought up again and again in the verses, especially 48.47 – 'if you stand still you are like fallen blossoms'. Certainly the training of the mind and spirit in the Shaolin temple was known to any martial artist who travelled, and there is an oblique reference to it in verse 36.36 – the 'scurrying of ants' – from the story that Da Mo was so connected that he could hear ants scurrying while meditating. I do not suggest that the masters of yesteryear did zazen, but perhaps if we approach our circle-walking with the same rigour we would not go wrong?

36.25.1 When the eyes arrive, the hands arrive, and the waist and legs arrive,

眼　　到　　手　　到　　腰　　腿　　到，
yǎn　dào　shǒu　dào　yāo　tuǐ　dào,

All sources have this line. Di Guoyong comments that the word 到 dào: 'arrive' is used in the sense of 达到 dá dào: 'achieve'. This would change the meaning to 'when your training achieves all the requirements for the eyes, hands, waist, and legs'. With this interpretation, the verse is more concrete, giving a goal for all your training.

36.25.2 The heart is true, the spirit is true, and the strength is also true.

心　　真　　神　　真　　力　　又　　真。
xīn　zhēn　shén　zhēn　lì　yòu　zhēn.

All but one source have exactly this line. Luo has 力亦真 lì yì dào: 'the strength is also true', which means the same thing. The heart is the heart/mind, intention, will, the part of the mind that intends to do something. It is not the intellectual mind. 真 zhēn: 'true' can also be translated as 'real', or 'genuine'.

36.25.3 When the 'three trues' and the 'four arrives' unite as one,

三　　真　　四　　到　　合　　一　　处，
sān　zhēn　sì　dào　hé　yī　chù,

All but one source have this exact wording. Zang has 三真四倒 sān zhēn sì dào, which looks to be a typo, as 倒 dào means 'upside down' or 'to move backwards'.

36.25.4 There is enough and to spare to defend oneself and control the adversary.

防　　已　　有　　余　　能　　制　　人。
fáng　yǐ　yǒu　yú　néng　zhì　rén.

All main sources have this exact wording.

Twenty-six

力要刚兮更要柔，
刚柔偏重功难收。
过刚必折真物理，
优柔太盛等于休。

Power should be hard but even more so should be pliant,
Emphasizing hardness or pliancy at the expense of one another makes it difficult to develop skill.
It is a law of nature that things that are too hard will break,
And that taking pliancy too far is tantamount to stopping.

  I call this verse Balance of Hardness and Pliancy. It is clear, concise, and well reasoned. It states clearly the basic principle of balancing hardness and pliancy, and the reasoning behind it. This understanding of hardness and pliancy is common to all styles that intend to develop deep skill. If 'hardness' is a firmness balanced with pliancy, it is not brittle. If 'pliancy' is a gentle yielding tempered with firmness, it is not weak. This is how a pliant defense can easily turn to a hard counter attack, and a counter attack meld into another technique if need be.

  This has been explained in many ways. Chang Naizhou's chapter on the interaction of hard and pliant in his work of the late 1700s gives a quite clear theoretical foundation for this practical observation. "Postures should be able to reach any point. *Qi* should reach everywhere without being exhausted. This is what is meant by 'when *yin* revolves to *yin*, *yang* is the intermediary. When *yang* revolves to *yang*, *yin* is the intermediary'. At the place of landing, where you are at the outmost place, this is where the *qi* accumulates and the blood condenses – this is where it stops in order to return. Using hard methods suitably, with a mix of *yang* and *yin*, enables the *qi* and blood to flow smoothly. Using pliant methods suitably is the same. If you only use a hard mode then the *qi* will fill the body but it will be harmfully stretched thin, and the placement/focal point of a hit will not be vigorous and fierce. If you only use a pliant mode then the *qi* will be scattered and not collect, there will be no returning, and the placement/focal point of a hit will not be solid. There must be pliancy as well as hardness. Then the *qi* will collect without stagnating. There must be hardness as well as pliancy. Then the *qi* will spread without being scattered. Everything must have the subtlety of this mutual benefit. Those who are skilled at using both hard and pliant are like the dragonfly dipping into the water – one touch and gone – the *qi* moves like a windmill, rotating and rolling continuously without stop. It must be like this, with hard and pliant just right. Only then do you avoid *qi* failure and *qi* stagnation."[33]

36.26.1 Power should be hard but even more so should be pliant,

力　　要　　刚　　兮　　更　　要　　柔，
lì　　yào　　gāng　　xī　　gèng　　yào　　róu,

Seven sources (Huan, Li, Lin, Liu, Luo, Tu, and Wu) have this line. Wang and the re-edited Li have 劲要柔 jìn yào róu: 'the power should be pliant', differentiating between 力 lì: 'hard strength', and 劲 jìn: 'trained power'. Most sources do not bother with this distinction, and use 力 lì: 'strength', to mean 'proper strength', not a stiff strength. It is fairly common to distinguish between 力 lì: 'brute strength' and 劲 jìn: 'trained power', but also fairly common to let context make the distinction. Many people use 发力 fā lì and 发劲 fā jìn: 'do a burst of power' interchangeably.

Zang has 更若柔 gèng ruò róu: 'even more so seems pliant', which seems like a typo. And Wang has another typo, with 力要分兮 lì yào fēn xī: 'strength should separate'.

36.26.2 Emphasizing hardness or pliancy at the expense of one another makes it difficult to develop skill.

刚　　柔　　偏　　重　　功　　难　　收。
gāng　　róu　　piān　　zhòng　　gōng　　nán　　shōu.

Most sources have this line. Liu and Xiang worded it slightly differently, 刚柔失调 gāng róu shī tiáo: 'if hardness and pliancy are imbalanced'.

36.26.3 It is a law of nature that things that are too hard will break,

过　　刚　　必　　折　　真　　物　　理，
guò　　gāng　　bì　　zhé　　zhēn　　wù　　lǐ,

All but one source have this line. Luo uses 万物理 wàn wù lǐ: 'the principles of the ten thousand things', which is essentially the same thing.

36.26.4 And that taking pliancy too far is tantamount to stopping.

优　　柔　　太　　盛　　等　　于　　休。
yōu　　róu　　tài　　shèng　　děng　　yú　　xiū.

Seven sources (Huan, Li, Lin, Luo, Tu, Wang, and Zang) have this line. Liu and Xiang have a slightly different phrase, with 过柔无力 guò róu wú lì: 'too pliant has no power'. Wu has 优柔太胜 yōu róu tài shèng: 'being pliant greatly winning', which seems a typo.

The Thirty-Six Verses

Twenty-seven

刚柔相济是何言，
刚柔相辅总无难。
刚柔当用乾坤手，
掀天揭地海波澜。

What does it mean to combine hardness and pliancy?
Coordinating hardness and pliancy isn't difficult.
(When you) use hardness and pliancy properly with *qian kun* (heaven and earth) hands,
You can shake heaven, expose the earth, and surge like waves in the ocean.

I call this verse Hard and Pliant *Qian Kun* Hands. The first lines are a simple statement of what we are aiming for in our training. The phrase 'surging like waves' is a standard metaphor for the wave breaking power used in Baguazhang and Xingyiquan. When the hands work as equal and opposite in positioning and power, and with the waist, they act as waves breaking on the shore. The rear hand must always be ready to take the place of the front hand, as is explained in verses 36.04, 36.05, and 36.06. The feeling of the waves breaking is that, even when waves are drawing back with an undertow they continue to roll forward. This is descriptive of the sucking in type of defense that snaps back with a hard counter.

This is the only reference to trigrams in the verses, and it refers to posture and feeling rather than theory. The trigram 乾 qián: 'heaven, sky, male', is represented by three solid (*yang*) lines and corresponds to the hard power of striking. The trigram 坤 kūn: 'earth, female', is represented by three broken (*yin*) lines and corresponds to the pliant power of deflecting. This does not have to refer to a specific posture, but can refer to the on guard posture the Old Monk Begs for Alms described in verse 36.17. The *qian kun* hands of the Old Monk have the arms well balanced, raised high and low, straight and angled, the palms turned up and down with hardness and pliancy, preparation for attack and defense balanced – the entire posture ready to trade places of the legs or arms, or change to defense or attack at any time. This power can apply to any posture or movement, as everything should balance all the time – especially *yin* and *yang*, hard and pliant. Simply saying *yinyang* hands would just mean one hand is facing down and one up, *qian kun* hands is more comprehensive. The key lies in the proper balance, not overdoing any one part at the expense of the whole body power and connectedness already explained in the verses.

36.27.1　　What does it mean to combine hardness and pliancy?

刚	柔	相	济	是	何	言，
gāng	róu	xiāng	jì	shí	hé	yán,

All sources have this exact wording.

36.27.2　　Coordinating hardness and pliancy isn't difficult.

刚	柔	相	辅	总	无	难。
gāng	róu	xiāng	fǔ	zǒng	wú	nán.

All sources have this exact wording.

36.27.3　　(When you) use hardness and pliancy properly with *qian kun* (heaven and earth) hands,

刚	柔	当	用	乾	坤	手，
gāng	róu	dāng	yòng	qián	kūn	shǒu,

All sources have this exact wording. *Qian kun* hands can be translated as 'heaven and earth' hands or 'full *yang* and full *yin* hands'. *Qian* is the full *yang*, three solid lines, and *kun* is the full *yin*, three broken lines. The use of the trigrams in the name encompasses more meaning, so I have left the Chinese terms to encompass more meaning than the English could manage.

36.27.4　　You can shake heaven, expose the earth, and surge like waves in the ocean.

掀	天	揭	地	海	波	澜。
xiān	tiān	jiē	dì	hǎi	bō	lán.

Seven sources (Huan, Li, Lin, Luo, Tu, Wang, and Wu) have this exact line. Zang differs in having 掀地 xiān dì: 'lift the earth', which also refers to ploughing the fields, and is a word often seen in descriptive phrases. Liu and Xiang also have a slight difference, 掀天翻地 xiān tiān fān dì: 'shake heaven, overturn the soil'. I think the phrase 揭地 jiē dì, is the best, as it is both descriptive of ploughing and forms the phrase 掀天揭地 xiān tiān jiē dì: 'shaking heaven and earth', which is a standard phrase meaning 'earth-shattering', 'achieve wonders', or 'exert a profound influence', which gives the sentence a double meaning.

Twenty-eight

人刚我柔是正方,
我刚人柔法亦良。
刚柔相遇腰求胜,
解此纠纷步法强。

If my adversary is hard and I am pliant, this is the conventional way,
If I am hard when my adversary is pliant, then this works too.
When both can use hardness and pliancy, use your waist to seek victory,
Strong footwork will resolve this issue.

I call this verse Hard and Pliant Waist and Footwork. It gives us quite a few options in using the balance of hardness and pliancy. We should use pliancy against hardness, and hardness against pliancy when appropriate. As the verse says, this is the conventional way, the concept is not new. Ming dynasty general Wang Minghe wrote in 1599, "On facing off, if he is soft I use strength, but if he uses strength then I am soft."[34] Using hard against hard doesn't usually work. This verse is suggesting that we should use pliant dissipating methods and footwork against a hard attack. Similarly, pliant against pliant is wasting time. We should take the opportunity to hit hard if our opponent is pliant. Examples of pliant neutralizing defenses are in verses 48.03, 48.04, 48.05, 48.07, and 48.12, among many. There are even more verses on using the pliant method of evasion to set up the hard counter attack – 48.18, 48.19, 48.22, 48.23, 48.31, 48.36, 48.43, and 48.47. Examples of hard are the spearing palms described in verses 48.06 and 48.28, and the continuing attack described in 48.10. Normally baguazhang does not favour the 正 zhèng: 'conventional' way, which consists largely of frontal attacks and common tactics, preferring the 奇 qí: 'unusual' or 'unconventional' way, which consists of surprise attacks and flanking tactics.

The second line is allowing that your adversary might also be skilled enough to use pliant power to defuse your attack. The third line gives even more credit to your adversary. When both are using pliancy and hardness well, then you really need to use your waist. Using pliancy and hardness in a well balanced way calls for good use of the waist, and if you have further difficulties because your opponent is also skilled at this, good footwork will decide the victory. Di Guoyong comments that of course other styles do understand the concept, but tend to depend on the waist, and the emphasis on the footwork is what makes baguazhang special.

36.28.1   If my adversary is hard and I am pliant, this is the conventional way,

人	刚	我	柔	是	正	方,
rén	gāng	wǒ	róu	shì	zhèng	fāng,

Most sources have this exact wording, except Liu, who has 相正方 <u>xiāng</u> zhèng fāng: 'this is the conventional way to <u>meet each other</u>'.

36.28.2   If I am hard when my adversary is pliant, then this works too.

我	刚	人	柔	法	亦	良。
wǒ	gāng	rén	róu	fǎ	yì	liáng.

Most sources have this line, except Huan, who reverses the order with the same meaning 人柔 我刚 <u>rén róu</u> wǒ gāng: '<u>my adversary is pliant</u> and <u>I am hard</u>'.

36.28.3   When both can use hardness and pliancy, use your waist to seek victory,

刚	柔	相	遇	腰	求	胜,
gāng	róu	xiāng	yù	yāo	qiú	shèng,

Seven sources have this exact phrasing (Li, Lin, Liu, Luo, Tu, Wu, and Zang). The re-edited Li uses the phrase 刚柔相济 gāng róu xiāng <u>jì</u>: '<u>coordinate</u> hardness and pliancy', for the same meaning.

There are two interesting variations in the 'use the waist to win' phrase. Huan has 腰求伸 yāo qiú <u>shēn</u>: '<u>extend</u> the waist', giving the phrase a more concrete action to do with the waist. Wang has 要求胜 <u>yào</u> qiú shèng: 'if you <u>want to</u> seek victory', which puts the phrase as an introduction to the following line, putting all the emphasis on the stepping instead of the waist. The pronunciations of all these versions are quite close, though the written characters are not. What to actually do with the waist is described in verses 48.42 and 48.44. This line is setting up for the following line, when you are dealing with an opponent who is quite skilled, you first try to win with your waist work, and if still in difficulty, your footwork should be better than his.

36.28.4   Strong footwork will resolve this issue.

解	此	纠	纷	步	法	强。
xiè	cǐ	jiū	fēn	bù	fǎ	qiáng.

Seven sources (Huan, Li, Lin, Tu, Wang, Wu, and Zang) have this line. Luo has 解决纠纷 jiě <u>jué</u> jiū fēn: '<u>resolve</u> the issue'. Liu has 能解纠纷 <u>néng</u> jiě jiū fēn: '<u>can</u> solve the issue'.

The Thirty-Six Verses

Twenty-nine

步法动时腰先提，
收缩合宜显神奇。
足欲动兮腰不动，
跟跄迈去误时机。

> When stepping, first lift the waist,
> Gather in just the right amount for the magical skill to be apparent.
> If, just before the foot moves, the waist does not move,
> Charging forward with huge steps, your timing will be off.

I call this verse Coordination of Stepping. It reinforces the idea that the footwork is not completely dependent on the feet and legs. The feet move because of a movement within the body, not simply from the thighs. It is not something different from what we do in everyday training of circle-walking. It just sounds tricky when put like this. Also, if done properly, it is scarcely or not at all visible.

Teachers vary between ascribing the gathering action to the hip joints or to within the waist or *dantian*. It can be explained as a slight retraction and release in the hip joint, coordinated with the waist, to lighten the steps. It is a lessening of the weight over the leg that is to move, to allow for agile stepping. It is not so much that the waist 'lifts', but that all stepping derives from the waist. Some see the lightening action more as a cutting action at the hip crease. When the thigh is drawn into the hip, any stepping or kicking action is easier. Gathering in at the abdomen and lifting in the back or *dantian* ensures that the hips remain level, which then ensures that the legs can move freely. The entire torso still needs to maintain the basic structure of straight and settled as described in verses 36.01 and 36.07. The Jiang school focuses within the *dantian* in front of the hips to enable free movement, while the Cheng style focuses behind to give more power to the stepping leg. Li Ziming's commentary says that this lifting action in the waist is very slight, more in the mind than visibly apparent – just enough, as the second line says. He quotes his teacher Liang Zhenpu, 'you shouldn't see the lift at all, it is all in the mind and power flow'. All commentators say that you shouldn't just charge in with big ungainly steps uncoordinated with the waist and hips.

36.29.1   When stepping, first lift the waist,

步	法	动	时	腰	先	提,
bù	fǎ	dòng	shí	yāo	xiān	tí,

All sources have this exact wording.

36.29.2   Gather in just the right amount for the magical skill to be apparent.

收	缩	合	宜	显	神	奇。
shōu	suō	hé	yí	xiǎn	shén	qí.

All sources have this exact wording. The magical skill, of course, is the marvelous stepping of baguazhang.

36.29.3   If, just before the foot moves, the waist does not move,

足	欲	动	兮	腰	不	动,
zú	yù	dòng	xī	yāo	bù	dòng,

Four sources (Li, Liu, Luo, and Wang) have this line. Lin and Tu have 如足动时 rú zú dòng shí: 'if the foot moves'. Wu and Zang have 足欲动时 zú yù dòng shí: 'when the foot is about to move'. Neither alternate version changes the meaning. For the final phrase, Huan has 腰先动 yāo xiān dòng: 'the waist first moves'. He would seem to be using this line to repeat what has been said, instead of as an introduction to the following line.

36.29.4   Charging forward with huge steps, your timing will be off.

跟	跄	迈	去	误	时	机。
liàng	qiàng	mài	qù	wù	shí	jī.

All sources have the meaning, with a variety of ways of phrasing the first four beats. Five sources (Huan, Li, Liu, Wu, and Zang) have 跟跄 liàng qiàng: 'charging'. Three sources (Lin, Tu, and Wang) have 跄跟 qiàng liàng: still meaning 'charging', just reversing the characters. Luo has 蹌脚 qiàng jiǎo: 'charge the feet', meaning the same thing. Huan and Luo use 迈出 mài chū: 'stride out', instead of 迈去 mài qù: 'stride', which emphasizes the striding out from yourself rather than striding towards your adversary. Liu uses 跨步 kuà bù: 'sidestep', instead of 迈去 mài qù, which usually implies a more sideways moving step.

The word 迈 mài or 迈步 mài bù is not usually used to mean a big step in the verses. Here it is used with modifiers 蹌跟 qiàng liàng: to indicate 'charging forward'. On its own, 迈 mài is used for 'walking' in the verses, and particularly for circle-walking (see verses 36.04 and 48.36).

Thirty

转身变法步莫长，
擦地而行莫要慌。
看准来路方伸手，
巧女穿针稳柔刚。

When turning and changing techniques the steps should not be long,
Rub the ground while walking, there is no need to get flustered.
Observe the attack and then extend the hand,
(Be like) a skillful woman threading a needle: steady, gentle, and firm.

I call this verse Short Steps. It emphasizes the use of small steps to move around with agility. The preceding verse implied that a long step is awkward, and the half step has been explained, but so far the use of small steps has not been explained. Small steps are further described in verses 48.22 and 48.36. The light, short steps give you time to stay calm, see what is going on, and deal with whatever comes.

The word 擦 cā: 'rub', refers to a short friction with the ground. Some commentators take this 'rub the ground' step to mean the natural action that happens when you push off the rear foot and land with the root of the front foot with a forward action in *tangnibu*, or 'mud stepping'. The use of the word 'rub' indicates that this is a short friction as you land. Some commentators take 'rub the ground' to mean that as you walk you do not take huge or high steps to move, just small, low steps, with the normal stepping that one uses in fighting. Most versions of circle-walking training build the habit of walking without lifting the knees or feet more than necessary, resulting in a silent, controlled walk even when relaxed to normal steps. A few small steps rather than one huge step moves the body quickly while remaining balanced and connected.

This tactic of first waiting and then taking the initiative is continually emphasized in the verses – see verses 48.2, 48.11, 48.15, 48.22, 48.24, 48.30, and 48.33. Li Ziming adds in his commentary that the fighter, like the woman threading the needle, needs accurate eyes, steady body and mind, and firm hands.

36.30.1 When turning and changing techniques the steps should not be long,

转　　身　　变　　法　　步　　莫　　长，
zhuàn　shēn　biàn　fǎ　bù　mò　cháng，

Most sources have this exact phrasing. Huan has 动兮变步 dòng xī biàn bù: 'when moving and changing footwork', which I suspect is partly a mis-copy, but it does not alter the key meaning that the footwork must not overextend, especially when turning. Wu has 转身变化 zhuàn shēn biàn huà: 'changes when turning'.

36.30.2   Rub the ground while walking, there is no need to get flustered.

擦　　地　　而　　行　　莫　　要　　慌。
cā　　dì　　ér　　xíng　　mò　　yào　　huāng.

Most sources have this exact wording. Only Huan has the same meaning with a slightly different phrase 莫须慌 mò xū huāng: 'no need to get flustered', which means exactly the same thing.

36.30.3   Observe the attack then extend the hand,

看　　准　　来　　路(势)　方　　伸　　手,
kàn　zhǔn　lái　lù (shì)　fāng　shēn　shǒu,

All sources agree on the meaning of this phrase. Five sources (Li, Lin, Luo, Tu, and Wang) have 看准来路 kàn zhǔn lái lù: 'observe the route of attack'. Four (Huan, Liu, Wu, and Zang) have 看准来势 kàn zhǔn lái shì: 'observe the incoming technique'.

36.30.4   (Be like) a skillful woman threading a needle: steady, gentle, and firm.

巧　　女　　穿　　针　　稳　　柔　　刚。
qiǎo　nǚ　chuān　zhēn　wěn　róu　gāng.

Most sources have this exact wording. Liu and Xiang have 柔中刚 róu zhōng gāng: 'hardness within pliancy'. The majority are more accurate about the action, which isn't simply pliant and hard – steadiness is key to threading a needle.

Thirty-one

人持利器我不忙，
飞剑遥遥到身旁。
看他来路哼哈避，
邪不胜正语颇良。

If an assailant is holding a sharp weapon I'm not bothered,
Even as his sword flies towards me from afar.
I watch his approach and avoid with a *heng* or *ha* sound,
It is an apt saying that the evil cannot beat the righteous.

The Thirty-Six Verses

I call this verse *Heng* and *Ha* Sounds. It would appear to be claiming that we can beat an opponent, even an armed one, by simply being a better person. This is patently not true. Up until now the advice in the verses has been practical, so we have to look at the practical advice here, which is – if we have confidence we will stay cooler under pressure, we will remain relaxed and better able to apprehend and react to our assailant's movements. When up against an opponent, wait to avoid the attack – there is no need to attack first. We need to stay calm and watch closely to see the preparation for an attack or even for throwing a weapon, and avoid it.

Li Ziming's commentary says that the *heng* or *ha* sound, introduced in verse 36.09, is meant to bolster your courage and to startle your opponent. Your righteous power, shown in the shout, overpowers his evil power. To be practical, as the verses are, the *heng* and *ha* sounds give you more power, as was explained in verse 36.09. If your shout also manages to startle your opponent this is a bonus. Verse 36.32 deals with swords, so it would make sense that this verse deals with thrown weapons, and your shout could put off their aim. The 'bad guys' are more likely to use hidden weapons, so this interpretation is entirely possible.

In addition to the use for generating power, 哼 Hēng and 哈 Hā are the names of two temple doorway guardians, fierce and invincible. *Heng*, 'the Snorter', is the Indian diety Narayana. He ejects two rays of light or energy from his nostrils. He has a closed mouth, and makes the sound *Hum*, which in Chinese became *Heng*. *Ha*, 'the Blower', is the Indian deity Guhyapada. He blows a gust of yellow gas or energy from his mouth. He has an open mouth, and makes the sound *Ah*, which in Chinese became *Ha*. The two sounds *Ah* and *Hum* represent the beginning and the end, or birth and

death, and put together make the chant '*Ohm*'. The sounds *Heng* and *Ha*, by association, are fierce and righteous.³⁵

36.31.1   If an assailant is holding a sharp weapon I'm not bothered,
        人　　持　　利　　器　　我　　不　　忙，
        rén　　chí　　lì　　qì　　wǒ　　bù　　máng,

Seven sources (Huan, Li, Lin, Luo, Tu, Wang, and Wu) have this line exactly. Zang has a slight difference in the first phrase, with 人持利剑 rén chí lì <u>jiàn</u>: 'if an assailant is holding a sharp <u>sword</u>'. For the final phrase, Liu has 心不慌 xīn bù <u>huāng</u>: 'my <u>heart/mind</u> is not<u> flustered</u>', which is really the same thing as the others.

36.31.2   Even as his sword flies towards me from afar.
        飞　　剑　　遥　　遥　　到　　身　　旁。
        fēi　　jiàn　　yáo　　yáo　　dào　　shēn　　páng.

Five sources (Li, Lin, Luo, Tu, and Wang) have this line exactly. Huan has 飞箭 fēi <u>jiàn</u>: 'flying <u>arrows</u>'. I would think that might be a mis-copy, as catching arrows is a bit beyond even baguazhang. The characters look nothing alike, but the pronunciation is the same, somewhat suggesting verbal transmission. For the final phrase Liu, Wu, and Zang have 到身强 dào shēn <u>qiáng</u>: 'coming towards me <u>strongly</u>'. Some commentators do interpret this line to refer to a thrown dagger.

36.31.3   I watch his approach and avoid with a *heng* or *ha* sound,
        看　　他　　来　　路　　哼　　哈　　避，
        kàn　　tā　　lái　　lù　　hēng　　hā　　bì,

Six sources (Li, Lin, Luo, Tu, Wang, and Wu) have this line. Huan has 看准来路 kàn <u>zhǔn</u> lái lù: 'watch <u>accurately</u> the approach'. Zang has 哼哈泄 hēng hā <u>xiè</u>: '<u>give vent to</u> the *heng* or *ha* sound', without apparently the need to avoid. Liu has the line as 看准来路闪身避 kàn <u>zhǔn</u> lái lù <u>shǎn</u> <u>shēn</u> bì: 'watch <u>accurately</u> his approach and <u>evade</u>, changing the '*heng* or *ha* sound' to simply 'evade'.

If line two is interpreted as a thrown weapon, then this line, whether implicitly or explicitly, will mean to evade. If you watch carefully you should be able to see your assailant's preparation for the throw.

36.31.4   It is an apt saying that the evil cannot beat the righteous.
        邪　　不　　胜　　正　　语　　颇　　良。
        xié　　bù　　shèng　　zhèng　　yù　　pō　　liáng.

Four sources (Li, Lin, Tu, and Wang) have this exact line. For the other sources, it is easiest to look at the two phrases separately, 邪不胜正 xié bù shèng zhèng: 'evil cannot beat the righteous', and 语颇良 yù pō liáng: 'it is a good saying'. Huan has a slightly different opening, 斜不正侵 xié bù zhèng qīn: 'the <u>angled</u> cannot <u>infringe</u> upon the upright'. Liu, Wu, and Zang also have a slightly different opening, with 邪不侵正 xié bù qīn zhèng: 'the evil cannot <u>infringe</u> upon the righteous'. Both alternate openings mean essentially the same thing. For the final phrase, Wu has 语话良 yù huà liáng: 'the saying is good'.

Thirty-two

短兵相接似难防，
哪怕锋利似鱼肠。
伸手取来探囊物，
指山打磨妙中藏。

It seems difficult to deal with a short weapon,
But what is there to be afraid of in a sharp blade like the 'fish gut sword'?
Extend your hand to fetch it, like reaching in to take something out of a pouch,
The secret is hidden in 'pointing at the mountain to get the millstone'.

I call this verse Disarming. It suggests that the task of disarming is more simple that we might think. We need to be calm and accurate, but it is not so terribly difficult. The first step is not to be afraid. The weapons described in the verses are the blades and sticks that martial artists used at the time of writing, and so there was a good chance of disarming our adversary.

The 'fish gut sword' is a very famous, short, sharp dagger from the Spring and Autumn period (770-476 BC). An assassin Zhuan Zhu 专诸 hid it in a cooked fish in order to kill King Liao of Wu during a banquet (so that the king's cousin, Prince Guang, whom he served, could take the throne). In addition to the dagger's own qualities, the thrust of the assassin was exceptionally well-timed, quick and direct. Of course the assassin was righteous – Prince Guang went on to become one of the great rulers, King Helü of Wu. And to pile image on image, the assassin went in knowing there was no hope of escape – he was of course killed by the guards – which indicates an intensity of purpose beyond the normal.

So, if your opponent has the intensity and skill of that assassin, you will not be able to simply disarm him. You need to distract him first.

This phrase Pointing at the Mountain to Get the Millstone is not a specific technique but a tactic. Li Ziming's commentary says that it is similar to Make Noise in the East and Attack the West. That is a feint that poses a threat that cannot be ignored, making your opponent react, thus giving you an opening. Verse 48.18 explains the method of Pointing at the Mountain to Get the Millstone as evasion followed by an immediate and relentless counter attack to the source of the problem. Di Guoyong says that it is a tactic that can be explained as pointing to the large (mountain) but hitting the small (stone), pointing far but hitting near, or searching through many stones to find the perfect one for your millstone (keep moving and chose the right target). I always thought of it as throwing out a hand high (to the mountain), causing the opponent to deal with your high attack, then hitting him low 'in the millstone'. Or, making it seem like you are going for a large target (the mountain) so that you can sneak into a small target (the millstone). The general principle refers to dealing calmly with an attack and taking what opportunity you can with feints, movement, pliancy, and the ability to adapt.

36.32.1   It seems difficult to deal with a short weapon,
　　　　　短　　兵　　相　　接　　似　　难　　防，
　　　　　duǎn　bīng　xiāng　jiē　sì　nán　fáng,

All sources agree on this exact wording, as indeed would anyone.

36.32.2   But what is there to be afraid of in a sharp blade like the 'fish gut sword'?
　　　　　哪(那)　怕　锋　利　似　鱼　肠。
　　　　　nǎ (ná)　pà　fēng　lì　sì　yú　cháng.

Four sources (Lin, Liu, Luo, Zang) use the clear interrogative 哪 nǎ: 'what', 'which', often used in rhetorical questions. Five sources (Huan, Li, Tu, Wang, and Wu) use the non-interrogative 那 nà or nǎ: 'that', and the re-edited Li is changed to 哪 nǎ: 'what'. Often 那 nà: 'that 'is used for 哪 nǎ: 'what' with the interrogative meaning, so the meaning of the phrase is clear with either.

Liu, Wu, and Zang have 那(哪)怕纯利 nǎ pà chún lì: 'what is there to be afraid of in a skillful and sharp blade'. Liu and Zang also have 是鱼肠 shì yú cháng: 'is the fish gut sword', just taking the metaphor a bit further.

36.32.3   Extend your hand to fetch it, like reaching in to take something out of a pouch,
　　　　　伸　　手　　取　　来　　探　　囊　　物，
　　　　　shén　shǒu　qǔ　lái　tàn　náng　wù,

There is basic agreement on what is going on here, but a variety of ways of saying it. To break it down into the four and three character parts, five sources (re-edited Li, Lin, Luo, and Tu, and Wang) have what I have picked as the standard, 伸手取来 shén shǒu qǔ lái: 'extend your hand to fetch it'. Zang reverses two characters, with 伸手来取 shén shǒu lái qǔ: 'extend your hand to fetch it'. Huan, Li, and Wu have 伸手来接 shén shǒu lái jiē: 'extend the hand to <u>intercept</u>'. Liu has 伸手<u>探取</u> shén shǒu <u>tàn qǔ</u>: 'extend the hand to <u>reach out to fetch</u>'.

In the three character part, most sources have 探囊物 tàn náng wù: 'reach in to take something out of a pouch or pocket'. Wang has 搽囊物 <u>chá</u> náng wù: '<u>smear</u> something in a pouch or pocket', which is a very nice way of putting it too. Four (Li, Liu, Wu, and Zang) using the verb from the preceding phrase, have simply 囊<u>中</u>物 náng <u>zhōng</u> wù: 'something <u>in</u> a pouch or pocket'.

36.32.4   The secret is hidden in 'pointing at the mountain to get the millstone'.

指　　山　　打　　磨　　妙　　中　　藏。
zhǐ　　shān　　dǎ　　mò　　miào　　zhōng　　cáng.

Almost all sources have this line. Only Lin has 妙中存 miào zhōng <u>cún</u>: 'the secret <u>lies in</u>' for the final phrase. This source consistently uses 存 cún: 'lies in', where the others use 藏 cáng: 'is hidden in'.

Thirty-three

人众我寡力难挡，
巧破千钧莫要忙。
一手不劳凭指力，
犁牛犹怕反弓张。

It is difficult to defend against the combined forces of a mob on your own,
With skill you can defeat ten hundredweight if you do not panic.
One hand is not needed, just the strength of one finger,
Even a plough ox is afraid when you draw the 'reverse bow'.

I call this verse One Finger to Beat Ten Hundredweight. It doesn't give much information considering the situation that you have found yourself in. A small force, used cleverly, using balance, timing, and pivot points, is very effective. Zang, and Liang Shouyu, in their commentaries, describe the 'reverse bow' as an unstrung bow that becomes a whip, which controls the ox through fear. Li Ziming and his student Di Guoyong, take this phrase to mean 'reverse the bow', as in turning the horn of the bull, which throws it to the ground. This makes more sense in terms of the sort of technique you would use, such as *ling* or *daishou*, making them pass by or preferably fall. The advice given is that you need to use skill, not strength, and save your energy, to beat multiple attackers.

36.33.1   It is difficult to defend against the combined forces of a mob on your own,

人	众	我	寡	力	难	挡，
rén	zhòng	wǒ	guǎ	lì	nán	dǎng,

All sources agree on the situation, just differing in one character. Four (Li, Lin, Liu, and Wang) have these exact words. Three (Luo, Wu, and Zang) have 力难强 lì nán <u>qiáng</u>: 'it is difficult to be <u>strong</u> against this strength'. Huan has 力难防 lì nán <u>fáng</u>: 'it is difficult to <u>defend</u> against'. Tu has 力难当 lì nán <u>dāng</u>: 'it is difficult to <u>match</u>'.

36.33.2   With skill you can defeat ten hundredweight if you do not panic.

巧	破	千	钧	莫	要	忙。
qiǎo	pò	qiān	jūn	mò	yào	máng.

Six sources have this line. Four (Liu, Luo, Wu, and Zang) have 莫要忘 mò yào <u>wàng</u>: which makes the line 'don't <u>forget that</u> with skill you can defeat ten hundredweight'. A thousand jun is about 15,000 kg, which just means 'a lot'. There is no such thing as a 'thousand weight' in English, but there is an old English weight measure of a 'hundredweight', which is 112 pounds, so I have used it to preserve the traditional feeling.

36.33.3   One hand is not needed, just the strength of one finger,

一	手	不	劳	凭	指	力，
yī	shǒu	bù	láo	píng	zhǐ	lì,

All but one source have this exact wording. Luo says 一手不劳凭借力 yī shǒu bù láo píng <u>jiè</u> lì: 'one hand needs no more work than to depend on <u>borrowing</u> strength'. This term is often used to refer to pliant defense such as *daishou*. It can also refer to qinna joint locking and controlling techniques.

36.33.4   Even a plough ox is afraid when you draw the 'reverse bow'.

犁	牛	犹	怕	反	弓	张。
lí	niú	yóu	pà	fǎn	gōng	zhāng.

All but one source have this exact line. Wang has 反弓强 fǎn gōng <u>qiáng</u>: 'the <u>strength</u> of the reverse bow'.

Thirty-four

伸手不见掌前伸，
又无油松照彼身。
收缩眼皮努睛看，
底盘掌使显奇神。

When you can't see your hand extended in front of you,
And you don't have a torch to illuminate your assailants.
Narrow your eyes and concentrate on seeing,
Go to a low stance and all will become clear.

I call this verse Fighting in Darkness. It gives good, practical advice about how to fight in the dark. Outdoors in the dark, if you crouch down you can quite often see your opponents against the natural light, which comes from above. Indoors, there could still be light coming in a window. The opponents have much less chance of seeing you, looking down into the darkness. This is described again in verse 48.25, which emphasizes that you need to move around, and stay low while moving around. Squinting is not to 'see better', but to help the eyes adjust to the dark by making it even darker for a brief moment, after which you will see better. Also, blocking the light temporarily to the eyes can serve to stimulate the other senses.

36.34.1 When you can't see your hand extended in front of you,
伸	手	不	见	掌	前	伸，
shēn	shǒu	bù	jiàn	zhǎng	qián	shēn,

All sources agree on the situation, with a few slight differences in description. Li just reverses the order 前掌伸 qián zhǎng shēn: 'your front hand extended'. Liu and Zang have 掌前人 zhǎng qián rén: 'the people in front of you'.

36.34.2 And you don't have a torch to illuminate your assailants.
又	无	油	松	照	彼	身。
yòu	wú	yóu	sōng	zhào	bǐ	shēn.

All sources agree on the situation, with most using these exact words. In olden days a torch was made of the pitch of the pine tree, so it was called simply 'pitch pine'. Minor differences in wording for this light source are: 松油 sōng yóu: 'pine pitch', 油灯 yóu dēng: 'an oil lamp', and 松明 sōng míng: 'light of the pine'.

36.34.3　　Narrow your eyes and concentrate on seeing.

收　　缩　　眼　　皮　　努　　睛　　看，
shōu　suō　yǎn　pí　nǔ　jīng　kàn,

Almost all sources have this line. Wu has a slight variation in the final phrase, 努眼看 nǔ yǎn kàn, just using the more common word for 'eyes'.

36.34.4　　Go to a low stance and all will become clear.

底　　盘　　掌　　使　　显　　奇　　神。
dǐ　pán　zhǎng　shǐ　xiān　qí　shén.

All but one source have the same initial phrase. Wu has 底盘手法 dǐ pán shǒu fǎ: 'go to low stance with your hand techniques', meaning the same thing. Almost all sources finish the line with 显神奇 xiān shén qí, which doesn't rhyme with lines one and two. Liu and Zang have 显奇神 xiān qí shén, reversing the last two characters. I have chosen this version because it makes the line rhyme.

Thirty-five

冰天雪地雨泞滑，
前脚横使且莫差。
翻身切忌螺丝转，
高低紧避乃为佳。

When it is icy, snowy, or muddy from rain so the ground is slippery,
　　Employ the front foot crossways and you can't go wrong.
　　When doing a full turn, by all means avoid pivoting,
Strictly avoid going high or low, and then you should be fine.

　　I call this verse Slippery Ground. Again, it gives good, practical advice for difficult conditions. In normal conditions, in addition to being more unstable than stepping, pivoting places the knees at risk of injury, and does not allow for changes mid-pivot. In icy conditions you are almost sure to slip. Turning the foot also helps to ensure that you do not take too long a step. The safest way to turn the front foot is a *koubu* step, which gives more control and keeps the knees stable, even if you slide. Some commentaries interpret 'avoid high and low' to mean avoiding bumps and irregularities in the surface, but most interpret this to mean your stance and techniques. Verse 48.34 also describes this situation, and specifically suggests avoiding

The Thirty-Six Verses

high stances or techniques, as they raise the centre of gravity and make it harder to stay steady.

36.35.1 When it is icy, snowy, or muddy from rain so the ground is slippery,

冰	天	雪	地	雨	泞	滑，
bīng	tiān	xuě	dì	yǔ	nìng	huá,

All but two sources have this exact wording. For the final pharse, Luo has simply 而泞滑 ér nìng huá: 'and muddy and slippery', and Wu has 雨泥泞 yǔ ní nìng: 'slippery with rain and mud'. Neither change the meaning.

36.35.2 Employ the front foot crossways and you can't go wrong.

前	脚	横	使	且	莫	差。
qián	jiǎo	héng	shǐ	qiě	mò	chà.

Four sources (Lin, Luo, Tu, Wang) have this exact wording. Liu, Wu, and Zang have 前脚横施 qián jiǎo héng shī: 'apply the front foot crossways', for the first phrase, really the same thing, but pronounced shī instead of shǐ. Huan, Li, Wu, and Zang have 切莫差 qiē mò chà: 'and indeed you can't go wrong', for the second phrase. The character 且 qiě is a grammatical connecter, 'moreover'. The character 切 qiē in this situation means 'be sure to', 'definite', so is essentially the same thing.

36.35.3 When doing a full turn, by all means avoid pivoting.

翻	身	切	忌	螺	丝	转，
fān	shēn	qiè	jì	luó	sī	zhuàn,

All but one source have this exact line. Zang has 翻身切记 fān shēn qiè jì: 'when doing a full turn, remember that', with the sense of 'keep in mind that you shouldn't do something'.

36.35.4 Strictly avoid going high or low, and then you should be fine.

高	低	紧	避	乃	为	佳。
gāo	dī	jǐn	bì	nǎi	wéi	jiā.

Five sources (Huan, Li, Luo, Tu, Wang) have these exact words. The others differ only on the 'strictly avoid' part. Liu, Wu, and Zang have 高低谨避 gāo dī jǐn bì: 'cautiously avoid'. I rather like the word 谨 jǐn, as 'cautious' is also with strict control, but has psychological meanings that fit as well. The characters 紧 and 谨 are both pronounced jǐn, so this could be an oral transmission variation. Lin has 高低紧闭 gāo dī jǐn bì: 'shut down with strict control'. The change in one word 闭 bì: 'shut down', changes the meaning of the phrase to 'cautiously defend whether in high stance or low stance'.

Thirty-six

用时最要是精神，
精神焕发耳目真。
任凭他人飞燕手，
蚁鸣我听龙虎吟。

In fighting, the most vital factor is spirit,
When the spirit shines the eyes and ears are true.
Even if an assailant flies at me as fast as a swallow,
The scurrying of ants sounds to me as the roar of dragons and tigers.

I call this verse Spirit. It refers to the sensitivity of your senses and mind, and thus your reactions, when you have clarity of spirit. So the final verse once again reminds us that the goal of our training is the full integration of mind and body. It reminds us that the collected spirit is a calm one. Once again, if we go back to our circle-walking, we can develop this calmness in movement.

The reference to the 'scurrying of ants' is a nod to Da Mo, who became so aware while sitting in meditation at the cave in the Shaolin temple that he 'could hear the scurrying of ants'. There is a danger of reading too much into these verses, taking this reference to mean that the spiritual result of circle-walking is equivalent to that of Ch'an sitting (zazen). The basic position is remarkably similar, but you should maybe say they came from the same root of effective body mechanics. There are not too many ways to seek a balanced, fully connected, fighting effective structure. For example, Musashi's *Book of Five Rings*, from 1640 Japan, describes an almost identical basic structure as that given in the thirty-six verses. "Adopt a stance with the head erect, neither hanging down, nor looking up, nor twisted. ... With your features composed, keep the line of your nose straight with a feeling of slightly flaring your nostrils. Hold the line of the rear of the neck straight: instil vigour into your hairline, and in the same way from the shoulders down through your entire body. Lower both shoulders and, without the buttocks jutting out, put strength into your legs from the knees to the tips of your toes. Brace your abdomen so that you do not bend at the hips."[36] I won't quote any more from it, because it is from another time and place, but there is much in it that is interesting to a baguazhang player.

36.36.1　In fighting, the most vital factor is spirit,

用	时	最	要	是	精	神，
yòng	shí	zuì	yào	shì	jīng	shén,

All but one source have exactly this line. Liu has 用是须要 yòng shí <u>xū</u> yào: 'in fighting there <u>must</u> have'.

36.36.2　When the spirit shines the eyes and ears are true.

精	神	焕	发	耳	目	真。
jīng	shén	huàn	fā	ér	mù	zhēn.

All but one source have this line. Tu has 耳目<u>新</u> ér mù <u>xīn</u>: the eyes and ears <u>are new</u>, but I suspect this is a typo.

36.36.3　Even if an assailant flies at me as fast as a swallow,

任	凭	他	人	飞	燕	手，
rèn	píng	tā	rén	fēi	yàn	shǒu,

All but one source have this line. Huan has 老熟手 lǎo shú shǒu: 'even if an opponent is a <u>really skilled</u> hand', which is the same essential meaning.

36.36.4　The scurrying of ants sounds to me as the roar of dragons and tigers.

蚁	鸣	我	听	龙	虎	吟。
yī	wū	wǒ	tīng	lóng	hǔ	yín.

Most sources have this line. Wu just reverses the final phrase to 虎龙吟 hǔ lóng yín: 'roar of tigers and dragons'. In my copy from Huan I have mistakenly written 老虎吟 <u>lǎo</u> hǔ yín: 'the roar of a tiger', and I clearly copied it wrong, expecting 老虎 lǎo hǔ: 'a tiger', not 龙虎 lóng hǔ: 'dragons and tigers'. This shows that sometimes the expectations of the copier can change a phrase or character, especially when what is written is a bit different from the normal phrase. The copier must have clarity of spirit to see what is really there.

In Praise of the Thirty-six Verses 歌赞

掌法拳法与岳议，
传出日久或忘记。
我歌我歌三十六，
字字句句有真意。

The palm methods and fighting methods are discussions from the mountains,
They have been transmitted for many years, and with the passing of time may have been forgotten.
The thirty-six verses that I wrote,
Each and every word and phrase has true meaning.

line 1   The palm methods and fighting methods are discussions from the mountains,

掌	法	拳	法	与	岳	议，
zhǎng	fǎ	quán	fǎ	yǔ	yuè	yì,

Not all sources have a verse of praise for the 36 verses. Some combine a longer verse of praise for the 36 and 48 methods together, which comes after the 48 methods verses.

Of those who have this verse, most sources have this line. For the first phrase, Wu has 拳法掌法 quán fǎ zhǎng fǎ, just reversing the order. For the final phrase, Luo has 与兵议 yǔ bīng yì: 'and weapons' (possibly a typo), and Zang has 云师传 yún shī chuán: 'are transmitted from the teacher in the clouds'.

line 2   They have been transmitted for many years, and with the passing of time may have been forgotten.

传	出	日	久	或	忘	记。
chuán	chū	rì	jiǔ	huò	wàng	jì.

All sources that have this verse of praise have this line.

line 3   The thirty-six verses that I wrote,

我	歌	我	歌	三	十	六，
wǒ	gē	wǒ	gē	sān	shí	liù,

Almost all sources that have this verse of praise have this exact line. Luo has 我歌八掌 wǒ gē bā zhǎng: 'my verses about the eight palms'.

line 4   Each and every word and phrase has true meaning.

字	字	句	句	有	真	意。
zì	zì	jù	jù	yǒu	zhēn	yì.

Almost all sources that have this verse of praise have this exact line. For the final phrase, Luo has 含深义 hán shēn yì: 'holds deep meaning', Wu has 有真义 yǒu zhēn yì: 'has true meaning', and Zang has 有深义 yǒu shēn yì: 'has deep meaning'.

Part Two

The Forty-Eight Methods Verses of Baguazhang

PART TWO

THE FORTY-EIGHT METHODS VERSES OF BAGUAZHANG

This is the text version that I have used in my translation. I compiled it by comparing the similarities and differences in text from eight sources.[37] In the discussion I point out these differences and similarities, and explain why I chose this version as the standard to translate. For modern characters see the discussion sections.

八卦掌四十八法歌訣

一。　　　身法
　　　　　手法步法要相隨，手到步到力必微。
　　　　　手腳俱到腰欠力，去時遲慢難抽回。
二。　　　相法
　　　　　對御群敵相法先，未曾進步退當然。
　　　　　退步審勢知變化，以逸待勞四兩牽。
三。　　　步法
　　　　　未從動梢先動根，手快不如半步跟。
　　　　　出入進退祇半不，制手避招而安神。
四。　　　邁法
　　　　　功夫本從彎步來，兩手變化隨步開。
　　　　　高挑低摟橫掩避，推托帶領不離懷。
五。　　　連步法
　　　　　連步必三費功夫，使手要簡自然無。
　　　　　搭手轉身是空手，機會恰巧是江湖。

六。　　囷步法
　　　　囷步不要兩相濟，前虛後實差相宜。
　　　　若要站濟前後仰，亦且腰短少靈機。
七。　　手法
　　　　偏沈則隨雙重滯，外硬裡軟拈槍勢。
　　　　橫推裡勾身有主，祇有吸手腰腹隨。
八。　　力法
　　　　人說冷彈脆快硬，我說冷快是一般。
　　　　脆硬細分無二致，發動全憑心力合。
九。　　存力法
　　　　祇會使力不會存，力過猶如箭離弦。
　　　　不但無功且有害，輕輪重折而傷身。
十。　　續力法
　　　　力著他人根已斷，若再續力彼難逃。
　　　　此時惟有衝前步，長膀長腰一齊交。
十一。　降人法
　　　　快打慢兮不足誇，強制弱兮不為佳。
　　　　最好比人高一招，顧盼中定不空發。
十二。　決胜法
　　　　彼力千鈞快如梭，避強用順快步挪。
　　　　千人祇有三五近，稍伸手腳不難遮。
十三。　運用法
　　　　高打矮兮矮打高，斜打胖兮不須搖。
　　　　若遇瘦長憑捋帶，年邁無功上下瞧。
十四。　封閉法
　　　　手講三關腳伸屈，一手三關腳直迁。
　　　　肩肘腕胯膝可用，縮頸空胸步帶驅。
十五。　接拳法
　　　　五花八門亂如麻，長拳短打混相加。
　　　　你越快兮我越慢，我若發時神鬼垮。
十六。　摘解法
　　　　多少拿法莫誇技，兩手拿一力固奇。
　　　　任他神拿怕過頂，穿鼻刺目勢難敵。

十七。　　接单补双法
　　　　　莫說兩手仗堅兵，一來一往是其能。
　　　　　閉住右手左無用，雙手棄來更無功。
十八。　　指山打磨法
　　　　　他人來手我不然，側身還擊彼自還。
　　　　　他若還時我入手，他若封時三手連。
十九。　　脱身化影法
　　　　　他不來時我叫來，他要來時我化開。
　　　　　不須手避憑身法，步步不離兩胯哉。
二十。　　背后轉身法
　　　　　伸手要小步要大，開步半跨貼身抓。
　　　　　跨步落地蹲身轉，他要轉時我鷹拿。
二十一。　磕砸劈撞法
　　　　　磕來還磕我要先，砸右換步左手粘。
　　　　　劈來疊肘樁橫立，撞來乾坤手搖圈。
二十二。　半圈手法
　　　　　他人手法多直線，跨上半步等如閑。
　　　　　即或指直打斜法，再跨半步不相干。
二十三。　整圈手法
　　　　　四面敵人我在中，穿花打柳任西東。
　　　　　八方憑勢風雲變，不守呆式不走空。
二十四。　心眼法
　　　　　心如大將眼如法，見景生情能制他。
　　　　　最忌心癡眼不準，手忙腳亂費周折。
二十五。　定眼法
　　　　　四面刀槍亂如麻，又當昏夜月無華。
　　　　　矮身定睛招路廣，步步彎行自贏他。
二十六。　接器法
　　　　　長短單雙器固精，算來不如兩手靈。
　　　　　鐵掌練來兵一樣，肉手偏找肱腕行。
二十七。　保身法
　　　　　以強勝弱不足誇，弱能勝強方是法。
　　　　　任他離弦箭快硬，左右磨身保無差。

二十八。　亂人法
　　　　　心亂先從眼上亂，千招不如掌一穿。
　　　　　對準鼻梁連環使，跨步制人左右換。
二十九。　開合法
　　　　　欲合先開是一般，見開防合不二傳。
　　　　　詐敗佯輸知捲土，指東打西意中含。
三十。　　定南法
　　　　　任他千手千眼快，守住中身是枉然。
　　　　　不到要時不伸手，伸手即要發手還。
三十一。　求近法
　　　　　封閉固是護身招，躲過他人自逍遙。
　　　　　切忌遠出尺步外，開門繞道法不牢。
三十二。　六路法
　　　　　他人六路是空言，我之掌法六路觀。
　　　　　動步既能八方顧，瞻前顧後身無難。
三十三。　不二法
　　　　　法不準兮不妄發，發不中兮第二發。
　　　　　任他鬼神多靈妙，不鉤魂兮亦裂牙。
三十四。　防滑法
　　　　　冰天雪地步難牢，前橫後直記心梢。
　　　　　轉動須用小開步，切忌挺身法打高。
三十五。　穩步法
　　　　　步不穩兮身必搖，腳踏實地勝千招。
　　　　　進取足趾退懸踵，不扣步兮莫回瞧。
三十六。　小步法
　　　　　回身轉步必須小，步大舍身不靈腳。
　　　　　欲要轉身邁半步，人難擒兮人不曉。
三十七。　掌法
　　　　　掌法雖有上中下，上下不過是掌架。
　　　　　圓轉自如惟中盤，高下全從此變化。
三十八。　忌俯法
　　　　　低頭如同眼不開，亦且身易往前栽。
　　　　　低頭貓腰中樞死，全步全掌使不來。

三十九。　　忌仰法
　　　　　　緊背空胸靜中求，挺胸坦腹悔難收。
　　　　　　疊肚吸腰來不及，最怕轉身不自由。
四十。　　　正身法
　　　　　　全身力量在中樞，自身歪斜力不周。
　　　　　　別看步彎身必正，發手如箭不停留。
四十一。　　輔身法
　　　　　　身如君王腰腿臣，君正臣強可制人。
　　　　　　進退躲閃憑身法，若無腰腿不生神。
四十二。　　扭（拗）身法
　　　　　　人來制我已貼身，此時手腳不贏人。
　　　　　　左右吸收用扭法，化險為夷把人擒。
四十三。　　跨步側身法
　　　　　　穿梭直入勢難停，先發制人顯他能。
　　　　　　若遇此手接連退，不如跨步側身靈。
四十四。　　左右甩身法
　　　　　　閃躲東方西又來，搖身一變甩身開。
　　　　　　左右連環皆如此，前推後捋腰安排。
四十五。　　蹲步沉身法
　　　　　　身高架大路上三，舉手招封勢所難。
　　　　　　蹲步沈身使就下，入我機關使法寬。
四十六。　　忌拿法
　　　　　　八卦之手不講拿，我拿人兮我亦差。
　　　　　　設若人多不方便，直出直入也堪誇。
四十七。　　忌站法
　　　　　　混元一汽走無涯，八卦真理是我家。
　　　　　　招招不離腳變化，站住即為落地花。
四十八。　　太上法
　　　　　　力要足活招要準，即或使空三不紊，
　　　　　　招套招兮無窮極，精神法術在乎純。
歌贊
　　　　　　四十八法意真切，練練說說不為神。
　　　　　　要得所傳純功到，幾人三年試驗深。

Translation of the Forty-eight Methods Verses of Baguazhang

One: Method of Using the Body
Hand techniques and footwork should work together,
If the hands arrive and then the feet land, power is slight.
And if the hands and feet arrive together but the waist lacks strength,
Then going in is delayed and slow, and drawing back is difficult.

Two: Method of Observing
To defend against a mob of assailants, first observe,
You should retreat before advancing.
Retreat to observe their situation and understand their fluctuations,
Keep at ease until they tire themselves, leading them along with a light touch.

Three: Method of Stepping
Before you move the tip, first move the root,
Using fast hands doesn't compare to using the half follow-step.
Just use the half step whether going in or out, advancing or retreating,
Then you can control your opponents, evade attacks, and remain safe.

Four: Method of Walking
Deep skill comes from walking with bent legs,
All the variations of the hands open out from stepping.
You can scoop high attacks, brush aside low attacks, cover and evade crossing attacks,
Push, lift, drag, and draw, all without (your hands) leaving your chest.

Five: Method of Continuous Steps
It takes time and training to develop the three continuous steps,
Good stepping enables hand techniques to be simple and natural.
When you engage with your opponent, turn so he enters into emptiness,
Take what opportunities present – this is the skill of 'the companions of rivers and lakes'.

Six: Method of the Gathering Stance

When in a gathering stance the feet must not be in line or together,

There should be an appropriate distinction: one in front and empty, one behind and solid.

If you stand up with the feet together you can too easily be leaned back or forward,

Moreover, this gives the waist a short reach and little agility or spontaneity.

Seven: Method of Using the Hands

When you are partially heavy you can follow (your opponent), but when you are double heavy you are sluggish,

Be hard on the outside and pliant on the inside, like when you hold a spear.

Whether pushing across or hooking in, the torso is always in charge,

You just need to absorb with the hands and the waist and belly will follow.

Eight: Method of Using Power

People talk about cold, springy, crisp, quick, and hard powers,

We say that cold and quick are the same.

Looking carefully at crisp and hard, they are the same, too,

Power depends completely on the harmony between heart and strength.

Nine: Method of Reserving Power

If you only know how to exert all your strength and not how to keep some in reserve,

Your strength will be excessive, like an arrow leaving the bowstring.

Not only will this achieve nothing, but it can also harm you,

If you get off lightly you will be defeated, but more seriously, you could be broken and injured.

Ten: Method of Continuing Power

When your power has contacted your opponent and he has already lost his root,

If you use continuous power he will have trouble getting away.

At this time you just need to charge forward with your footwork,

Lengthen the shoulder girdle, lengthen the waist, and deliver all in unison.

Eleven:	How to Subdue Opponents
There is nothing to boast about in the quick beating the slow,
There is nothing fine about the strong beating the weak.
It is best to be more highly skilled than your opponents,
Then you can watch both sides and keep centered, and not issue any empty attacks.

Twelve:	How to Ensure Victory
If your adversary has massive strength and is as quick as a weaver's shuttle,
Avoid his strength by using smooth following methods, and shifting your stance quickly.
If there are a thousand people, only three to five can get close to you,
It isn't difficult to impede them by slightly extending your hands and feet.

Thirteen:	How to Apply Tactics
Hit short people high and tall people low,
Angle in on fat people, and you won't flounder.
Up against a lanky person depend on a pulling drag,
Against the old or unskilled, just look them up and down.

Fourteen:	How to Seal Off
In the upper limbs we talk of the three passes, and for the lower limbs the extension and flexion,
The upper limbs can use three passes, while the lower limbs can go straight or circuitously.
You can use your shoulders, elbows, wrists, hips, and knees,
Retract your neck, empty your chest, and your footwork will lead the whole body.

Fifteen:	How to Meet an Attack
(If I meet assailants acting as) 'five blossoms and eight doors' as chaotic as tangled hemp,
Long and short styles all mixed up.
The faster they go the more leisurely I'll react,
Once I initiate my attack, even gods and ghosts will praise me.

Sixteen: How to Release Grabs
Knowing a lot of grab and control methods is nothing to boast about,
Once two hands grab one, the strength is fixed and stuck.
No matter how good someone is at grabbing, they still fear going up over the head,
Add a spear to the nose and pierce to the eyes, and your momentum is difficult to resist.

Seventeen: How to Take a Single to Remedy a Double
Let's say an assailant attacks with a weapon in both hands,
All he can do is send one hand in while the other goes back.
Shut down one hand and his other hand becomes useless,
If he comes in with both hands then he has nothing at all.

Eighteen: The Tactic of Pointing at the Mountain to Get the Millstone
If someone attacks me I don't bother much,
I turn to the side, counter attacking, so he himself counter attacks.
As he counters I begin another attack,
If he tries to seal off (that attack) I do three continuous palm strikes.

Nineteen: How to Trade your Body for a Shadow
If he doesn't attack I call him in,
Just as he attacks I dissolve away.
I don't need my hands to evade, but depend on bodywork,
My stepping never leaves (the width of) my hips.

Twenty: The Tactic of Turning and Getting Behind the Back
The hands should extend a small distance while the footwork should be large,
Step out with a half sidestep, keeping the body in close to grab.
As my sidestep lands, I squat down and turn,
If he tries to turn I do an eagle grasp.

Twenty-one: Tactics against Hard Attacks
When a knock comes I need to be first with a countering knock,
When a pound comes on my right I switch my stance and stick with my left hand.
When a chop comes I fold my elbow and cut across with an upright forearm,
When a ram comes I use both hands in balance and swing on the circle.

Twenty-two: How to Use Half-Circle Hands
>   Someone from another fighting style usually attacks in a straight line,
>   Take a half sidestep forward and wait at ease.
>   If he tries a straight fake with an angled strike,
>   Take another half sidestep and (what he is doing) becomes irrelevant.

Twenty-three: How to use Full-Circle Hands
>   If I am surrounded on four sides by assailants,
>   I move freely East and West like threading through blossoms to hit willow trees.
>   Even if completely encircled with the momentum (of the enemy) changing like clouds in the wind,
>   I don't guard in a dull-witted posture and I don't take a pointless step.

Twenty-four: Method of using the Heart and Eyes
>   The heart is like a commander and the eyes are his aides,
>   They scan the scene to observe the battle array in order to beat the enemy.
>   The worst case would be if the heart became stupid and the eyes didn't see clearly,
>   Then the hands would become frenzied and the feet chaotic, wasting a lot of effort.

Twenty-five: The Tactic of Fixing the Regard
>   All around you are blades and spears, as chaotic as tangled hemp,
>   And it is a dark evening unadorned by moonlight.
>   Lower the body and fix the eyes open to see the route widely,
>   Flex and curve at every step, and you can beat them.

Twenty-six: How to Disarm
>   Long or short, single or double, weapons are undoubtedly proficient,
>   But they really don't compare in dexterity to two (empty) hands.
>   An iron palm can be forged to become like a weapon,
>   Bare hands, contrary to expectations, can find the arms and wrists.

Twenty-seven: How to Protect the Body
   Beating someone weaker than you is nothing to boast about,
   But with our method you can beat someone stronger.
   Even if someone attacks as fast and hard as an arrow leaving the bowstring,
   Rub with your body left and right and you won't fall short in defense.

Twenty-eight: How to Confuse your Adversary
   A confused mind begins in the eyes,
   A thousand techniques don't compare to one spearing palm.
   Hit the bridge of the nose accurately and continuously,
   Step around to control your adversary, switching to left and right.

Twenty-nine: Method of Opening and Closing
   It is quite common to open up before closing,
   Seeing (your opponent) open and preventing his closing – it is not taught otherwise.
   (If he) fakes defeat and feigns loss, be aware of (a comeback like) rolling dust,
   He is planning to 'point East and hit West'.

Thirty: The Tactic of Setting in the South
   If your opponent is so quick he strikes as if with a thousand hands and a thousand eyes,
   Defend your midline and his attacks are futile.
   Do not extend your hand until the right moment,
   When you do extend your hand, he will have to pull back his attack.

Thirty-one: The Tactic of Getting in Close
   Shutting down is of course a method of defending oneself,
   Dodge your opponent and you are free and unfettered.
   But be sure to avoid stepping more than a foot away (from him),
   Just opening the doors and taking detours won't beat your opponent.

Thirty-two: Method of the Six Directions
   When others say they can take care of six directions this is empty talk,
   In our style we can look to the six directions.
   When we step we can already see to eight directions,
   We have no difficulties at all watching both before and behind.

Thirty-three: The Tactic of One and Only
>   Don't attack rashly if you don't (think you can) land a well aimed technique,
>   If you do an inaccurate hit then hit again.
>   No matter if your opponent has supernatural skills,
>   If you don't panic him you will at least make him rend his teeth.

Thirty-four: How to Prevent Slipping
>   It is difficult to keep to your feet in a world of ice and snow,
>   Pay close attention – turn the front foot across and keep the back foot straight.
>   When turning you must use small steps,
>   Avoid being stiff and erect, or hitting high.

Thirty-five: Method for Stable Footwork
>   If the footwork isn't stable the body will certainly be unstable,
>   Having firmly grounded feet will win more than knowing a thousand techniques.
>   Grab with the toes to advance and lift the heel to retreat,
>   Don't look back or turn around without using a hook-in step.

Thirty-six: Method of Small Steps
>   To turn back you must take small turning steps,
>   If your steps are large then you give up your body and your feet are maladroit.
>   If you want to turn around then take a half step,
>   No one will be able to catch you or figure you out.

Thirty-seven: Methods for the Palms
>   Although our palms have upper, middle and lower,
>   The upper and lower are just different frames for the palms.
>   Only the middle basin moves freely when turning on the circle,
>   The high and low are variations unfolding from it.

Thirty-eight: Avoid Slouching
>   Hanging your head is the same as closing your eyes,
>   And moreover, the body then tends to slouch forward.
>   Hanging your head and hunching your back like a cat deadens the Central Pivot,
>   None of your footwork or hand techniques will come off.

Thirty-nine: Avoid Arching Back
  Tauten the upper back and empty the chest to seek a still centre,
  With a puffed up chest and flattened abdomen, you will regret your difficulty receiving (an attack).
  You won't have time to fold your belly and suck in your waist,
  What we fear most is not being able to turn around freely.

Forty: Method of an Upright Body
  The power of the whole body lies in its central axis,
  A misaligned body has fragmentary power.
  Even when you bend your legs your body must remain upright,
  Then you can attack like shooting arrows nonstop.

Forty-one: Method of Supplementing the Body
  The body is like the sovereign with the waist and legs as his ministers,
  An upright sovereign with strong ministers can control the people.
  Advancing, retreating, dodging and evading all depend on the bodywork,
  But without the waist and legs, the spirit cannot grow.

Forty-two: Method of Twisting the Body
  If someone tries to control me and has already gotten in close,
  At this point I can't win using my hands and feet.
  Suck in and gather left or right, using the twisting method,
  Turn danger into safety, grabbing him.

Forty-three: The Tactic of Sidestepping and Turning Sideways
  It is difficult to stop spearing palms coming straight in like a weaver's shuttle,
  Your opponent has attacked first to gain control, and shown his ability.
  If you meet this opponent, continuously retreat,
  But it is more effective to sidestep and turn your body sideways.

Forty-four: Method of Shaking Off Side to Side
  If you evade an attack from the East and there comes another from the West,
  Change shape in a single shake, shaking the body free.
  Repeat continuously side to side like this,
  Push forward and pull back, all set up from the waist.

Forty-five: The Tactic of Hunkering Down
>If you meet a tall, massive opponent who attacks your upper three (passes),
>You will be in trouble if you raise your hands to block the attack.
>Squat down to lower your body, inducing him to come down,
>Once he enters your space you have a wide range of applications.

Forty-six: Avoid Grabbing
>The techniques of bagua do not stress grabbing,
>If I grab someone then I am also at a disadvantage.
>I am inconvenienced if there are a lot of attackers,
>'Straight out and straight in' also rates praise.

Forty-seven: Avoid Standing Still
>When your original *qi* is full then you can walk without boundaries,
>The truth of the eight trigrams is in our school.
>Every single technique comes from the changes of the feet,
>If you stand still you are like fallen blossoms.

Forty-eight: The Supreme Method
>Power must be full and lively and moves must be accurate,
>Even if you miss, 'the three' must not get confused.
>Inexhaustible moves within moves,
>Your spirit and technique depend on your mastery of them.

In Praise of the Forty-eight Methods Verses
>The meaning of the forty-eight verses is clear,
>If you just train and train, discuss and discuss, you will not achieve their essence.
>If you want to achieve what they transmit and gain pure skills,
>You need to train three years with others and gain much experience.

One: Method of Using the Body

身法   shēn fǎ

手法步法要相随，
手到步落力必微。
手脚俱到腰欠力，
去时迟慢难抽回。

Hand techniques and footwork should work together,
If the hands arrive and then the feet land, power is slight.
And if the hands and feet arrive together but the waist lacks strength,
Then going in is delayed and slow, and drawing back is difficult.

To sum up this verse, the whole body needs to work together, with the root of the movement coming from the feet, the power coming from the waist, and the connection going through to the hands. The title suggest that the bodywork is the foundation for the footwork and everything else. This is the goal in training and fighting. If the hands, feet, or waist is missing or mis-timed, the whole body is sluggish and weak and movement is awkward. This is why we need to be careful that the hands not arrive before the feet. The power is a whole body power, but the feet are the root of that power. If we do a mis-timed hit it takes some adjustment before we can change to something else.

48.01.1   Hand techniques and footwork should work together,

手	法	步	法	要	相	随，
shǒu	fǎ	bù	fǎ	yào	xiāng	suí,

All sources have this line.

48.01.2   If the hands arrive and then the feet land, power is slight.

手	到	步	落	力	必	微。
shǒu	dào	bù	luò	lì	bì	wēi.

Six sources (Li, Lin, Tu, Wang, Wu, and Zang) have this line. Liu has 手到步差 shǒu dào bù chà: 'if the hands arrive and the feet fall short', which makes the line's meaning much clearer.

For the final phrase, Huan has 心力催 xīn lì cuī: 'the mind urges the strength'. This line takes on a different sense – when the hands and feet arrive at the same time, the mind can urge the power – which is a desired outcome. This interpretation is possible because the line does not actually say the hands arrive 'before' the feet, it actually just says the hands arrive and the feet land, which could be understood as together. The interpretation of mis-timing is taken from context and word order.

48.01.3   And if the hands and feet arrive together but the waist lacks strength,

手	脚	俱	到	腰	欠	力，
shǒu	jiǎo	jù	dào	yāo	qiàn	lì,

All sources have this line.

48.01.4   Then going in is delayed and slow, and it difficult to draw back.

去	时	迟	慢	难	抽	回。
qù	shí	chí	màn	nán	chōu	huí.

Four sources (Li, Lin, Tu, and Wang) have this exact line. Huan has 走时迟慢 zǒu shí chí màn: '<u>moving</u> is delayed and slow', which is essentially the same thing, but emphasizing the walking nature of baguazhang. Zang has 迟缓 chí huǎn: also meaning 'delayed and slow' and reverses the final phrase to 抽难回 chōu nán huí. Liu and Wu have also reversed order in the final phrase. The order does not change the meaning, as long as the line ends in huí to rhyme.

Two: Method of Observing

相法   xiāng fǎ

对御群敌相法先，
未曾进步退当然。
退步审势知变化，
以逸待劳四两牵。

To defend against a mob of assailants, first observe,
You should retreat before advancing.
Retreat to observe their situation and understand their fluctuations,
Keep at ease until they tire themselves, leading them along with a light touch.

The tactic given in this verse is to save your energy and stay calm in a multiple attack situation. Even with many assailants, there is no need for haste. It is better to observe the situation clearly before reacting – the placement, feelings, movement, and apparent skill levels of the assailants, the lay of the land, and whatever is there that may help you. Do not attack blindly, but step back to observe the various factors and find out more about each of the assailants. Move to draw them out, so you can observe what each of them does, assessing who are stronger and who weaker, seeing their reactions and their placement, so that you can pick and chose who you deal with. Use drawing and leading in defensive techniques to keep them at bay or throw them until they tire themselves in the attack.

This verse makes reference to two of the thirty-six stratagems of Chinese generals. The fourth stratagem of Wait Leisurely and Tire the Enemy is to wait and gather strength, avoiding the fight until you chose to engage. Take time to observe the enemy and figure out his or their strengths and weaknesses, watching for a moment of weakness before attacking. In addition to gaining you time, the key lies in the fact that the opponent loses morale with the delay. They will be tiring from moving around, but will more importantly become mentally tired. The Art of War states that the soldiers have high morale at the beginning of a battle, but lose morale gradually as the fighting continues. The twelfth stratagem of Take the Opportunity to Pilfer a Goat, or Lead a Sheep Along, is to draw the opponent in, watching for every opportunity and being ready at any time to react to any mistake or weakness on his part. This tactic is often used as retreating steps followed by an aptly timed sidestep and drag.

48.02.1 To defend against a mob of assailants, first observe,

对　　御　　群　　敌　　相　　法　　先，
duì　　yù　　qūn　　dì　　xiāng　　fǎ　　xiān,

All sources have this line.

48.02.2 You should retreat before advancing.

未　　曾　　进　　步　　退　　当　　然。
wèi　　céng　　jìn　　bù　　tuì　　dāng　　rán.

All but one sources have this line. Zang has 未从进步 wèi <u>cóng</u> jìn bù: which still means 'before advancing'.

48.02.3 Retreat to observe their situation and understand their fluctuations,

退　　步　　审　　势　　知　　变　　化，
tùi　　bù　　shěn　　shì　　zhī　　biàn　　huà,

Four sources (Li, Lin, Tu, and Wang) have this exact line. Four (Huan, Liu, Wu, and Zang) have 退则审势 tuì <u>zé</u> shěn shì: 'retreat <u>and then</u> observe their situation'.

48.02.4   Keep at ease until they tire themselves, leading them along with a light touch.

以	逸	待	劳	四	两	牵。
yǐ	yì	dài	láo	sì	liǎng	qiān

All sources have this line, and they are tactics that most martial artists would know. The first, 以逸待劳 yǐ yì dài láo: 'keep at ease until they tire themselves' is the fourth stratagem. The second, 四两牵 sì liǎng qiān: 'lead along with a light touch' is a common tactic. The weight measure 四两 sì liǎng, four 'liang' is about two grams, often used in martial verses with the sense of 'not much force'.

Three: Method of Stepping
步法   bù fǎ

未从动梢先动根，
手快不如半步跟。
出入进退只半步，
制手避招而安神。

Before you move the tip, first move the root,
Using fast hands doesn't compare to using the half follow-step.
Just use the half step whether going in or out, advancing or retreating,
Then you can control your opponents, evade attacks, and remain safe.

The verses 36.14 and 36.23 have explained the use of the shoulder as the root of the hands. This verse is explaining the footwork, so the root and tips in this case are not the roots and tips of the segments, but of the whole body. The feet are the roots of the whole body, and the hands are the tips. The tactic given in this verse is that we must move from our feet, and use the controlled, agile, and powerful half stepping to move around either in defensive moves or for attacking. The basic footwork has been described in verse 36.12, and the half-step is added here. This footwork is not that common, but Ming dynasty general Wang Minghe wrote in 1599, "On facing off, if you don't move your front foot and then shift your rear foot, you can't win."[38]

The half follow-in step is not actually defined. We are meant to know what it is from our training, the verse is just reminding us to use it. The 'half step follow-up' refers to following up the rear foot a half step after the front foot has advanced, or following back the front foot a half step after the rear foot has retreated, or following over when you sidestep. This ensures that we remain in a comfortable and balanced stance during and after movement, and that we gain distance with a stealing step. This can be done staying on the same side, which is a driving step. As a three step advance, you advance the front foot, then step through the rear foot, and then follow in with what is now the rear foot, which is a stealing step. Instead of taking one large step, two or three half steps are taken to cover more distance with more control and power, and the body is able to remain stable and strong. Wu quotes Guo Gumin as saying, "A large step is three feet, a small step is three inches. You want to shift your body into a position that is advantageous to you and disadvantageous to your opponent, to both avoid his attack and control him."[39] The feet deliver the body and hands effectively without over reaching.

48.03.1   Before you move the tip, first move the root,

未　从　动　梢　先　动　根，
wèi　cóng　dòng　shāo　xiān　dòng　gēn,

Five sources (Huan, Li, Lin, Wang, and Zang) have this exact line. Liu and Wu have 未曾动梢 wèi <u>céng</u> dòng shāo: 'before <u>already</u> moving the tip', which doesn't change the meaning. Tu has a typo, with 未从动梢 wèi cóng dòng <u>shāo</u>: 'before you move <u>a bit</u>'.

48.03.2   Using fast hands doesn't compare to using the half step follow-up.

手　快　不　如　半　步　跟。
shǒu　kuài　bù　rú　bàn　bù　gēn.

All sources have this exact line.

48.03.3   Just use the half step whether going in or out, advancing or retreating,

出　入　进　退　只　半　步，
chū　rù　jìn　tuì　zhǐ　bàn　bù,

Five sources (Li, Lin, Tu, Wang, and Wu) have this exact line. Three sources (Huan, Liu, and Zang) have 进退出入 <u>jìn tuì</u> chū rù, just a reversed phrase for the 'back and forth'. One source has a different last phrase – Huan has 走半步 <u>zǒu</u> bàn bù: '<u>walk</u> with half steps', which is a bit more descriptive of the action.

48.03.4   Then you can control your opponents, evade attacks, and remain safe.

制	手	避	招	而	安	神。
zhì	shǒu	bì	zhāo	ér	ān	shén.

Al but one sources have this line. Liu has 以安神 yǐ ān shén: <u>in order to remain safe</u>.

Four: Method of Walking
迈法   mài fǎ

功夫本从弯步来，
两手变化随步开。
高挑低搂横掩避，
推托带领不离怀。

Deep skill comes from walking with bent legs,
All the variations of the hands open out from stepping.
You can scoop high attacks, brush aside low attacks, cover and evade crossing attacks,
Push, lift, drag, and draw, all without (your hands) leaving your chest.

This verse describes the results of circle-walking. It explains 迈法 mài fǎ: 'stepping'. The term 功夫 gōng fǔ: 'deeply trained skill' is used, so 'walking with bent legs' means more than just moving around, and more than walking on a curving route, but refers specifically to circle-walking. Although this verse emphasizes that the deep skill comes from circle-walking, neither the verse itself nor anywhere else in the verses describes what circle-walking actually is – we know from our teachers. The closest you can get in the verses to circle-walking is to combine the posture described in the verses 36.01 and 36.02 with the movement described in 36.03 and 36.08. This is reinforcing the explanation in verse 36.03 of always using footwork. So basically, this verse is saying 'do your circle-walking and trust it to develop your body connections and skills so that you can use your footwork to make your hand techniques effective'.

When the circle-walking has built the foundation and the connection, the feet are able to deliver the hands where they need to go. It does not mean literally that you keep your hands at your chest, just generally in a comfortable position in front of your body. Placement of the

THE FORTY-EIGHT METHODS VERSES   119

body by walking and the connection you have developed in the circle-walking allows the hands to stay in front of the body while doing techniques, so that you do not lean or overreach. The hands can stay quite still when you use your feet to move your body to the right place to get the techniques done. The hands are thus more effective, and the verse lists some defensive options made available by good connections. The technique 推 tuī: 'push' is used for striking forward. The technique 托 tuō: 'lift' us used for striking up, it is your rising defense/attack. The technique 带 dài: 'drag' is used for pulling smoothly (if left foot is forward, the right hand pulls to the right side). The technique 领 lǐng: 'draw' is used for pulling across (two handed pull: if left foot is forward, the right hand crosses the body, the left hand pulls to the left). The four techniques mentioned in the last line are four standards – by no means an exhaustive list – but generally regarded as core techniques of baguazhang. The verses sometimes suggest techniques in the manner of presenting options, which gives us the principles of fighting without overwhelming us with the details.

48.04.1   Deep skill comes from walking with bent legs,

　功　　　夫　　　本　　　从　　　弯　　　步　　　来，
　gōng　　fū　　　běn　　cóng　　wān　　bù　　　lái,

Six sources (Li, Lin, Tu, Wang, Wu, and Zang) have this line. The phrase 弯步 wān bù: 'bent legs', was the term used in verse 36.03 that described the circle-walking method. Huan has 功夫求从弓步来 gōng fū qiú cóng gōng bù lái: 'we seek deep skill in the arced legs walking'. Huan referred to this posture as 弓步 gōng bù: 'arced legs' in that verse, so 'circle-walking' is also the intended meaning. Liu uses 工夫 gōng fū: which also means 'workmanship, effort'.

48.04.2   All the variations of the hands open out from the stepping.

　两　　　手　　　变　　　化　　　随　　　步　　　开。
　liǎng　shǒu　biàn　huà　　suí　　bù　　　kāi.

All sources have this line.

48.04.3   (You can) scoop high attacks, brush aside low attacks, cover and evade crossing attacks,

　高　　　挑　　　低　　　搂　　　横　　　掩　　　避，
　gāo　　tiǎo　　dī　　　lōu　　héng　　yǎn　　bì,

Most sources (Huan, Li, Lin, Liu, Wang, and Zang) have with this line. Tu and Wu have 横掩闭 héng yǎn bì: 'cover and close off crossing attacks'.

48.04.4   Push, lift, drag, and draw, all without (your hands) leaving your chest.

| 推 | 托 | 带 | 领 | 不 | 离 | 怀。 |
| tuī | tuō | dài | lǐng | bù | lí | huài. |

Six sources (Li, Lin, Liu, Wang, Wu, and Zang) have this line. Tu has 推托带擰 tuī tuō dài nǐng: 'push, lift, drag, and twist'. Huan has 不离根 bù lí gēn: 'without leaving your root'. Unfortunately, this doesn't rhyme, because it ties nicely to the previous verse of the hands never leaving your feet.

Five: Method of Continuous Steps

连步法   lián bù fǎ

连步必三费功夫，
使手要简自然无。
搭手转身是空手，
机会恰巧是江湖。

It takes time and training to develop the three continuous steps,
Good stepping enables hand techniques to be simple and natural.
When you engage with your opponent, turn so he enters into emptiness,
Take what opportunities present – this is the skill of 'the companions of rivers and lakes'.

This verse doesn't so much explain continuous stepping as say that we need to train it (a lot – the term 功夫 gōng fǔ: 'deeply trained skill' is again used). Together with the front foot step, explained in previous verses, you then step through, and then the follow-up step prepares for the next step. The lively stepping allows you to attack and then turn to disappear. When we do straight line drills we practise a three step advancing pattern, and combine it with hand techniques so they become as one. Immediately on contact, turn – perhaps with a drawing pull to assist him into emptiness. This is another recommendation for moving evasion to keep your opponent off balance, and the final line recommends that evasion is always in conjunction with a counter. If you can count on your stepping, then the techniques don't need to be fancy. Simple methods keep the power clear.

The phrase 江湖 jiāng hú: 'rivers and lakes', refers to the brotherhood of martial artists who lived in the margins of society –

THE FORTY-EIGHT METHODS VERSES   121

figuratively 'in the land of rivers and lakes'. Bandits usually had their lairs in areas that were difficult to access such as in the rivers, lakes, and marshes. Wandering knight errants, of 'the world of rivers and lakes', were supposed to be chivalrous and were expected to come to the aid of the unfortunate and powerless. Novels throughout history, such as The Water Margin (Outlaws of the Marshes), and modern films recount many stories of such honourable bandits and heroes.[40] Dong Haichuan had spent a lot of time travelling around China, so would also be very familiar with the *jianghu* world. Cruel bandits and thugs were not considered among the brotherhood. The *jianghu* society followed a slightly different code than normal Confucian society in giving first allegiance to the martial brotherhood (and sisterhood – skilled women were respected), and giving allegiance to the king only if he were honourable. The ties made between martial artists were of loyalty to each other and friendship, irrespective of social position, and not particularly caring about lawfulness. This is one reason Chinese governments vacillate between discouraging the martial world and trying to incorporate it to serve their purposes.

The *jianghu* includes martial artists on both sides of the law, as long as they follow the martial code. In the time of the development of baguazhang in Beijing, martial arts were more about fighting skills than health, and there were not much proper work available – teacher, guard, or the more marginal busker. Many Bagua and Xingyi masters (such as Yin Fu, Liang Zhenpu, and Liu Bin) in the late 19th century worked as security guards. Mid 19th century China was in constant conflict, while at the same time the commodity economy was rapidly developing, so 镖局 biāo jú: 'security agencies' flourished. Many martial artists earned their living as 保镖 bǎo biāo: 'bodyguards', either as 护院 hù yuàn: 'security guards in compounds' or 走镖 zǒu biāo: 'armed escorts', who travelled the country escorting merchants' caravans. Although on the side of the law, guards were also of the *jianghu* world. Armed escorts, particularly, would have many opportunities to meet and exchange with other martial artists in their travels. This served

to open up and bring interchange between styles. The fun image on the preceding page, called 'In Jiyang town', is from an old 'book of heroes' that recounts the story of a travelling busker who made friends with the local martial artist of the town. Buskers, performing in the streets, were not looked down on by other martial artists, as long as they held to the code. It says "Our hero, while performing in the street, met a certain master Song, who was an honourable person, not a vicious bandit. They swore brotherhood on the banks of the Xunyang River."[41]

48.05.1　　It takes time and training to develop the three continuous steps,

连　　步　　必　　三　　费　　功　　夫，
lián　bù　bì　sān　fèi　gōng　fū,

Five sources (Li, Lin, Liu, Tu, and Wang) have this line. Wu has 用步连三 yòng bù lián sān: '<u>using</u> three <u>continuous</u> stepping'. Zang has 连步法三 lián bù <u>fǎ</u> sān: 'continuous steps <u>method</u> three', which seems to be a typo. Huan has 连步必须 贵功夫 lián bù bì <u>xū guì</u> gōng fū: 'if you use continuous steps you <u>must have excellent</u> skill' (without the 'three steps').

48.05.2　　Good stepping enables hand techniques to be simple and natural.

使　　手　　要　　简　　自　　然　　无。
shǐ　shǒu　yào　jiǎn　zì　rán　wú.

All sources have this line.

48.05.3　　When you engage with your opponent, turn so he enters into emptiness,

搭　　手　　转　　身　　是　　空　　手，
dā　shǒu　zhuàn　shēn　shì　kōng　shǒu,

All sources have this exact line. The term 转身 zhuàn shēn: 'turn' sometimes is a generalised term that refers to a variety of turning methods. When used specifically, it means a stepping turn, doing a *koubu* step with the front foot. As a general term, it could refer to a waist turn without a step, but that is usually called 拧身 níng shēn: 'twist the body'.

48.05.4　　Take what opportunities present – this is the skill of 'the companions of rivers and lakes'.

机　　会　　恰　　巧　　是　　江　　湖。
jī　huì　qià　qiǎo　shì　jiāng　hú.

All sources have this exact line.

Six: Method of the Gathering Stance

囤步法　　tún bù fǎ

囤步不要两相齐，
前虚后实差相宜。
若要站齐前后仰，
亦且腰短少灵机。

When in a gathering stance the feet must not be in line or together,
There should be an appropriate distinction: one in front and empty, one behind and solid.
If you stand up with the feet together you can too easily be leaned back or forward,
Moreover, this gives the waist a short reach and little agility or spontaneity.

A gathering step or stance is a pause during a fight – basically standing still, but only for an instant while gathering potential energy for the next move. This is the stance referred to in the verses that describe pausing to observe the situation (36.31, 48.02, 48.11, 48.12, 48.15, 48.24, 48.30). The gathering stance, as described, is a stable but agile position with the legs front and back, a bit more weighted to the rear.

The briefly held stance described in this verse refers to a weighting of about 70/30, which is not an empty stance. From this stance you can step in any direction easily while keeping the body stable. This is similar to Xingyiquan's *santi* stance, with the feet about a shin length apart, but in Baguazhang it is a momentary stance, a pause, and so is lighter and more mobile. A 'suitable distinction' between the feet means the combination of neither too close and nor too far, with a good balance of empty and solid, so that they can move easily. If you just stand up with the feet together you lose balance, reach, speed of reaction, and the ability to move freely. Simply standing up is not an option. Neither is setting firmly into a deep or long stance that restricts mobility. The verse doesn't say so, but I think *qian kun* hands would be a good balance with the momentary pause while watching, having the same sort of balance.

48.06.1　　When in a gathering stance the feet must not be in line or together.

囤	步	不	要	两	相	齐,
tún	bù	bù	yào	liǎng	xiāng	qí,

Four sources (Huan, Lin, Tu, and Wang) have this exact wording. Liu and Zang call the stance a 顿步 dùn bù : 'pausing stance', both in the title and the line. Wu calls the stance a 屯步 tún bù: 'collection stance', or 'storing stance'. Li calls the stepping 固步 gù bù: 'fixed stance', but describes it as a pause during movement in his commentary. This is most likely a typo, especially as the re-edited Li has 囤步 tún bù: 'gathering stance'.

A similar pausing stance is called 霎步 shà bù: 'momentary stance' in Shaolin materials.

48.06.2　　There should be an appropriate distinction: one in front and empty, one behind and solid.

前　虚　后　实　差　相　宜。
qián　xū　hòu　shí　chā　xiāng　yí.

Four sources (Li, Lin, Tu, and Wang) have this exact line. The slight variations are in the final phrase. Liu has 互参差 hū cān chā: 'mutually uneven'. Huan has 不远离 bù yuán lí: 'should not be too far apart'. Wu has 两相差 liǎng xiāng chā: 'two different'. Zang has 至参差 zhì cēn cī: 'so they are not uniform'. These variations agree with the meaning of having the feet just the right distance apart and weighted just right.

48.06.3　　If you stand up with the feet together you can too easily be leaned back or forward,

若　要　站　齐　前　后　仰，
ruò　yào　zhàn　qí　qián　hòu　yǎng,

All main sources (Huan, Li, Lin, Liu, Tu, Wang, Wu, and Zang) have this exact line.

48.06.4　　Moreover, this gives the waist a short reach and little agility or spontaneity.

亦　且　腰　短　少　灵　机。
yì　qiě　yāo　duǎn　shǎo　líng　jī.

Five sources (Li, Lin, Tu, Wang, and Zang) have this exact line. Liu has 亦且腰裹 yì qiě yāo guǒ: 'moreover, the waist is wrapped', perhaps meaning 'bound up'. Wu has 亦且腰腿 yì qiě yāo tuǐ: 'moreover, the waist and legs'. My copy of Huan is a bit of a mess here.

The Forty-Eight Methods Verses

Seven: Method of Using the Hands

手法　shǒu fǎ

偏沉则随双重滞，
外硬里软拈枪势。
横推里勾身有主，
只有吸手腰腹随。

When you are partially heavy you can follow (your opponent), but when you are double heavy you are sluggish,
Be hard on the outside and pliant on the inside, like when you hold a spear.
Whether pushing across or hooking in, the torso is always in charge,
You just need to absorb with the hands and the waist and belly will follow.

The main idea of this verse is that it is best to use deflective techniques combined with the work of the waist. To achieve this, the hands need to operate in a certain way. The first prerequisite is the correlation that is made between the hand techniques and the foot techniques – that of keeping both hands and feet apart and unequal in weighting and power. The first line makes the same point as the previous verse – that the body should be held ready to fight, a bit uneven in the stance, not set solid into a double weighted stance.

The second line gives perhaps one indication why the forty-eight methods are said to be for more advanced students. Normally the spear is an advanced weapon, so this analogy isn't that much use to a beginner. The touch to play with a spear is a subtle one, but you can hit very hard due to the suppleness of the spear's shaft. The hands are also one forward, one back when holding a spear, and using a spear takes perfect coordination between them, connected through the body. Most importantly, as Ming dynasty general Wang Minghe wrote, "the power of the waist is most vital, then that of the rear hand, and then that of the front hand."[42]

What is meant by being 'double heavy' is being 'caught flat footed' in a fight, without any intention to move. Jiang Rongqiao, in his unpublished manuscript, wrote that baguazhang does not worry about 'double heavy' in the feet – that having even weighting is not an error if the body is all together, the mind is collected, and the power and movement remains lively. A worse error is putting too much weight on one leg, which makes movement less agile.⁴³

Some of the training of baguazhang involves 'double heavy' stances such as the horse stance. Moreover, the title indicates that the power balance of the hands is key, not the stance. Yin Yuzhang's book has many examples of horse stance as in integral part of the techniques. The baguazhang horse stance is a short one – you must be able to step in and out of it.

The second idea is the balance of hardness and pliancy, which has been explained in verses 36.19, 36.20, 36.26, 36.27, and 36.28. The third idea is the connection of the hands through the waist, which has also been explained in the thirty-six verses. The techniques named in line three are defensive ones that completely use the turning of the torso, absorbing an opponent's incoming hand or weapon by following with the back and hips, sucking in the belly. Yan Dehua's book of applications often refers to this method. In the seventh application, for example, sucking in is used with the push across. "My opponent twists his stance to enter his body and dissipate the attack of my right hand. He quickly pulls his left hand away then hits to my left ribs with his right hand. I quickly absorb with my body then roll my left arm down and out, sticking to his right arm to press it outwards."⁴⁴ Yan often refers to 'sucking in the chest' as the initial response to an attack to the body, "My opponent strikes at my chest with his right hand. I quickly suck in my chest to evade while twisting my body and sliding my right hand along the outer edge of his arm to stab downward."⁴⁵

48.07.1   When you are partially heavy you can follow (your opponent), but when you are double heavy you are sluggish,

偏　　　沉　　　则　　　随　　　双　　　重　　　滞，
piān　　chén　　zé　　　suí　　shuāng　zhòng　zhì,

THE FORTY-EIGHT METHODS VERSES 127

There is full agreement on this line except for one character, with a split on the word in the first phrase for the character for 'heavy'. Three (Huan, Liu, and Wu) use 沉 chén, and five (Li, Lin, Tu, Wang, and Zang) use 重 zhòng. Both mean 'heavy'. Usually 沉 chén has a more positive connotation of 'sinking heaviness' and 重 zhòng is used when something is just heavy. I picked 沉 chén as it helps make the meaning clearer.

48.07.2   Be hard on the outside and pliant on the inside, like when you hold a spear.

外　　硬　　里　　软　　拈　　枪　　势(式)。
wài　 yìng　 lǐ　 ruǎn　nián　qiāng　shì (shì).

All sources have this line (although Liu has what is probably a typo of 裹 guǒ: 'wrap' for 离(里) lǐ: 'inside').

48.07.3   Whether pushing across or hooking in, the torso is always in charge,

横　　推　　里　　勾　　身　　有　　主，
héng　 tuī　 lǐ　 gōu　 shēn　yǒu　 zhǔ,

Six sources (Huan, Li, Lin, Tu, Wang, and Wu) have this exact line. Liu and Zang use the character 钩 gōu for 'hook'. The character 勾 gōu is a common shorthand for 钩 gōu: 'hook'. This line suggests a couple of deflecting defenses, by no means exhaustive. Liu again has 裹 guǒ: 'wrap' instead of 离 lǐ: 'in', but this time it is a valid move in the context.

48.07.4   You just need to absorb with the hands and the waist and belly will follow.

只　　有　　吸　　手　　腰　　腹　　随。
zhǐ　 yǒu　 xī　 shǒu　yāo　 fù　 suí.

Five sources (Li, Lin, Tu, Wang, and Zang) have this exact line. Liu has 只有呼吸 zhǐ yǒu hū xī: 'you just need to breathe'. Huan has 只有平手 zhǐ yǒu píng shǒu: 'you just need to keep the hands level'. He might be taking the spear holding analogy further. Wu has 腰腹助 yāo fù zhù: 'the waist and belly assist'.

The technique of 吸 xī : 'absorbing', is a bit more than giving in, but is sucking in your opponent in preparation for a dragging throw, which uses the waist to gain power.

Eight: Method of Using Power

力法　　　lì fǎ

人说冷弹脆快硬，
我说冷快是一般。
脆硬细分无二致，
发动全凭心力合。

People talk about cold, springy, crisp, quick, and hard powers,
We say that cold and quick are the same.
Looking carefully at crisp and hard, they are the same, too,
Power depends completely on the harmony between heart and strength.

Baguazhang is known for these five powers – cold, springy, crisp, quick, and hard – but this verse is saying that they really are all the same thing. Baguazhang's power comes from deep inside – a whole body power based on the internal and external harmonies. These 'five powers' are really attempts to describe this one power. Cold power is the ability to strike with no apparent preparation. Springy power is a snapping force that shoots out from a 'pod pop' within the waist. Crisp power is the ability to pop a short hard power within a smooth movement. A hard strike comes out cold, springs crisply, and is quick. If the strike is cold or springy it is, of course, quick, or if it is cold and quick it is, of course, springy. Zang comments that springy power is the combination of cold and quick powers. Both Li and Zang comment that since crisp must hit hard, there isn't any point in differentiating between these two powers. Wu comments that cold and quick both refer to speed, and crisp and hard both refer to hardness. The point is that there is no purpose in making such fine distinctions between what is essentially whole body power.

The 'harmony between heart and strength' points to the three internal harmonies, which are usually listed as the heart 心 xīn harmonized with awareness 意 yì, the awareness harmonized with qi 气 qì, and the qi harmonized with power 力 lì. These fit together with the three external harmonies of the shoulders harmonized with hips, elbows harmonized with knees, and hands harmonized with feet, or the more general 'hands, eyes, bodywork'. Another version of the internal harmonies is 'optic nerves, central nervous system, and nerve endings throughout the body', which places the unities at the level of perception rather than thought. This fits together with three external harmonies of hands with waist, waist with feet, and feet with hands.[46] Baguazhang uses whole body power, the power of the mind combining with the body. As described in verse 36.25, the heart, spirit, and strength unite with the eyes, hands, waist, and legs for one true power. If the mind and body are connected then there is no need to analyse a lot of different types of power. Hair splitting about what power is being used, or what is harmonizing with what, is pointless.

48.08.1   People talk about cold, springy, crisp, quick, and hard powers,
人　　说　　冷　　弹　　脆　　快　　硬，
rén　shuō　lěng　tán　cuì　kuài　yìng,

All sources agree on the list of powers, and five (Lin, Liu, Tu, Wang, and Zang) have this order. Three sources have a slightly different order. Huan has 快脆硬 kuài cuì yìng: 'quick, crisp, and hard'. Li and Wu have 快硬脆 kuài yìng cuì: 'quick, hard, and crisp'. The line in any order doesn't rhyme well anyway, so it doesn't really matter. The essential meaning is the same.

48.08.2   We say that cold and quick are the same.
我　　说　　冷　　快　　是　　一　　般。
wǒ　shuō　lěng　kuài　shì　yī　bān.

Four sources (Huan, Liu, Wu, and Zang) have this line, and four (Li, Lin, Tu, and Wang) have 冷弹 lěng tàn: 'cold and snapping' as the same. Although Li Ziming's text has 'cold and snapping', his commentary says that 'cold and quick' powers combined make up snapping power, so cold and quick are essentially the same. This suggests that the line should be 'cold and quick'.

48.08.3   Looking carefully at crisp and hard, they are the same, too,
脆　　硬　　细　　分　　无　　二　　致，
cuì　yìng　xī　fēn　wú　èr　zhì,

All sources have this line.

48.08.4   Power depends completely on the harmony between heart and strength.
发　　动　　全　　凭　　心　　力　　合。
fā　dòng　quán　píng　xīn　lì　hé.

Five sources (Huan, Li, Lin, Liu, and Zang) agree with this word for word. Tu uses the phrase 发力 fā lì instead of 发动 fā dòng, which is essentially the same in this context. Wang mixes the order 心合力 xīn hé lì: 'heart in harmony with strength'. In Chinese, the word order often doesn't change the meaning, but the other order is more normal for this phrase. Wu has 心力含 xīn lì hán: 'is contained in the heart and strength'.

Nine: Method of Reserving Power

存力法　　cún lì fǎ

只会使力不会存，
力过犹如箭离弦。
不但无功且有害，
轻输重折而伤身。

If you only know how to exert all your strength and not how to keep some in reserve,
Your strength will be excessive, like an arrow leaving the bowstring.
Not only will this achieve nothing, but it can also harm you,
If you get off lightly you will be defeated, but more seriously, you could be broken and injured.

This verse doesn't so much tell us how to store power as tell us that we should. Since the metaphor of shooting power like shooting a bolt from a crossbow has been used in verse 36.08 as a 'good power', this verse reminds us that we are indeed neither a crossbow and nor an arrow. A key tactic of baguazhang is to make your opponent over reach so that you can counter. You do not want to fall into this trap yourself. You must be balanced as you strike or throw, and not overextend, over commit, or let yourself get caught out. You need to have something held back in reserve, so you can change at the last instant. You need to be able to use the elasticity in your body to quickly change or strike again.

This relates to the 'one inch' burst of power of some schools of baguazhang. If each joint in the body, combined with the segments surrounding it, has an inch of leeway on extension, then at any moment this inch can be completed. Throughout the body, each segment gives its inch, generating a tremendous burst of power instantaneously with very little effort. This works in conjunction with the united fascial chains that run through the body.

This verse can be taken short term or long term, in relation to your training or in relation to fighting. If you over exert in your techniques, you may injure yourself. In the short term, with a small injury, but in the long term with internal injuries. If you over exert in a fight, you will lose. In the short term, by overextending and leaving yourself open, and in the long term, by running out of energy before your opponent.

THE FORTY-EIGHT METHODS VERSES 131

48.09.1 If you only know how to exert all your strength and not how to keep some in reserve,

只	会	使	力	不	会	存,
zhǐ	huì	shǐ	lì	bù	huì	cún,

Most sources have this exact line. Wu has 只会用力 zhǐ huì yòng lì: 'if you only know how to use force'.

48.09.2 Your strength will be excessive, like an arrow leaving the bowstring.

力	过	犹	如	箭	离	弦。
lì	guò	yóu	rú	jiàn	lí	xián.

Six sources (Li, Lin, Liu, Tu, Wang, and Wu) have this exact line. Huan has 箭离位 jiàn lí wèi: 'an arrow leaving its place', and Zang has 箭出弦 jiàn chū xián: 'an arrow going out from the bowstring'.

48.09.3 Not only will this achieve nothing, but it can also harm you,

不	但	无	功	且	有	害,
bù	dàn	wú	gōng	qiě	yǒu	hài,

All sources have this line.

48.09.4 If you get off lightly you will be defeated, but more seriously, you could be broken and injured.

轻	输	重	折	而	伤	身。
qīng	shū	zhòng	zhé	ér	shàng	shēn.

All sources agree with the meaning of this line. Four (Li, Lin, Tu, and Wang) have the exact line. Wu has a possible typo in the initial phrase, repeating the word broken for both consequences, 轻折重折 qīng zhé zhòng zhé: 'lightly will be broken, seriously will be broken'. Huan agrees with the defeat and breaking, but the final phrase is 且失勇 qiě shī yǒng: 'and moreover, loss of courage'. Liu, Wu and Zang have the final phrase consequences a bit more drastic, 且失身 qiě shī shēn: 'even leads to death'.

This can be understood in two ways. The first as I have translated it. Another possibility is: if you emit too lightly you will lose for sure. If you emit too strongly you can hurt yourself.

Ten:　　Method of Continuing Power
　　　　续力法　　　　xù lì fǎ

力着他人根已断，
若再续力彼难逃。
此时惟有冲前步，
长膀长腰一齐交。

When your power has contacted your opponent and he has already lost his root,
　If you use continuous power he will have trouble getting away.
　At this time you just need to charge forward with your footwork,
　Lengthen the shoulder girdle, lengthen the waist, and deliver all in unison.

　　　This is a nice practical verse, with a tactic and a method to go with it. They depend on the ability to lengthen within the body. The method of lengthening needs to be understood and practiced, in combination with the footwork and various techniques. In a situation where you have put your opponent off balance with your entry, it is best to keep stepping into him rather than backing off or changing to another technique. Li Ziming adds in his commentary that this is why you keep the reserve power described in the preceding verse. If you manage to get your opponent back on his heels but not yet fallen over, just keep going forward with your footwork (the follow-up step works well here) to continue whatever it is that you are doing. If you try to change to something else, that will give your opponent time to adjust as well. For this to be effective you need to keep connected through the body and expand into the attack. If you step forward but do not consciously expand and extend your waist and shoulder girdle, you risk collapsing under the pressure that you are putting on your opponent. This method will work particularly well with throws and takedowns. This means that the body must stay connected during all your training, so that you do not collapse in on yourself when you drive in and expand.

48.10.1　　When your power has contacted your opponent and he has already lost his root,
　　　　力　　着　　他　　人　　根　　已　　断，
　　　　lì　　zháo　tā　　rén　　gēn　　yǐ　　duàn,

All sources have this line, although Liu, Wu, and Zang have 跟 gēn: heel instead of 根 gēn: 'root'. Once he shifts his heel his root is lost, so this means the same thing.

48.10.2　　If you use continuous power he will have trouble getting away.
　　　　　若　　再　　续　　力　　彼　　难　　逃。
　　　　　ruò　zài　xù　　lì　　bǐ　　nán　táo.

All sources have this line.

48.10.3　　At this time you just need to charge forward with your footwork,
　　　　　此　　时　　惟　　有　　冲　　前　　步，
　　　　　cǐ　　shí　wéi　yǒu　chòng　qián　bù,

Six sources (Li, Lin, Liu, Tu, Wang, and Zang) have this exact line. for the initial phrase, Wu has 此时唯有 cǐ shí <u>wéi</u> yǒu: 'at this time you <u>only</u> need to'. For the final phrase, Huan has 冲<u>箭</u>步 chòng <u>jiàn</u> bù: 'charge forward with <u>arrow stepping</u>'.

48.10.4　　Lengthen the shoulder girdle, lengthen the waist, and deliver all in unison.
　　　　　长　　膀　　长　　腰　　一　　齐　　交。
　　　　　cháng　bǎng　cháng　yāo　yī　　qí　　jiāo.

Most sources have the gist of this line, with a bit of variation. Four (Li, Lin, Tu, and Wang) have this exact line. Three (Huan, Liu, and Zang) have a reversed order, with 长腰长膀 cháng <u>yāo</u> cháng <u>bǎng</u>: 'lengthen the <u>waist</u>, lengthen the <u>shoulder girdle</u>'.

In the final phrase, Huan has 一齐<u>发</u> yī qí <u>fā</u>: '<u>give a burst</u> in unison'.

　　　　　　　　Eleven:　　How to Subdue Opponents
　　　　　　　　降人法　　jiàng rén fǎ

　　　　　　　快打慢兮不足誇，
　　　　　　　强制弱兮不为佳。
　　　　　　　最好比人高一招，
　　　　　　　顾盼中定不空发。

　　There is nothing to boast about in the quick beating the slow,
　　　There is nothing fine about the strong beating the weak.
　　　　It is best to be more highly skilled than your opponents,
Then you can watch both sides and keep centered, and not issue any empty attacks.

This verse suggests that the best way to subdue opponents is to be better than them. While this seems a bit obvious, the verse clarifies itself by explaining that this is in the sense of being more skillful, and with deeper skills. This belief is not unique to baguazhang. An old text from the Shaolin temple says, "Accomplished fighters must have highly refined skills. It is said that a highly skilled person is courageous, and this confidence is not misplaced."[47] Similarly, Ming dynasty general Wang Minghe wrote in 1599, "Someone with unrefined sword skills will not have courage."[48]

This verse continues the idea from verse 36.31 of watching and taking your time before reacting to attackers. Waiting is an classic tactic, but it requires a confidence in your ability to react properly at the right time. This is easier to do when confident of your deep skill. This verse is saying that it is better to train our circle-walking, footwork, and body connections than to train specific drills for strength or speed. If we are well trained, centered, well connected, and in harmony, we can beat opponents who are quicker and stronger than us.

48.11.1 There is nothing to boast about in the quick beating the slow,

快　　打　　慢　　兮　　不　　足　　誇，
kuài　dǎ　　màn　xī　　bù　　zú　　kuā,

All sources have this line. Some sources use 夸 kuā, the simplified character for 誇 kuā.

48.11.2 There is nothing fine about the strong beating the weak.

强　　制　　弱　　兮　　不　　为　　佳。
qiáng　zhì　ruò　xī　　bù　　wéi　jiā.

Most sources have this exact line. Wu has 強胜弱兮 qiáng shèng ruò xī: 'the strong beating the weak'. For the final phrase, Huan has 不为德 bù wéi dé: 'there is nothing virtuous'.

48.11.3 It is best to be more highly skilled than your opponents,

最　　好　　比　　人　　高　　一　　招，
zuì　　hǎo　bǐ　　rén　gāo　yī　　zhāo,

Most sources have this line. Huan has 取如此人高一招 qǔ rú cǐ rén gāo yī zhāo: 'taken in such a way, be more highly skilled than your opponents'. For the final phrase, Liu has 高一着 gāo yī zhāo, with the same meaning.

48.11.4 Then you can watch both sides and keep centered, and not issue any empty attacks.

顾　　盼　　中　　定　　不　　空　　发。
gù　　pàn　zhōng　dìng　bù　　kōng　fā.

Almost all sources have this exact line.

Both 顾 gù and 盼 pàn mean to watch. Taken together they are short for the phrase 顾左盼右 gù zuǒ pàn yòu: 'look to the left and right', which is a phrase also used to refer to deflecting and taking care of what is coming from left and right.

Twelve: How to Ensure Victory

决胜法   jué shèng fǎ

彼力千钧快如梭，
避强用顺快步挪。
千人只有三五近，
稍伸手脚不难遮。

If your adversary has massive strength and is as quick as a weaver's shuttle,
   Avoid his strength by using smooth following methods and shifting your stance quickly.
   If there are a thousand people, only three to five can get close to you,
   It isn't difficult to impede them by slightly extending your hands and feet.

This is another straightforward verse with practical tactics that work with a variety of techniques. Remember that no matter how much you seem to be overpowered, conserve your strength by remaining calm and by using softer deflecting moves. Smooth following methods include drawing and dragging, which take the force of an incoming attack and continue it smoothly in the same direction 'with the grain', 'down river', 'with the wind at your back', veering it slightly off so that it misses you, without wasting a lot of energy or movement. Using stillness and smooth methods to beat strong attacks, staying still to give yourself time to look, analyze, and deal with the situation, is a time honoured method. Ming dynasty general Qi Jiguang wrote, "You need to go along smoothly with the opponent's structure and borrow his strength. You need to be able to quickly use the situation, and to appear to be advancing when in reality you are retreating. Then you advance and win a great victory."[49]

This works for a lone attacker, but can also be used with multiple assailants. The verse reminds us that in a crowd only a few people can get to you, so you can take care of them and not bother with the others until they move in. Endurance rather than strength will win, so you need to use the smooth methods to save energy.

48.12.1   If your adversary has massive strength and is as quick as a weaver's shuttle,

彼	力	千	钧	快	如	梭，
bǐ	lì	qiān	jūn	kuài	rú	suō,

Most sources have this line exactly. Only Wang has 快如棱 kuài rú léng: 'quick as a <u>ridge</u>', obviously a typo for 梭 suō: 'shuttle'. The measure 千钧 qiān jūn: 1000 jun, is about 15000 kg, but this just means 'a lot'. At this point the explanation could be about a lone attacker.

48.12.2   Avoid his strength by using smooth following methods and shifting your stance quickly.

避	强	用	顺	快	步	挪。
bì	qiáng	yòng	shùn	kuài	bù	nuó.

Five sources have the character 步 bù: 'stance' or 'footwork' in the last phrase, (re-edited Li, Liu, and Wu) 快步挪 kuài <u>bù</u> nuó: 'quick <u>footwork</u> moving, and (Lin and Tu) 步快挪 <u>bù</u> kuài nuó: '<u>footwork</u> quick moving'. Four sources (Huan, Li, Wang, and Zang) have 快不挪 kuài <u>bù</u> nuó: 'quickly <u>do not</u> shift', which doesn't make a lot of sense, unless the intended meaning is 'do the techniques quickly without shifting around in your stance'.

Generally, the term 挪步 nuó bù: 'shifting step', means to pivot one foot in preparation for the other to step, or to shift the feet around a bit without stepping. Technically, a *nuobu* pivot pushes the heel back (lengthening the stance) as opposed to a *koubu* pivot, which turns the toes in (shortening the stance). This is one time that a real split in the sources makes for some confusion, giving two opposite resulting meanings. Li Ziming's commentary says that the footwork is coordinated with the drawing in methods, and that you are generally quite still, using the tactic of leading the sheep along. Wu comments that 挪 nuó is a shifting body technique.

48.12.3   If there are a thousand people, only three to five can get close to you,

千	人	只	有	三	五	近，
qiān	rén	zhǐ	yǒu	sān	wǔ	jìn,

All but one source have this exact line. Huan has 只有三五进 zhǐ yǒu sān wǔ <u>jìn</u>: 'only three to five can <u>get in towards</u> you'. This attitude is vital to anyone in a multiple attack situation, and is the key to this verse.

48.12.4   It isn't difficult to impede them by slightly extending the hands and feet.

稍	伸	手	脚	不	难	遮。
shāo	shēn	shǒu	jiǎo	bù	nán	zhē.

All sources have this line. I have seen this translated as 'it isn't difficult to protect yourself', but this is not the exact meaning of 遮 zhē: 'impede'. When fighting multiple attackers, looking for the weaker ones, tripping the closer ones up and messing them around, you can use them to impede the others. When many people surround you, they are essentially impeding each other in trying to get to you. In Aikido randori it is a common tactic not just to see who is closest, but to see who is weakest and move to ensure they become the closest, and then go for them, throwing them into the others. You could also go with the eighteenth stratagem, In Order to Catch the Bandits Catch the Leader, and take out the leader, thus taking the enthusiasm for a fight out of his followers.

Thirteen: How to Apply Tactics
运用法　　yùn yòng fǎ

高打矮兮矮打高，
斜打胖兮不须摇。
若遇瘦长凭拧带，
年迈无功上下瞧。

Hit short people high and tall people low,
Angle in on fat people, and you won't flounder.
Up against a lanky person depend on a pulling drag,
Against the old or unskilled, just look them up and down.

If you follow the advice of this verse, you can use your body proportions to your own advantage. Striking to the legs of tall people, you use your lower height to your advantage. Striking to the heads of short people takes the initiative away from them, should they want to attack you low. You prevent tall or short people from using their height to their advantage. Stepping around to flank larger people, who are usually fairly stable but not agile, you use your superior agility. Also, you don't need to reach so far, as fat people are usually larger in the front than the sides and back. Lanky people are relatively easy to topple, so a pulling technique works well against them.

I like the last line about not fighting with people with whom you don't really need to fight. Martial virtue comes in here, as it is not proper to beat someone who is clearly weaker than you.

48.13.1　　Hit short people high and tall people low,

高	打	矮	兮	矮	打	高，
gāo	dǎ	ǎi	xī	ǎi	dǎ	gāo,

All sources have this line, although Huan and Wang use 短 duǎn: 'short', instead of 矮 ǎi: 'short in stature'.

48.13.2　　Angle in on fat people, and you won't flounder.

斜	打	胖	兮	不	须	摇。
xié	dǎ	pàng	xī	bù	xū	yáo.

Most sources have this line. Liu has 不动摇 bù dòng yáo: 'you won't sway'. Wu has 不须劳 bù xū láo: 'you don't need to work hard'.

48.13.3　　Up against a lanky person depend on a pulling drag,

若	遇	瘦	长	凭	捋	带，
ruò	yù	shòu	cháng	píng	lǔ	dài,

All sources have a line that says it is relatively easy to topple a tall thin person with a pull. Five sources (Li, Lin, Tu, Wu, and Zang) have this exact line. Wang has the technique 采带 cǎi dài: 'a plucking drag'. Huan has 巧捋带 qiǎo lǔ dài: 'use a skillful pulling drag'.

48.13.4　　Against the old or unskilled, just look them up and down.

年	迈	无	功	上	下	瞧。
nián	mài	wú	gōng	shàng	xià	qiáo.

All sources have the same final phrase 上下瞧 shàng xià qiáo: 'look them up and down'. All sources have some descriptor of an older opponent. Five (Li, Lin, Liu, Tu, and Zang) have the phrase above. Wang has 年迈不功 nián mài bù gōng: 'old or unskilled'. Huan has 无功手老 wú gōng shǒu lǎo, and Wu has 无功年老 wú gōng nián lǎo: both meaning 'without skill or old'. These are all essentially the same.

Di Guoyong has 年迈无攻 nián mài wú gōng: 'don't attack the old'. He interprets this line as recommending that you keep your distance from older people until you wear them out. Perhaps speaking from experience, he says that you need to watch old people carefully, as they are more likely to try to surprise you with quick and vicious guerrilla tactics.

The Forty-eight Methods Verses

Fourteen: How to Seal Off
封闭法　　fēng bì fǎ

手讲三关脚伸屈，
一手三关脚直迂。
肩肘腕胯膝可用，
缩颈空胸步带躯。

In the upper limbs we talk of the three passes, and for lower limbs the extension and flexion,
The upper limbs can use three passes, while the lower limbs can go straight or roundabout.
You can use your shoulders, elbows, wrists, hips, and knees,
Retract your neck, empty your chest, and your footwork will lead the whole body.

  The title of this verse is how to seal off, and it explains how to close the three passes of the arms to seal off the body. The term 闭 bì means to cut off an attack before it is fully launched, so is best translated as 'jam' or 'shut down'. A 关 guān: 'pass' is a term used in martial arts for the joints in the limbs, short for the full word in Chinese, which is 关节 guān jié: a 'pass node'. In the upper limbs they are the shoulders, elbows, and wrists. In the lower limbs they are the hips, knees, and ankles. Like mountain passes, although they are weak points, they are also where you set up your defenses and ambushes. In other words, the joints are points that your adversary can use to control you, but they can also be used to strike. When referring to the striking capability of the area around the joints, they are often called the seven stars (the six striking surfaces of the shoulders, elbows, hands, hips, knees, feet, plus the head). The forward hand is called the 虎口关 hǔ kǒu guān: 'tiger's mouth pass', so if someone enters 'the tiger's mouth pass', he is in big trouble. The term 关 guān: 'passes' uses a similar concept but is not the same as the 门 mén: 'doors', which I discuss with verse 48.31.

  The verse says that you can hit with most of your upper and lower three passes. All the parts that need to be defended can also be used to attack, remembering that the actual focal point of the strike is usually the segment on either side of the joint. When the three passes in the upper and lower limbs are listed, the ankles are not included in the list. The main use of the ankles is to move around to enable defense and attack with the other segments, unless you count shin techniques. Usually you keep your feet for walking, not kicking, although kicks are an important tool of baguazhang. Li Ziming's commentary says that the three passes of the legs are brought into account with the bending and flexing of the legs during walking and moving around, and thus, the action of the legs closes off the three passes throughout the whole body.

In addition, the verse reminds us to keep our body structure so that our feet can better move the body around to enable us to bring all of our potential weapons into play.

48.14.1   In the upper limbs we talk of the three passes, and for lower limbs the extension and flexion,

手   讲   三   关   脚   伸   屈，
shǒu jiǎng sān guān jiǎo shēn qū,

Almost all the sources have this line. Wu has 手脚三关 shǒu jiǎo sān guān: 'the upper and lower limbs each have three passes'. As mentioned above, in Chinese a joint is 关节 guān jié: 'pass node'.

48.14.2   The upper limbs can use three passes, while the lower limbs can go straight or roundabout.

一   手   三   关   脚   直   迂。
yī shǒu sān guān jiǎo zhí yù.

Four sources (Liu, Tu, Wang, and Wu) have this exact line, which uses the character 迂 yù: 'circuitous'. Three (Li, Lin, and Zang) have 脚直遇 jiǎo zhí yù: 'the feet go straight to meet'. I wonder if these sources thought they were using the traditional character for 迂 yù? But the other sources also have straight line walking. Huan has 脚直迈 jiǎo zhí mài: 'stride directly'. It could be a mis-copy, as the characters 迂 and 迈 are pretty close, and 迈 mài doesn't rhyme. Li Ziming's commentary says that the protection of the upper three passes depends entirely on the footwork, so one would think that the stepping should vary. The re-edited Li has 脚直迂 jiǎo zhí yù: 'the feet go straight or circuitously', so I have gone with that character, as what makes most sense overall. With Wu's lines, the idea is that both upper and lower limbs have three passes, and you use the lower limbs to ensure the safely of the upper limbs. Alhtough this makes more sense, he is the only one with a different first line.

This line seems to just be repeating the first line, which is not usual for the verses. Di Guoyong also didn't like these two lines, and we thought perhaps the 脚 jiǎo: 'feet' could be supposed to be 叫 jiāo: 'called'. This would make the first line 'when we talk of three passes of the arms they are called that which extends and flexes'. The second line would then be 'each of the three passes of the arms are called what lets them go straight or roundabout'. I don't like the idea of changing lines, so have not done this, and also this doesn't take care of the repetition or take into account the lower limbs in the third line.

48.14.3 You can use your shoulders, elbows, wrists, hips, and knees,
　　肩　　肘　　腕　　胯　　膝　　可　　用，
　　jiān　zhǒu　wàn　kuà　xī　kě　yòng,

Most sources have this line. Only Wang has a slightly different order 肩腕膝胯肘 jiān wàn xī kuà zhǒu: 'shoulders, wrists, <u>knees</u>, hips, <u>elbows</u>'. That order is a bit random, while the usual order goes nicely from proximal to distal in the upper and lower passes.

48.14.4 Retract your neck, empty your chest, and your footwork will lead the whole body.
　　缩　　颈　　空　　胸　　步　　带　　躯。
　　suō　jǐng　kòng　xiōng　bù　dài　qū.

All sources have this line. This line is restating the basic body structure that allows the body to be stay in repose and go along with the feet.

Fifteen:　　How to Meet an Attack

接拳法　　jiē quán fǎ

五花八门乱如麻，
长拳短打混相加。
你越快兮我越慢，
我若发时神鬼誇。

(If I meet assailants acting as) 'five blossoms and eight doors' as chaotic as tangled hemp,
Long and short styles all mixed up.
The faster they go the more leisurely I'll react,
Once I initiate my attack, even gods and ghosts will praise me.

　　This verse describes the tactic (also explained in verses 48.02, 48.11, 48.22, 48.24, 48.30, and 48.33) of waiting patiently for opportunities to present themselves in a fight, then seizing the initiative with a devastating attack. It does not mean to move slowly, to hesitate, or to 'think', but to take your time to wait and watch, to not allow your opponents to fluster you. This tactic is an old one – indeed the thirtieth of the thirty-six the stratagems – Turn the Guest into the Host. Ming dynasty general Wang Minghe described a favourite tactic of a general Li, "If they come at you all disorderly, you must patiently retreat and settle in a balanced posture, waiting for them to come, then use a knocking technique to enter and win. This principle is called 'to use stillness to wait for movement, to wait at ease until they tire'."[50] You can't know what the assailants might do, so you need to take your time and observe, not getting sucked in to a panicked response. The more the assailants rush about the less effective will be their attack. When you take the initiative you are using your own way, not reacting to theirs. If you can force your rhythm on your assailants they are thrown off.

The phrase 五花八门 wǔ huā bā mén: 'five blossoms and eight doors', means 'a wide variety'. It also means to go all over the place, 'scattered like blossoms and heading for all doors', the direct opposite tactic of waiting calmly. This is a conventional phrase, not specific to martial arts – it is not a coded reference to five phases or eight trigrams. The term 门户 mén hù: 'doorway to a house' is used for martial schools, however, which makes this phrase an excellent one to also describe a variety of styles.

The phrase 乱如麻 luàn rú má: 'random like hemp', is a common metaphor for messiness or a chaotic situation, and is also used in verse 48.25. Hemp fibres are notoriously difficult to work with when being made into textile. I have left the translation with the more evocative phrases rather than translating it into 'if I'm attacked by a lot of people doing a lot of different things'. Within this verse is also an assumption that your attacks will be tremendous, not just because you waited for the right time, but because the baguazhang training has developed your whole body power.

48.15.1 (If I meet assailants acting as) 'five blossoms and eight doors' as chaotic as tangled hemp,

五　　花　　八　　门　　乱　　如　　麻，
wǔ　　huā　　bā　　mén　　luàn　　rú　　má,

All sources have this line.

48.15.2 Long and short styles all mixed up.

长　　拳　　短　　打　　混　　相　　加。
cháng quán　duǎn　dǎ　　hùn　xiāng　jiā.

All sources have this line. This is simply referring to the variety of styles and methods that you may have to deal with. Because you do not know their styles, you cannot predict their actions.

48.15.3 The faster you go the more leisurely I'll react,

你　　越　　快　　兮　　我　　越　　慢，
nǐ　　yuè　　kuài　　xī　　wǒ　　yuè　　màn,

Six sources (Li, Lin, Liu, Tu, Wu, and Zang) have this line. There are some slight differences in the grammar. Wang has 就越慢 jiù yuè màn: 'then the slower (I'll) go', which is alright, as Chinese grammar does not need the

THE FORTY-EIGHT METHODS VERSES 143

subject. My copy of Huan seems to be a mis-copy, 我越快 wǒ yuè <u>kuài</u>: 'the <u>faster</u> I'll go'. I have picked the most balanced line from the choices.

48.15.4   Once I initiate my attack, even gods and ghosts will praise me.

我	若	发	时	神	鬼	誇。
wǒ	ruò	fā	shí	shén	guī	kuā.

All sources agree on the meaning of this line. Seven have the exact first phrase 我若发时 wǒ ruò fā shí: 'when I attack'. Huan has 我拳发时 wǒ quán fā shí: 'when <u>my fists</u> attack'.

The descriptor of what happens to the assailant varies, but not in its essential meaning. Six (Huan, Li, Lin, Liu, Tu, and Zang) have 誇(夸) kuā: 'gods and ghosts will <u>praise</u>'. Two have a different reaction from the gods and ghosts – Wang has them 垮 kuǎ: '<u>collapse</u>', and Liang Shouyu has them 怕 pà: '<u>afraid</u>'. Wu just has them reversed 鬼神夸 guī shén kuā: '<u>ghosts and gods</u> will praise me'.

Sixteen: How to Release Grabs

摘解法   zhāi jiě fǎ

多少拿法莫誇技，
两手拿一力固奇。
任他神拿怕过顶，
穿鼻刺目势难敌。

Knowing a lot of grab and control methods is nothing to boast about,
Once two hands grab one, the strength is fixed and stuck.
No matter how good someone is at grabbing, they still fear going up over the head,
Add a spear to the nose and pierce to the eyes, and your momentum is difficult to resist.

If you are grabbed there is nothing to fear at all. Your opponent, especially if he grabbed you with both hands, is just as stuck as he is trying to make you. This also serves as a warning to you to not depend on grabbing. This is the rotational rising movement that breaks a grab and descends while gaining control, and in baguazhang we practice it a lot – one of the most repeated moves in baguazhang while doing the changes is drilling up from Hide a Flower Under a Leaf and turning to the Dragon Stretches its Talons posture (Wild Goose Leaves the Flock). The body turns and rolls, the arms twist and coil, and the power settles down, while the hands drill up over the head then roll down. Doing the changes, one may think the change is done when one gets to Hide a Flower Under a Leaf and perhaps turn sloppily. This verse serves to remind the student of the importance of training this method – putting intensity into the forearm twist drilling up, then equal intensity into the roll and placement downwards. The rising drill and rolling drop, along with the waist rolling turn, must be done with purpose, and this verse gives one reason why.

Yan Dehua's drawing of this method shows the drilling up with just a bit of shifting in the stance. If you are in more trouble, stepping will be even more effective.

Timing and moving would be key, because once you are well grabbed it is more difficult to bring off a release. If you are grabbed well enough that the drill up cannot work, you still have the other hand free to strike, loosening his grip. The spearing palm is emphasized throughout the verses, and this is one of its uses. This is where the cold power of baguazhang comes in – even in an awkward position you can still strike hard.

48.16.1 Knowing a lot of grab and control methods is nothing to boast about,

多	少	拿	法	莫	誇	技,
duō	shǎo	ná	fǎ	mò	kuā	jì,

All sources have this line (either with 夸 kuā or 誇 kuā).

48.16.2 Once two hands grab one, the strength is fixed and stuck.

两	手	拿	一	力	固	奇。
liǎng	shǒu	ná	yī	lì	gū	qí.

Most sources have this exact line. Huan has 力故挤 lì gù qí: 'strength <u>must be lined up purposefully</u>'. Wu has 力故奇 lì gù qí: 'strength <u>must be wrong</u>'.

48.16.3 No matter how good someone is at grabbing, they still fear going up over the head,

任	他	神	拿	怕	过	顶，
rén	tā	shén	ná	pà	guò	dǐng,

All sources have this line.

48.16.4 Add a spear to the nose and pierce to the eyes, and your momentum is difficult to resist.

穿	鼻	刺	目	势	难	敌。
chuān	bī	cì	mù	shì	nán	dí.

Almost all sources have this line. For the final phrase, Wu has 自难敌 zì nán dí: 'and you are difficult to resist'.

Seventeen: How to Take a Single to Remedy a Double

接单补双法　　jiē dān bǔ shuāng fǎ

莫说两手仗坚兵，
一来一往是其能。
闭住右手左无用，
双手齐来更无功。

Let's say an assailant attacks with a weapon in both hands,
All he can do is send one hand in while the other goes back.
Shut down one hand and his other hand becomes useless,
If he comes in with both hands then he has nothing at all.

  This verse offers practical advice against weapons held in both hands – either a long weapon or double weapons. Someone with a long weapon held in both hands has one forward and one back, and needs to wield the weapon with both hands balanced. When moving the weapon the hands will work together, even if he swings the weapon or switches the hands, they will still be one forward and one back. Someone with double weapons will usually move one back when the other moves forward to keep balance. In either case, you just need to go for one hand – 'receive a single' – and both hands are put out of commission – 'remedy a double'. The technique 闭住 bì zhù: 'shut down', means to jam an attack, preferably at the root, to shut it down before it is fully expressed. This is commonly done in baguazhang, turning your defense into an attack. As Cao Zhongsheng defines the technique, "I advance throwing out my arm to shut down my opponent's extended arm, so that he can't close in on me, but instead is hit by me."[51]

If the whole unit of weapon and both hands comes in, just dodge. You know where your opponent's weapon and both hands are, and he has nothing left. With both hands on his weapon or weapons, if you get out of the way he has his hands stuck with the weapon or weapons, and can't really do much at all. Double weapons become awkward if they come in together. Long weapons are quite easy to slide in on once they are close to you, once you have stepped out of the way of the immediate threat.

In his book on tactics, Ming dynasty general Wang Minghe has a section in his training manual describing how to use long weapons as if they were short weapons, recognizing the danger of entering and missing, or getting in and being unable to get back out, and the ease with which the enemy can then deal with your spear if you don't know how to react.[52]

48.17.1   Let's say an assailant attacks with a weapon in both hands,
莫　　说　　两　　手　　仗　　坚　　兵，
mò　　shuō　liǎng　shǒu　zhàng　jiān　bīng,

All sources agree on the meaning of this line, five (Huan, Li, Lin, Tu, and Zang) with this exact wording. For the final three character phrase, Wang has 掌坚兵 zhǎng jiān bīng: 'a weapon in his <u>palms</u>', possibly a mistake instead of 仗 zhàng: 'to hold a weapon'. Liu has 使坚兵 shǐ jiān bīng: '<u>making use of</u> a weapon'. Wu has 似坚兵 sì jiān bīng: '<u>are like</u> a weapon'.

48.17.2   All he can do is send one hand in while the other goes back.
一　　来　　一　　往　　是　　其　　能。
yī　　lái　　yī　　wáng　　shì　　qí　　néng.

All sources agree on the coming and going. Five sources (Li, Lin, Liu, Tu, and Zang) have 是其能 shì qí néng: 'is his ability'. Wang has 是真能 shì <u>zhēn</u> néng: 'is the <u>real</u> ability'. Huan has 是步能 shì <u>bù</u> néng: 'is the <u>footwork's</u> ability'. Wu has 是奇能 shì <u>qí</u> néng: 'is the <u>unusual</u> ability'.

48.17.3   Shut down one hand and his other hand becomes useless,
闭　　住　　右　　手　　左　　无　　用，
bì　　zhù　　yòu　　shǒu　　zuǒ　　wú　　yòng,

Five sources (Huan, Li, Liu, Wang, and Wu) have the same phrasing, which says 'if you shut down his right hand, his left hand becomes useless'. They agree that if you get control of the strongest hand holding the weapon his other hand can't do much. Three sources (Lin, Tu, Zang) switch the hands 闭住左手右无用 bì zhù <u>zuǒ</u> shǒu <u>yòu</u> wú yòng: 'if you close off the <u>left</u> hand, his right hand becomes useless'. For them this line means that if you control the forward hand on a spear, the back hand holding the butt can't do anything. Once either hand is gone from a long weapon the control is gone. In light of this difference, and that both versions work, I have allowed for both in my translation.

48.17.4   If he comes in with both hands then he has nothing at all.

双   手   齐   来   更   无   功。
shuāng shǒu   qí   lái   gēng   wú   gōng.

Most sources have this line. Tu has 更无能 gēng wú néng: 'he is helpless'.

Eighteen: The Tactic of Pointing at the Mountain to Get the Millstone

指山打磨法   zhǐ shān dǎ mò

他人来手我不然，
侧身还击彼自还。
他若还时我入手，
他若封时三手连。

If someone attacks me I don't bother much,
I turn to the side, counter attacking, so he himself counter attacks.
As he counters I begin another attack,
If he tries to seal off (that attack) I do three continuous palm strikes.

    This verse describes the tactic of evasion and strong unrelenting counter attack. Feints are described in the verses, but they take second seat to evasion, direct counter attack, distracting attacks, and unrelenting attacks. Tactics rely on not getting caught up in reacting directly to the opponent's attack by blocking. A turn or step to the side is enough for many situations, and allows you a counter attack without a block. The counter is powerful because the turn is already using the hips, so the counter comes out directly with the turn, not after. This sets you up for further attacks. Wu comments that Guo Gumin taught seventy-two 'three strike combinations', so that this tactic would be well trained and spontaneous.

    In his commentary on this verse, Li Ziming says that it refers to the second of the thirty-six stratagems – Besiege Wei to Rescue Zhao. This stratagem was used to relieve a besieged army (Zhao) by attacking the home base of the besiegers (Wei), instead of attacking the strong besieging Wei army directly. The Wei army had to abandon the siege to go protect their home base. This stratagem is often called diversionary, which is not quite right. It attacks to the root of the problem. It could also be seen as the tactic of 'just one hit', that is, dealing with an attack by attacking, not blocking. The evasion and counter 'just one hit', well described in a Shaolin book from the 1850s – "don't posture, don't block, just one hit"[53] – is one of the main tactics used in Baguazhang. The Shi lineage verses refers to this tactic in almost the same words: "Don't block: If your adversary is brave and fierce, you needn't be afraid, When he (goes to) hit you, you hit him. Turn and move to counter, moving in close, Don't block low, don't block high, just one hit."[54] Baguazhang's solid and quick footwork makes this particularly effective.

The title of this verse is named as a method in verse 36.32, which references disarming opponents. That verse describes remaining calm under attack and thus being able to use this method, without explaining it. The phrase 指山 zhǐ shān means to 'point to the mountain'. The phrase 打磨 dǎ mò normally means to 'grind with a millstone', but here can mean '(take stone from the mountain to) make a millstone'. This verse clarifies what was meant, but still leaves some ambiguity. This is one of those phrases that sound really cool, but are not so clear. Everyone thinks they know exactly what it means, but they don't all agree, which leaves room for personal interpretation and the development of your own favourite techniques and methods. The Li and Zang commentaries describe the meaning as 'if you want a stone with which to make a millstone you need to point out and go to the mountain'. Di Guoyong's commentary says that it is simply to point at the mountain, which is far away, and strike the millstone, which is close. The verses sometimes say 指上打下 zhǐ shàng dǎ xià: 'point high and hit low', treating this as about the same tactic.

48.18.1   If someone attacks me I don't bother much,

他	人	来	手	我	不	然，
tā	rén	lái	shǒu	wǒ	bù	rán,

Six sources (Li, Lin, Liu, Tu, Wang, and Wu) have this exact phrase. Huan has 他人手来 tā rén shǒu lái: 'comes with his hands', just reversing the word order. Zang has 他人采手 tā rén cǎi shǒu: 'if someone pulls me', which makes the following line a more specific counter to a pull.

48.18.2   I turn to the side, counter attacking, so he himself counter attacks.

侧	身	还	击	彼	自	还。
cè	shēn	huán	jī	bǐ	zì	huán.

Most sources have this line, except Liu and Zang, who have 彼身还 bǐ shēn huán: 'his body counters'.

THE FORTY-EIGHT METHODS VERSES   149

48.18.3   As he counters I begin another attack,

| 他 | 若 | 还 | 时 | 我 | 入 | 手, |
| tā | ruò | huán | shí | wǒ | rù | shǒu, |

Most sources have this exact line. Wang has 我八手 wǒ bā shǒu: 'I eight hands', which I suspect is a typo.

48.18.4   If he tries to seal off (that attack) I do three continuous palm strikes.

| 他 | 若 | 封 | 时 | 三 | 手 | 连。|
| tā | ruò | fēng | shí | sān | shǒu | lián. |

Six sources (Li, Lin, Liu, Tu, Wu, and Zang) have 'if he tries to seal off'. Wang has 他若致时 tā ruò zhì shí: 'if he tries to stop me'. Huan has 他不还时 tā bù huàn shí: 'if he doesn't pull back'.

         Nineteen: How to Trade your Body for a Shadow
                  脱身化影法   tuō shēn huà yǐng

                      他不来时我叫来，
                      他要来时我化开。
                      不须手避凭身法，
                      步步不离两胯哉。

              If he doesn't attack I call him in,
              Just as he attacks I dissolve away.
      I don't need my hands to evade, but depend on bodywork,
              My stepping never leaves (the width of) my hips.

     This verse once again explains using quick evasive footwork and bodywork to evade and counter, rather than blocking with the arms. This tactic was described in verse 36.21, and here it reinforces the idea of using small steps. Along with waiting for your opportunity, evasion with counter attack is one of the main topics of the tactical verses. This verse suggests baiting with a movement or a placement that makes your opponent want to attack. The timing needs to be tight with an evasive maneuver that simply steps aside, so you also must remember the protective arm position described in verse 36.17. The overall pattern of advice is not to attack until you have to – move to dissolve an attack, hopefully drawing out the opponent until he over extends. Then when the time is right, finish it with a quick and relentless counter attack.

The name of the verse is a technique known to baguazhang practitioners. In Yin Yuzhang's book, he describes it as a single quick technique, "If the opponent strikes to my face with his right hand, I withddraw my body and dodge behind him, using my left hand to hit his right ear. This is called Trade Your Body for a Shadow."[55] Other branches also say that it is 'such and such' a move or combination, but it is better to think of it as a general tactic. You move to the most advantageous place for you to counter attack – you do not move to escape. Changing to a Shadow refers to the two aspects of this tactic. One, to disappear leaving only your shadow. Two, to stick to your opponent like a shadow.

In this photo we accidentally caught the shadow effect of the speed of the half-step moving to the outside door of the opponent.

48.19.1 If he doesn't attack I call him in,
他 不 来 时 我 叫 来,
tā bù lái shí wǒ jiào lái,

Most sources have this exact line. Huan has 我引来 wǒ yīn lái: 'I draw him in'. Drawing him in is a more normal way to say it, but 'calling him in' is a nice way to put it.

48.19.2 Just as he attacks I dissolve away.
他 要 来 时 我 化 开。
tā yào lái shí wǒ huā kāi.

Four sources (Li, Lin, Tu, and Wang) have this exact line. The difference is in a slight grammatical variation of the setup phrase. Four sources (Huan Liu, Wu, and Zang) have 他若来时 tā ruò lái shí: 'if he attacks'. All sources use the term 我化开 wǒ huā kāi: 'I dissolve away'.

48.19.3　　I don't need my hands to evade, but depend on bodywork,

不	须	手	避	凭	身	法，
bù	xū	shǒu	bì	píng	shēn	fǎ,

Four sources (Li, Lin, Tu, Wang) have this exact line. For the first phrase, Huan has 不凭手力 bù píng shǒu lì: 'I do not depend on the strength of my hands'. For the second phrase, Liu, Wu, and Zang have 凭身段 píng shēn duàn: 'depend on body posture'.

48.19.4　　My stepping never leaves (the width of) my hips.

步	步	不	离	两	胯	哉。
bù	bù	bù	lí	liǎng	kuà	zāi.

Most sources have this exactly this line. Huan has 步子 bù zǐ: also meaning 'stepping'. Liu has 手步不离 shǒu bù bù lí: 'neither the hands nor the feet leave'. I understand this line to refer both to using small steps and to staying close, and I feel the Liu version backs up this interpretation.

Twenty:　　The Tactic of Turning and Getting Behind the Back
背后转身法　bèi hòu zhuàn shēn fǎ

伸手要小步要大，
开步半跨贴身抓。
跨步落地蹲身转，
他若转时我鹰拿。

The hands should extend a small distance while the footwork should be large,
Step out with a half sidestep, keeping the body in close to grab.
As my sidestep lands, I squat down and turn,
If he tries to turn I do an eagle grasp.

This verse describes the tactic of grabbing as you step around, flanking to get in beside or behind with control. You can take your opponent directly down from there. If he spins with you, though, grab firmly and continue to spin and drop, you spin him down face first into the ground. I see the eagle grasp as the same as Xingyiquan's eagle or Aikido's ikkyo – grabbing the wrist and cupping or cutting to control the elbow to immobilize and takedown with a smooth follow and spin. The grab from a close position of control, especially alongside or behind, seems to be the exception to the 'do not grab' rule of verse 48.46. No rule is set in stone.

Verse 36.12 said that the sidestep should be well away from the centre. This verse seems to be correcting mistakes that might have occurred from people stepping too far away, reminding us that it is a big step, but not to go too far if we want to remain effective. The general advice is the verses is to use small steps to move and turn around (verses 36.30, 36.34 and 36.36) but large steps are recommended to get in with an attack or around to the side of your opponent (in order that the hands do not need to reach out too far). Since the main goal is to flank the opponent, or move into him to put him off balance, you keep the hands reserved, moving along with the body. It is always better to stay upright and under control by stepping than to reach out with the arms. You settle down to stabilize yourself enough to take the opponent down, and only go fully down if you need to. If you do go down, do so with your legs, squatting into the dragon riding stance, not leaning.

48.20.1 The hands should extend a small distance and the footwork should be large,

伸	手	要	小	步	要	大，
shēn	shǒu	yào	xiǎo	bù	yào	dà,

All sources have this line.

48.20.2 Step out with a half sidestep, keeping the body in close to grab.

开	步	半	跨	贴	身	抓。
kāi	bù	bàn	kuà	tiē	shēn	zhuā.

Four sources (Huan, Li, Lin, and Liu) use the phrase 开步半跨 kāi bù bàn kuà: 'step out with the half sidestep'. The word 跨步 kuà bù: 'sidestep', is a step aside. The 'half step' says that although this is a large step, as said in the first line, it does not travel far from your adversary. Four sources (Tu, Wang, Wu, and Zang) use 开步半胯 kāi bù bàn <u>kuà</u>: 'step out a half <u>hip</u>', which also means to keep close. Both versions say that although you are taking relatively big steps, you are not moving away from your adversary, but trying to get to a side door. The step 开步 kāi bù: 'open step' is a general term for stepping to the side, but can also mean 'start out', or 'your first step'. That would make this line, 'on your first step, take a half sidestep'. Wu comments that since 跨步 kuà bù: 'side step' is a sideways step, and you are entering and staying close, it isn't a full sidestep, and this is why it is referred to as 开步半跨 kāi bù bàn kuà: 'open half side step'.

For the final phrase, four sources have the phrase 'stick to the body to grab'. Lin has 贴心抓 tiē <u>xīn</u> zhuā: 'stick to the <u>heart</u> to grab', which is the same as sticking to the body. Huan has 贴身跟 tiē shēn <u>gēn</u>: 'stick to the body and follow in'. Wang has 贴手抓 tiē shǒu zhuā: 'stick with the hands and grab'. Wu has 贴耳抓 tiē ěr zhuā: 'stick to the ears and grab', meaning to stick closely.

48.20.3   As my sidestep lands, I squat down and turn,

跨	步	落	地	蹲	身	转，
kuà	bù	luò	dì	dūn	shēn	zhuàn,

Almost all sources have this line. Wu has 跨步拖地 kuà bù tuō dì: 'drag the feet on stepping', meaning to keep the feet low.

48.20.4   If he tries to turn I do an eagle grasp.

他	要	转	时	我	鹰	拿。
tā	yào	zhuàn	shí	wǒ	yīng	ná.

All sources agree with the meaning of this line. Five (Li, Lin, Liu, Tu, and Wang) use 他要转时 tā yào zhuàn shí, and three (Huan, Wu, and Zang) use 他若转时 tā ruó zhuàn shí. These two words 要 yào and 若 ruó are used practically interchangeably throughout the verses. The character 要 yào makes the meaning more 'when he wants to…' or 'when he is going to', and 若 ruó makes the meaning more 'supposing that he…'. Wang has 我应拿 wǒ yìng ná: 'I grab in response'. I wonder if this was the intended word, especially considering all the other typos in that book.

Twenty-one: Tactics Against Hard Attacks
磕砸劈撞法   kē zá pī zhuāng fǎ

磕来还磕我要先，
砸右换步左手粘。
劈来叠肘椿横立，
撞来乾坤手摇圈。

When a knock comes I need to be first with a countering knock,
When a pound comes on my right I switch my stance and stick with my left hand.
When a chop comes I fold my elbow and cut across with an upright forearm,
When a ram comes I use both hands in balance and swing on the circle.

This verse gives the principles of countering specific hard attacking methods. Chang Naichou in the late 1700s explained the logic behind this defense reaction, in his chapter on aligning *qi*, explaining defense as a natural corollary to the power being applied, "You should understand the route of each technique. Once the hand is sent out its *qi* is directed in one way. It can't be applied in all four directions. A straight line attack has no crossing strength, so I cut across it. A crossing attack has no straight line strength, so I intercept it directly. A rising attack has no lowering strength, so I lift it. A dropping chop has no rising strength, so I hit on top of it. This applied to all attacks, whether angled, straight, bent, or extended. This is called 'muffling the void' – you attack the line that is ill prepared."[56] It is interesting to note that his comment was written well before the distinction between 'external' and 'internal' styles was made. Explaining fighting by *qi* lines referring to lines of force is just the normal vocabulary used.

A knock is a short abrupt strike, often with the forearm. It also means a bumping kind of hit, like you do in arm and leg bumping exercises with a partner. If you haven't done these, using a bump against a bump might hurt you more than it hurts your opponent. A countering knock does not mean you use exactly the same technique, but that you hit before he has reached his point of focus. A well timed abrupt forearm or elbow knock cuts off an attacking knock.

A pound is a hard hit, and heavy. It is usually downward, with a back fist or a strike with the heel of the fist. The verse recommends moving out of the way and sticking to deflect this punch, as it is safest to make sure it misses its target.

A chop is a quick downward strike with the forearm or palm edge. It is usually a fairly straight arm strike, so cutting across it with your forearm would deflect it from its line if timed just right. Tucking the elbow in gives a spiraling power so that this is a deflection rather than a block.

A ram, also translated as a shove, is a hard barging strike with the ends of the arms or charge with the body. It is a strong strike, and best dealt with not head-on, but by pliantly connecting, circling, and shifting to dissipate the force. The use of both hands in the *qian kun* position described in verses 36.17 and 36.27 indicates that the hands are apart and well balanced. With both hands circling in full coordination, even a very strong attack can be dissipated.

Yan Dehua's drawing on the following page shows the deflection of a chopping attack, and how that sets you up for your counter attack.

The Forty-eight Methods Verses

48.21.1   When a knock comes I need to be first with a countering knock,

磕　　　来　　　还　　　磕　　　我　　　要　　　先，
kē　　　lái　　　huán　　　kē　　　wǒ　　　yào　　　xiān,

Six sources (Lin, Liu, Tu, Wang, Wu, and Zang) have this exact line. Liu Jingru has 彼来迅疾我更先 bǐ lái xùn jí wǒ gèng xiān: 'when the adversary comes quickly I am even quicker'. The meaning is essentially the same, but the specific technique is missing. Most sources refer to four specific techniques in this verse, but his version is quite different, giving four defenses but not to specific attacks.

48.21.2   When a pound comes on my right I switch my stance and stick with my left hand.

砸　　　右　　　换　　　步　　　左　　　手　　　粘。
zá　　　yòu　　　huàn　　　bù　　　zuǒ　　　shǒu　　　zhān.

Most sources have this exact line. My copy of Huan is a bit messed up for these two lines. Wu repeats 磕 kē: 'knock' as the attack, which I suspected as a typo, but he comments that the knock can also be dealt with by switching feet and hands.

48.21.3   When a chop comes I fold my elbow to cut across with upright forearm,

劈　　　来　　　迭(叠)　　　肘　　　椿(桩)　　　横　　　立，
pī　　　lái　　　dié　　　zhǒu　　　zhuāng　　　héng　　　lì,

Seven sources (Li, Lin, Liu, Tu, Wang, Wu, and Zang) have this line. Once again, Liu Jingru's version does not name a specific attacking technique. He doesn't specify the attack and uses a different verb for the elbow technique, 左来加肘 zuǒ lái jiā zhǒu: 'if he comes on the left I add my elbow'. Huan has 劈来坚时 pī lái jiān shí: 'when he chops hard'.

The use of 迭 dié or 叠 dié: for 'fold', and 椿 zhuāng or 桩 zhuāng: for 'stance', do not change the meanings. They are not specific simplified and traditional characters, but tend to be used as such throughout the verses.

48.21.4　　When a ram comes I use both hands in balance and swing on the circle.

撞	来	乾	坤	手	摇	圈。
zhuàng	lái	qián	kūn	shǒu	yáo	quān.

Most sources have this line. Liu Jingru, once again, does not have a specific attack, 双来 shuāng lái: 'when he attacks <u>with both hands</u>'.

The 乾坤手 qián kūn shǒu: *qian kun* hands, is the 'heaven and earth hands' – one forward one back, one hard one pliant, one high one low, one straight one slightly crossing, described in verses 36.17 and 37.27.

Twenty-two:　　How to Use Half-Circle Hands

半圈手法　　　bàn quān shǒu fǎ

他人手法多直线，
跨上半步等如闲。
即或指直打斜法，
再跨半步不相干。

Someone from another fighting style usually attacks in a straight line,
　　Take a half sidestep forward and wait at ease.
　　If he tries a straight fake with an angled strike,
Take another half sidestep and (what he is doing) becomes irrelevant.

This whole verse is a bit cocky, but the verses are meant for baguazhang practitioner's ears only. 'Half-circle Hands' sounds like a hand technique, but of course it describes the principle of using footwork to evade – keeping the hands ready for defense and counter, and keeping connected through the body. With the half-circle stepping we put ourselves into a situation where we take the initiative, not controlled by our opponent. A sidestep is a step a bit to the side, with either foot, and can go a bit forward or backward, wherever is best. Used to evade, as here, it is usually used as a half step. Used to attack it is a bigger step, as described in verse 48.20. It is an agile repositioning step, like straddling a creek, which, as here, is used to get to an advantageous position. The half-circle hands would use the *qian kun* hands to go along with the stepping.

Ming dynasty general Wang Minghe described this tactic well, "If he attacks with a raised staff I gradually encroach on his space. If he comes at me face on I stay face on ('big door', squaring up with the same feet forward), receiving slightly and shifting an inch. If he comes at me shoulder to shoulder I stay shoulder to shoulder ('small door', angling in sideways with different feet forward), receiving slightly and shifting an inch. I wait to see what door he will take then I enter with my utmost attack."[57]

48.22.1 Someone from another fighting style usually attacks in a straight line,

他　　人　　手　　法　　多　　直　　线，
tā　　rén　　shǒu　　fǎ　　duō　　zhí　　xiàn,

Almost all sources have this line. Wu has 他人打法 tā rén dǎ fǎ: 'other people's fighting methods', with the same meaning.

48.22.2 Take a half sidestep forward and wait at ease.

跨　　上　　半　　步　　等　　如　　闲。
kuà　　shàng　　bàn　　bù　　děng　　rú　　xián.

Almost all sources have this line. For the final phrase, Wu has 只等闲 zhǐ děng xián: '<u>just</u> wait at ease'. The use of 上 shàng: 'forward' indicates that the rear foot sidestep is not a retreating technique – the rear foot, as it sidesteps, moves forward a bit.

48.22.3 If he tries a straight fake with an angled strike,

即　　或　　指　　直　　打　　斜　　法，
jí　　huò　　zhǐ　　zhí　　dǎ　　xié　　fǎ,

Most sources have this line. Huan has 即二 jí <u>èr</u>: 'if he tries a <u>second</u> hit'.

48.22.4 Take another half sidestep and (what he is doing) becomes irrelevant.

再　　跨　　半　　步　　不　　相　　干。
zài　　kuà　　bàn　　bù　　bù　　xiāng　　gān.

All sources have this line.

Twenty-three: How to Use Full-Circle Hands
整圈手法　　　zhěng quān shǒu fǎ

四面敌人我在中，
穿花打柳任西东。
八方凭势风云变，
不守呆式不走空。

If I am surrounded on four sides by assailants,
I move freely East and West like threading through blossoms to hit willow trees.
Even if completely encircled with the momentum (of the enemy) changing like clouds in the wind,
I don't guard in a dull-witted posture and I don't take a pointless step.

Often the more poetic lines tend to be passed on exactly as they are. 'Threading through blossoms to hit willow trees' suggests that if you are surrounded but not completely hemmed in you can put the continual spearing palm to good use, moving back and forth through the crowd unpredictably. In his commentary, Li Ziming adds the image of a butterfly fluttering freely amongst the flowers. The verses were transmitted within each lineage but Li Ziming was the first to publish them. It is interesting how his influence is seen in the commentaries of others – other commentators and translators often use the butterfly allusion, although it is not said in the verse. I like to think of slipping through waving willow fronds full of blossoms to arrive at the trunk without being touched.

When completely encircled, on all eight points of the compass, this is where the full circle comes in – you change more randomly so that they cannot get a fix on you. If you are completely surrounded there is still no need to worry, just more care is needed. This is the tactic of keeping moving without getting flustered. You can't just run around – you will get as confused as your assailants. You use the space within the full circle to evade your assailants – you do not run around in a circle. The suggestion in the verse is that we cannot just defend, but must be proactive. Again, changeable footwork is the key. Practising the changes adapt us to moving around in all sorts of directions, so we are perhaps better able to use this full circle tactic than those who usually practice on the straight line.

48.23.1　　If I am surrounded on four sides by assailants,
　　　　　四　　面　　敌　　人　　我　　在　　中，
　　　　　sì　　miàn　　dí　　rén　　wǒ　　zài　　zhōng,

The Forty-eight Methods Verses

All sources have exactly this line.

48.23.2 I move freely East and West like threading through blossoms to hit willow trees.

穿	花	打	柳	任	西	东。
chuān	huā	dǎ	liú	rèn	xī	dōng.

All sources have this line.

48.23.3 Even if completely encircled with the momentum changing like clouds in the wind,

八	方(面)	凭	势	风	云	变,
bā	fāng (miàn)	píng	shì	fēng	yún	biàn,

Most sources have this line, either with 八方 bā fāng or 八面 bā miàn, both of which mean the eight compass directions, or 'all around'. Lin and Tu have 八面恶势 bā miàn è shì: 'surrounded on all eight sides by evil momentum', which is evocative but does differ from the others. Wu has 八方形势 bā fāng xíng shì: 'surrounded on all eight sides by postures'. Wang has another probable typo, with 风去变 fēng qù biàn: 'wind go change'.

48.23.4 I don't guard in a dull-witted posture and I don't take a pointless step.

不	守	呆	式(势)	不	走	空。
bù	shǒu	dāi	shì	bù	zǒu	kōng.

Most sources have for the final phrase 不守空 bù shǒu kōng: 'I don't do a pointless defensive move'. I have used the version from Huan and Wu 不走空 bù zǒu kōng: 'I don't take a pointless step', as this phrase has the benefit of saying that you neither stand still nor run about blindly. The character 守 shǒu: 'defend' twice in the same line is repetitive and doesn't add to the meaning. You can see how the verses sometimes change in transmission, as I have picked my preferred phrase and will transmit that.

Twenty-four: Method of Using the Heart and Eyes

心眼法　　xīn yán fǎ

心如大将眼如法，
见景生情能制他。
最忌心痴眼不准，
手忙脚乱费周折。

The heart is like a commander and the eyes are his aides,
They scan the scene to observe the battle array in order to beat the enemy.
The worst case would be if the heart became stupid and the eyes didn't see clearly,
Then the hands would become frenzied and the feet chaotic, wasting a lot of effort.

This verse reminds us to keep our wits about us and look for opportunities as we move. It reminds us of the connection between the eyes and the mind, and the need for calmness and the courage of a battle commander in any situation. The 'heart' is the heart/mind, awareness, focus, the part of the mind that intends to do something, rather than the intellectual thinking part of the mind. If either the heart/mind or thinking mind is stuck or flustered the eyes won't see clearly. We need to react quickly; there is not time to think about things too much, to 'sit stupidly'.

This is also a reminder to focus during solo training, always looking and moving deliberately as if there were an opponent. The movements of the eyes should be trained along with the movements of the body. Too often, people look at the ground, especially when concentrating on a feeling or trying to remember a move.

The metaphor of 'scanning the scene' gives a nice image of the commander and his aides standing on the hilltop calmly surveying the enemy's battle array, looking for weaknesses. This is a common image in Chinese warfare, well described in the metaphor, "The heart is the Field Marshal, the eyes are the vanguard, the hands are the weapons, and the feet are the war horses."[58] The Field Marshal needs to stay calm, while the vanguard scouts out enemy displacement, builds bridges, and opens roads to prepare the way for the soldiers and cavalry.

The drawing on the following page is from a comic book about the battle of Red Cliff. These types of stories and story books are common in China, and the image called to mind is still relevant in our time. The caption is "Every day Zhou Yu and the others stood on the Southern bank and observed the movements of Cao's camp."

The Forty-eight Methods Verses

48.24.1 The heart is like a commander and the eyes are his aides,

心	如	大	将	眼	如	法，
xīn	rú	dà	jiàng	yǎn	rú	fǎ,

All sources have this line. Usually in discussions of warfare 法 fǎ means 'the rules of the army', but that doesn't make sense in this context.

48.24.2 They scan the scene to observe the battle array in order to beat the enemy.

见	景	生	情	能	制	他。
jiàn	jǐng	shēng	qíng	néng	zhì	tā.

Six sources (Huan, Li, Liu, Wang, Wu, and Zang) have this exact line. The four character phrase 见景生情 jiàn jǐng shēng qíng means 'to observe the battle array and adapt to it'. The battle array in this case is 敌情 dī qíng: 'the enemy's deployment', or 'disposition of troops'. Lin and Tu have 见机 jiàn jī: 'watch for opportunities', instead of 见景 jiàn jǐng: 'watch the scene', which makes it clear that you look for opportunities as they present, and brings it to the more personal level of fighting.

48.24.3 The worst case would be if the heart became stupid and the eyes didn't see clearly,

最	忌	心	痴	眼	不	准，
zuì	jì	xīn	chī	yǎn	bù	zhǔn,

Five sources (Huan, Li, Liu, Wang, and Wu) have this exact line. Three (Lin, Tu, and Zang) have 最忌心迟 zuì jì xīn chí: 'the worst would be if heart were slow'.

48.24.4 Then the hands would become frenzied and the feet chaotic, wasting a lot of effort.

手　　忙　　脚　　乱　　费　　周　　折。
shǒu　máng　jiǎo　luàn　fèi　zhōu　zhé.

All but my copy of Huan have this line. I have copied 费周章 fèi zhōu zhāng: 'wasting orders', and am pretty sure it is a mistake, but could be going with the metaphor of the general. The phrase 费周折 fèi zhōu zhé is a set phrase, meaning 'to spend much effort', or 'to go through a lot of trouble'.

Twenty-five:　The Tactic of Fixing the Regard

定眼法　　　dìng yǎn fǎ

四面刀枪乱如麻，
又当昏夜月无华。
矮身定睛招路广，
步步弯行自赢他。

All around you are blades and spears, as chaotic as tangled hemp,
　And it is a dark evening unadorned by moonlight.
Lower the body and fix the eyes open to see the route widely,
　Flex and curve at every step, and you can beat them.

　　　The setup - you are surrounded on a dark night by armed assailants - sets up a pretty bad situation, but once again, keeping calm and moving is the key to getting out of it. We know that in the late 1800s quite a few Xingyi and Bagua men were in the security business, so this is practical advice. The tactic particular to darkness is to drop down to make as much use of the available light as you can. Even on a dark night there is usually some ambient light from the sky, and being lower you might be able to catch sight of your assailants' silhouettes. Lowering yourself also keeps them from seeing you and reduces the target area. This has already been described in verse 36.34. The additional detail of this verse is to keep moving in unpredictable lines in the lowered stance. Just lowering yourself is not enough if you stop moving. And you can't just drop down to catch a

The Forty-eight Methods Verses

glimpse then rise up again to move. You need to keep yourself in the advantageous position and your assailants in the disadvantage position.

48.25.1 All around you are blades and spears, as chaotic as tangled hemp,

四	面	刀	枪	乱	如	麻，
sì	miàn	dāo	qiāng	luàn	rú	má,

All sources have this exact line. Usually 面 miàn: 'side' is used with the phrase 四面 sì miàn: 'four sides' and 方 fāng: 'direction' is used with the phrase 八方 bā fāng: 'eight directions', as in verse 36.23. In these contexts they both mean you are surrounded.

48.25.2 And it is a dark evening unadorned by moonlight.

又	当	昏	夜	月	无	华。
yòu	dāng	hūn	yè	yuè	wú	huá.

Most sources have these exact words. Liu has 夜晚 yè wǎn: 'late evening'.

48.25.3 Lower the body and fix the eyes open to see the route widely,

矮	身	定	睛	招	路	广，
ǎi	shēn	dìng	jīng	zhāo	lù	guǎng,

All sources have this exact line.

48.25.4 Flex and curve at every step, and you can beat them.

步	步	弯	行	自	赢	他。
bù	bù	wān	xíng	zì	yíng	tā.

Five sources (Huan, Lin, Liu, Tu, and Wu) have this exact line. The use of the character 弯 wān: 'flex; curved' gives the phrase two meanings. One, that the legs are flexed and remain flexed while moving. Two, that the stepping pattern is a turning and curving line – not straight and predictable. Zang has 步步变行 bù bù biàn xíng: 'change on every step'. Li and Wang have 必赢他 bì yíng tā: 'you will certainly beat them'.

Twenty-six: How to Disarm
接器法　　　jiē qì fǎ

长短单双器固精，
算来不如两手灵。
铁掌练来兵一样，
肉手偏找肱腕行。

Long or short, single or double, weapons are undoubtedly proficient,
But they really don't compare in dexterity to two (empty) hands.
An iron palm can be forged to become like a weapon,
Bare hands, contrary to expectations, can find the arms and wrists.

There are many verses that mention weapons in a general way, usually 'surrounded by armed assailants'. Verses 36.31 and 36.32 are a bit general, but verse 48.17 and this verse give the practical tactic of going for the hands and arms. Empty hands can always move more freely than hands holding a weapon, and can be put to more varied use. Holding a weapon you have to use the weapon or drop it to do something else. The first generation of bagua masters were living in a challenging and changing world – remember that Cheng Tinghua, armed with a sabre, was able to take out some German soldiers before being shot and killed in the streets of Beijing in 1900. This advice is still relevant, though, to fighting most regular bandits, who would probably still be traditionally armed.

This verse raises the question of whether or not baguazhang uses 'iron palm' training. My teachers would say that it does not, and Li's and Zang's commentary say that it is simply a metaphor for the palms being forged by meticulous training, not being forged into iron. The hands can poke a pressure point, cut with a palm edge, strike with the wrist or arm, ram with the heel of the palm, or grab. None of these techniques use the palm itself, and so no iron palm training would be necessary. Cao Zhongsheng's 1942 book contained a considerable number of training methods, some of them using apparatus, and they focused on solid forearms and a good grip, not hard hands. One of the main tactics of baguazhang is the dissipation of oncoming force, which calls for some sensitivity of the arms and hands, and iron palm training takes away this sensitivity. The last line gives the tactic of striking the opponent's arm or wrist holding the weapon, aiming for sensitive points to numb the arm or cause enough pain to make the assailant drop his weapon. Solid forearms, good grip strength, and abundant *qi* would be sufficient for this.

The Forty-eight Methods Verses

48.26.1 Long or short, single or double, weapons are undoubtedly proficient,

长	短	单	双	器	固	精，
cháng	duǎn	dān	shuāng	qī	gù	jīng,

All sources have this exact line.

48.26.2 But they really don't compare in dexterity to two (empty) hands.

算	来	不	如	两	手	灵。
suàn	lái	bù	rú	liǎng	shǒu	líng.

All sources have this exact line.

48.26.3 An iron palm can be forged to become like a weapon,

铁	掌	练(炼)	来	兵	一	样，
tié	zhǎng	liàn	lái	bīng	yī	yàng,

All but two sources have this exact line. Huan has 铁掌穿出 器一样 tié zhǎng <u>chuān chù</u> <u>qì</u> yī yàng: 'an iron palm <u>can spear</u> like a <u>weapon</u>'. Both 兵 bīng and 器 qì mean 'weapon', and in common speech, a weapon is usually called 兵器 bīng qì. Wu has 铁掌练就 tié zhǎng liàn <u>jiù</u>: 'an iron palm can be trained <u>to become</u>'.

48.26.4 Bare hands, contrary to expectations, can find the arm and wrists.

肉	手	偏	找	肱	腕	行。
ròu	shǒu	piān	zhǎo	gōng	wàn	xíng.

The sources agree on the use of bare hands to attack the arms and wrists of the assailant holding the weapon, just with some slightly different phrasing. Only two sources (Wang, and Zang) have this exact line. To break it into its phrases, six sources have 肉手 ròu shǒu: 'bare hands', while two (Lin, Tu) have 伸手 <u>shēn</u> shǒu: '<u>reach out</u> the hands', and one (Liu) has 两手 <u>liǎng</u> shǒu: '<u>both</u> hands'.

Five sources have 偏找 piān zhǎo: 'seek'. Two (Huan and Li) have 偏我 piān wǒ: '<u>I</u>', which makes the phrase more '<u>I go for</u> his arm and wrist'. 偏 piān has many meanings, but here it the best meaning is in the sense of 'contrary to expectations'. Wu has 专找 zhuān zhǎo: '<u>specialize</u> in seeking'.

All but one source have the final phrase 肱腕行 gōng wàn xíng: 'go along the arm and wrist'. Liu has 横腕行 <u>héng</u> wàn xíng: 'go <u>across</u> the wrist'.

Twenty-seven: How to Protect the Body

保身法　　　bǎo shēn fǎ

以强胜弱不足誇，
弱能胜强方是法。
任他离弦箭快硬，
左右磨身保无差。

Beating someone weaker than you is nothing to boast about,
But with our method you can beat someone stronger.
Even if someone attacks as fast and hard as an arrow leaving the bowstring,
Rub with your body left and right and you won't fall short in defense.

This verse continues with the idea introduced in other verses, especially 48.22, of flanking your adversary, getting in and keeping close to control him and take away his ability to control you, even if you are weaker. Size and strength do matter – you definitely need skill to beat someone bigger and stronger than you. Rubbing refers to the tactic of using turning techniques in close contact. One could be to make full contact with your opponent, stick and turn like a millstone, spinning him around the outside. Combined with a controlling technique, he is taken down or spun out. Another could be moving in to stick and applying a technique to either side that twists and rotates him. Another is quickly turning and moving – hitting if possible, getting away if not.

48.27.1　Beating someone weaker than you is nothing to boast about,

以	强	胜	弱	不	足	夸(誇)，
yǐ	qiáng	shèng	ruò	bù	zú	kuā,

Six sources (Huan, Li, Liu, Wang, Wu, and Zang) have this line. Two (Lin and Tu) have 以强制弱 yǐ qiáng zhì ruò: 'controlling someone weaker than you'.

48.27.2　But with our method you can beat someone stronger.

弱	能	胜	强	方	是	法。
ruò	néng	shèng	qiáng	fāng	shì	fǎ.

Three sources (Li, Wang, and Zang) have this line. Four (Huan, Lin, Liu, and Tu) have 弱能制强 ruò néng zhì qiáng: 'the weak can control the strong'. I chose to use the same word 胜 shèng: 'defeat' in both lines, to balance them. Wu has 以弱胜强 yǐ ruò shèng qiáng: 'when you beat the strong using the weak'.

48.27.3 Even if someone attacks as fast and hard as an arrow leaving the bowstring,

任	他	离	弦	箭	快	硬，
rèn	tā	lǐ	xián	jiàn	kuài	yìng,

Five sources (Li, Lin, Tu, Wang, and Wu) have this line. Three (Huan, Liu, and Zang) reverse the final two characters 箭硬快 jiàn <u>yìng kuài</u>: '<u>hard as fast</u> as an arrow', with no change in meaning. This is not a rhyming line, so word order doesn't matter.

48.27.4 Rub with your body left and right and you won't fall short in defense.

左	右	磨	身	保	无	差。
zuǒ	yòu	mó	shēn	bǎo	wú	chà.

All sources have this line. The character 磨 mó: 'rub', is also translated as 'grind' in the context of a millstone grinding. With two bodies in contact, rather than stone, rubbing seems the more appropriate word. The term 磨身 mó shēn: 'rub the body' is the name of one of the palm changes in many branches, 磨身掌 mó shēn zhǎng: 'body rubbing change'. To rub with the body is a close range technique.

Twenty-eight: How to Confuse your Adversary

乱人法   luàn rén fǎ

心乱先从眼上乱，
千招不如掌一穿。
对准鼻梁连环使，
跨步制人左右换。

A confused mind begins in the eyes,
A thousand techniques don't compare to one spearing palm.
Hit the bridge of the nose accurately and continuously,
Step around to control your opponent, switching to left and right.

As verse 48.24 explained, a calm mind allows your eyes to see clearly. Attacking your opponent's eyes with the spearing palm disturbs his mind. To this aim, this verse recommends successive spearing palms to the nose. It states very clearly that this is a nose strike, not a strike directly to the eyes. The eyes are well protected by the bone structure, but punching or striking towards them can cause swelling and disorientation even if you don't get into the eyes themselves. Also, in a normal fight there is no need to maim your opponent by stabbing him in the eyes. If you strike to the nose, which is an easier target, his eyes will water and your attack is just as effective as if you had gone for his eyes. Moving around ensures that he won't get you if he blindly hits out. It adds detail to the attack given in verse 36.16.

Stabbing the eyes is recommended in verse 48.16, but only after your releasing action has failed. Some baguazhang writings do, however, suggest going straight for the eyes. Three of Yan Dehua's thirty-four applications in his book use eye strikes. As the caption for his drawing says, "I step my left foot forward and use my right fingers to poke his eyes."

A direct eye strike is encouraged in verse 48.34 of the Shi lineage: "Controlling someone depends on stabbing the eyes, When the eyes are injured your adversary can no longer defy you. A light strike will injure and a hard strike will blind him, A poke to the eyes is better than a thousand techniques."[59]

The Gao lineage verses also adds to the lore of spearing palm with more specific applications verses such as: "The technique of the walking spearing palm is agile. Spear left and right like a dragon. Spear down with Push Aside the Grass to Search for a Snake. Spear up with Two Dragons Pluck the Pearl Eyeballs. Spear on the outside with Step Forward Push the Mountain into the Sea. Spear on the inside with Single Ram Hits the Chest. If you see that you can't put the best use to the spearing technique, then step back with a spearing palm to return to your on guard stance."[60] You can see they include strikes to the eyes.

48.28.1   A confused mind begins in the eyes,

心　　乱　　先　　从　　眼　　上　　乱,
xīn　luàn　xiān　cóng　yǎn　shàng　luàn,

All but one source have this exact line. Huan has 心乱是从眼上乱 xīn luàn shì cóng yǎn shàng luàn: 'a confused mind is from the eyes'.

48.28.2   A thousand techniques don't compare to one spearing palm.
　　　　千　　招　　不　　如　　掌　　一　　穿。
　　　　qiān　zhāo　bù　　rú　　zhǎng　yī　　chuān.

All but one source have this line. Wu has a reversed order for the final phrase, 一掌穿 yī zhǎng chuān, not changing the meaning.

48.28.3   Hit the bridge of the nose accurately and continuously,
　　　　对　　准　　鼻　　梁　　连　　环　　使，
　　　　duì　zhǔn　bī　　liáng　lián　huán　shǐ,

All but one source have this line. Wang has 对着鼻梁 duì zháo bī liáng: 'aim to hit the nose'.

48.28.4   Step around to control your opponent, switching to left and right.
　　　　跨　　步　　制　　人　　左　　右　　换 (还)。
　　　　kuà　bù　　zhì　　rén　　zuǒ　you　huàn (huán).

All sources have this line. The characters 换 huàn (Huan, Lin, Tu, and Wu) and 还 huán (Li, Liu, Wang, Zang) are often used as about the same thing. The character 换 huàn means 'to change, exchange', so usually means changing sides or stances. The character 还 huán means 'to go back or return', so usually means a riposte. In this case, either one means to continue the attack from both sides.

　　　　　　　Twenty-nine: Method of Opening and Closing
　　　　　　　　　　　开合法　　　kai hé fǎ

　　　　　　　　　　欲合先开是一般，
　　　　　　　　　　见开防合不二传。
　　　　　　　　　　诈败佯输知卷土，
　　　　　　　　　　指东打西意中含。

It is quite common to open up before closing,
Seeing (your opponent) open and preventing his closing – it is not taught otherwise.
(If he) fakes defeat and feigns loss, be aware of (a comeback like) rolling dust,
He is planning to 'point East and hit West'.

This verse explains a bit of what we are watching for when we use the tactic of 'waiting and watching' – we watch our opponent's bodywork, not just his gross movements. Opening refers to a number of small hints given by the opponent – a small body movement before a strike, a fake opening given to draw you in, or a gathering of force. Closing refers to the strike. You see the hint to his attack and you need to shut him down.

Faking a defeat to prepare a counter is a time honoured tactic. Ming dynasty generals Qi Jiguang and Wang Minghe warned against this, "A spear pulled back and down is trying to fool me into driving forward. He will quickly snap it up and kill me. Remember this!"[61], and "Facing off with staffs, if he pulls his back and sets on the ground, opening his small door (goes side on, shoulder to shoulder, opposite feet forward), I raise my staff and wait patiently for him to shoot out a killing technique, then I either lead him along or enter with a shearing killing strike."[62]

48.29.1   It is quite common to open up before closing,

欲	合	先	开	是	一	般，
yù	hé	xiān	kāi	shì	yī	bān,

All but one source have this line. Wu has a reversed 欲开合先合 yù kāi xiān hé: 'to close before opening up'. This reverses the meaning of opening and closing, to a closing body movement in preparation for an opening strike.

48.29.2   Seeing (your opponent) open and preventing his closing – it is not taught otherwise.

见	开	防	合	不	二	传。
jiàn	kāi	fáng	hé	bù	èr	chuán.

All sources have this line.

48.29.3   (If he) fakes defeat and feigns loss, be aware of (a comeback like) rolling dust,

诈	败	佯	输	知	卷	土，
zhà	bài	yáng	shū	zhī	juǎn	tǔ,

Five sources (Li, Lin, Wang, Wu, and Zang) have this exact line. The phrase 卷土 juǎn tǔ: 'rolling dust', is short for the metaphor 卷土重来 juǎn tǔ chóng lái: 'come back like rolling dust', which means to stage a comeback (like dust that blows back in your eyes). Liu and Tu, using traditional characters, have 捲土 juǎn tǔ: 'roll dust', but this is not necessary. For the last phrase Huan has 如燕平 rú yàn píng: 'like a swallow' instead. If my copying was correct, this would mean 'to be quick and agile like a swallow'.

48.29.4   He is planning to 'point East and hit West'.

指	东	打	西	意	中	含。
zhǐ	dōng	dǎ	xī	yì	zhōng	hán.

All sources have this line. This is a warning against chasing an apparently retreating opponent, who could well be feigning retreat to set up his counter attack. The tactic of 'making noise in the East and attacking West' was described in verse 36.15. The text here says 'point East' instead of 'make noise in the East', but it is certainly the same strategy. Mixing up 'sound' and 'point' here indicates that perhaps there was not that much distinction between the tactics Sounding East and Hitting West and Pointing to the Mountain to Get the Millstone.

Thirty: The Tactic of Setting in the South

定南法   dìng nán fǎ

任他千手千眼快，
守住中身是枉然。
不到要时不伸手，
伸手即要发手还。

If your opponent is so quick he strikes as if with a thousand hands and a thousand eyes,
Defend your midline and his attacks are futile.
Do not extend your hand until the right moment,
When you do extend your hand, he will have to pull back his attack.

This verse repeats the uses of waiting and using up the energy of the opponents, and trusting in your superior power developed from your training. This has already been explained in verses 48.2, 48.11, 48.15, 48.22, 48.24, and 48.33. The best structure for defending the midline has been explained in verse 36.02, 36.05, and many others. Waiting and patience is a classic tactic, described by Chang Naizhou in the 1700s, "If my opponent doesn't move, neither do I. When my opponent prepares to move, I move first."[63] We see once again the tactic of Changing from Guest to Host – taking matters into your own hands, not simply reacting to the attack.

As for the title, it suggests two possibilities. One, is the suggestion that we should set ourselves with the sun behind us so that the sun in in our opponent's eyes. It does not mean literally to always put your back to the south, but to keep the sun at your back. Two, it could be referring to Sun Zi's tactic from the Art of War of, in hazardous territory, setting up in the best position before the enemy arrives – up in the high ground, on the sunny side of the slope – forcing the attacker to make the first move.[64] The tactic means to take all the advantages that we can, and waiting, which seems to suit the title to the verse. Wu comments that the tactic of the verse is the principle of waiting until you have to hit, which fits with the tactic in the Art of War.

48.30.1   If your opponent is so quick he strikes as if with a thousand hands and a thousand eyes,

任　　他　　千　　手　　千　　眼　　快，
rèn　　tā　　qiān　shǒu　qiān　yǎn　　kuài,

All sources have this line. It could also literally mean that there are many assailants. The following tactic would be the same in either case.

48.30.2   Defend your midline and his attacks are futile.

守　　住　　中　　身　　是　　枉　　然。
shǒu　zhù　zhōng　shēn　shì　wǎng　rán.

Six sources (Lin, Liu, Huan, Tu, Wu, and Zang) have this line. Two (Li and Wang) have 守住中心 shǒu zhù zhōng <u>xīn</u>: 'defend your <u>centre</u>'.

48.30.3   Do not extend your hand until the right moment,

不　　到　　要　　时　　不　　伸　　手，
bù　　dào　　yào　　shí　　bù　　shēn　shǒu,

All sources have this line.

48.30.4   When you do extend your hand, he will have to pull back his attack.

伸　　手　　即　　要　　发　　手　　还。
shēn　shǒu　　jí　　yào　　fā　　shǒu　huán.

Five sources (Huan, Lin, Tu, Wang, and Wu) have exactly this line. The opening phrase is just a matter of grammatical differences between sources. Li has 伸手就要 shēn shǒu <u>jiù</u> yào: 'extend your hand <u>and he will have to...</u>'. Liu and Zang have 伸手即教 shēn shǒu jí <u>jiào</u>: 'when you extend your hand you <u>teach</u>', perhaps as in 'teach him a lesson'.

For the final phrase all have the 发手还 fā shǒu huán: 'he will pull back his attack'. Because of the lack of 'he' and 'I', this could also be interpreted as you should pull back your hand after your strike.

Thirty-one: The Tactic of Getting in Close
求近法   qiú jìn fǎ

封闭固是护身招，
躲过他人自逍遥。
切忌远出尺步外，
开门绕道法不牢。

Shutting down is of course a method of defending oneself,
Dodge your opponent and you are free and unfettered.
But be sure to avoid stepping more than a foot away (from him),
Just opening the doors and taking detours won't beat your opponent.

   This verse is clarifying that guarding yourself or evading are not goals in and of themselves. Other verses, even the immediately preceding one, have pointed out the value of guarding your midline, so this is a valid technique. Dodging and evasion are explained in verses 48.18, 48.19, 48.22, 48.23, 48.36, and 48.47. Enough verses extol the virtues of evasion that we can take line two as a valid technique. As quite often in the verses, lines one and two are the setup, and lines three and four are the lesson. Line three is reminding us not to go too far from your target. If you get too far away you can't counter and you give an equal chance to your opponent to regroup. Whatever you do, you need to stay close enough to be attacking as you evade or at least launching an effective counter attack. If you evade and gain openings you should not just ignore them, and you should not be so far away that you cannot take the opportunity presented.

   The 门 mén: 'doors' refer to the doorways into your body and the ways in to the chest, ribs and groin. Setting up against the opponent, standing chest to chest (you each have the same foot forward) is 'big door' facing off – that is, giving a large frontal surface. Setting up a bit sideways, standing shoulder to shoulder (you have your opposite feet forward) is 'small door' facing off – that is, giving a small frontal surface. Going to the 'inside door' is to the inside of an outstretched arm or leg, into the body. Going to the 'outside door' is to the outside of an outstretched arm or leg. Getting to the 'front door' is arriving forward of an outstretched elbow. Getting to the 'back door' is getting in past the elbow into the body. The 'upper door' is above an outstretched hand, and the 'lower door' is below an outstretched arm. Chang Naizhou, in the late 1700s, described this very well, "The upper limbs have three doors. The wrist is the first. This is the main door. The core of the elbow is the second. When you get in here you have mounted to the outer second door. The root of the arm is the third. When you get into here you are at the third door. Once you are past the three doors you approach the inner courtyard – you can pass through the hall into the inner chamber."[65] You can see how the concepts of the 'doorways' and the 'passes' explained in verse 48.14 overlap a bit.

This verse emphasizes one, that our evasion should be opening our opponent's doors – making him react in some way that weakens his defense structure – so that we can get our target, not just getting out of the way, and two, that evasion needs to remain close enough to take advantage of openings.

48.31.1 Shutting down is of course a method of defending oneself,

封 闭 固 是 护 身 招，
fēng bì gù shì hū shēn zhāo,

Five sources (Li, Lin, Tu, Wang, and Zang) have this line. Three (Huan, Liu, and Wu) have 封躲 fēng duǒ: 'closing off and dodging', which are still in the light of defending without attacking, but don't fit that well considering the next line.

48.31.2 Dodge your opponent and you are free and unfettered.

躲 过 他 人 自 逍 遥。
duǒ guò tā rén zì xiāo yáo.

All sources have this line.

48.31.3 But be sure to avoid stepping more than a foot away (from him),

切 忌 远 出 尺 步 外，
qiè jì yuǎn chū chǐ bù wài,

All sources have the same meaning, but the exact wording varies phrase by phrase. Four sources (Huan, Li, Liu, and Wu) have 切忌 qiè jì: 'avoid'. Four (Lin, Tu, Wang, and Zang) have 切记 qiè jì: 'remember that', which is used to admonish in the negative sense of 'remember not to do'.

All sources have 远出 yuǎn chū: 'go far away'. Most sources have 尺步外 chǐ bù wài: 'outside a foot length'. Wang has 尺步远 chǐ bù yuǎn: 'if you go further away than a foot'.

48.31.4 Just opening the doors and taking detours won't beat your opponent.

开 门 绕 道 法 不 牢。
kāi mén ráo dào fǎ bù láo.

All sources have this exact line, except Wang, with another probable typo 开门绕到 kāi mén ráo dào: 'open the door and go around to'.

Thirty-two: The Method of the Six Directions
六路法   liù lù fǎ

他人六路是空言,
我之掌法六路观。
动步既能八方顾,
瞻前顾后自无难。

When others say they can take care of six directions this is empty talk,
In our style we can look to the six directions.
When we step we can already see to eight directions,
We have no difficulties at all watching both before and behind.

This verse points out the practicality of circle-walking, and especially the training of turning in the changes and in technique drills, which habituates us to looking all around. In addition to circle-walking, baguazhang extensively trains the use of *koubu* and *baibu*, which enables quick turning in any direction. The *koubu* and *baibu* stepping brings us around with the body straight and the head up, so we can see a full circle even as we turn. The 'six directions' are to the front, back, left, right, up, and down. The 'eight directions' are the eight points of the compass, all around you. Because baguazhang was so good at using the eight directions, this may have lead to its name eventually becoming 'eight trigrams' palm. Most styles practice in straight lines, and so are used to looking forward. Our changes go off in many directions, so we become used to that. This verse can be taken as a reminder to watch not just where we are going but all around when we circle-walk and do the changes and drills, to take full advantage of the training effect.

Another somewhat cocky verse, but they were written for insiders. And to be honest, other styles do tend to train this type of turning a bit less than does baguazhang, and people not used to turning can get dizzy doing just a few full turning techniques in a row.

This simple illustration shows how the sight lines while circle walking take in a new direction with each step. Even with

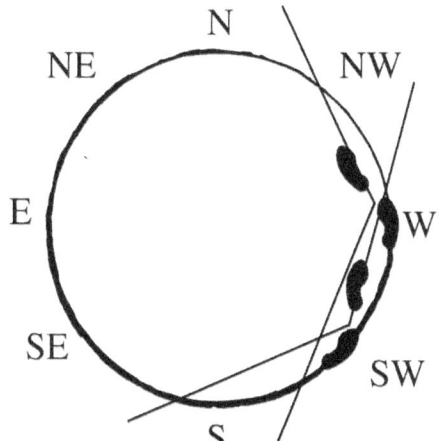

conservatively estimated peripheral vision and not turning the head, we can see behind where we were within a couple of steps.

48.32.1 When others say they can take care of six directions this is empty talk,

他	人	六	路	是	空	言，
tā	rén	liù	lù	shì	kōng	yán,

All sources have this line.

48.32.2 In our style we can look to the six directions.

我	之	掌	法	六	路	观。
wǒ	zhī	zhǎng	fǎ	liù	lù	guān.

Four sources (Li, Lin, Tu, Wang) have this line. Three (Huan, Wu, and Zang) have 我之掌式 wǒ zhī zhǎng shì: 'our style's postures'. Liu has 我之掌势 wǒ zhī zhǎng shì: also meaning 'our style's postures'.

48.32.3 When we step we can already see to eight directions,

动	步	既	能	八	方	顾，
dòng	bù	jì	néng	bā	fāng	gù,

Most sources have this line. Wang has 八方倾 bā fāng qīng: 'leans in the eight directions', another typo. This particular book has a lot of typographical errors, I suspect it was not proof read. Wu has 八方按 bā fāng àn: 'presses down to the eight directions', but makes a comment about watching.

48.32.4 We have no difficulties at all watching both before and behind.

瞻	前	顾	后	自	无	难。
zhān	qián	gù	hòu	zì	wú	nán.

Six sources (Huan, Li, Liu, Wang, Wu, and Zang) have this line. Lin and Tu have 身无难 shēn wú nán: 'the body has no difficulties', which is the same meaning.

Thirty-three: The Tactic of One and Only

不二法　　bù èr fǎ

法不准兮不妄发，
发不中兮第二发。
任他鬼神多灵妙，
不勾魂兮亦裂牙。

Don't attack rashly if you don't (think you can) land a well aimed technique,
If you do an inaccurate hit then hit again.
No matter if your opponent has supernatural skills,
If you don't panic him you will at least make him rend his teeth.

    The title of this verse is 'one and only' and it is about the tactic of continuous attack, so it is your intent that is 'one and only'. You cannot be of two minds when fighting. You see a target and shoot for it. If you miss you keep shooting. You shouldn't miss, but if you do, you should turn that into a barrage of attacks, each one as fierce as the other, so that your opponent is overwhelmed, if not panicked. The first line reiterates the tactic of waiting for the right opportunity before striking. Li Ziming comments 'if you don't have a target then don't shoot the arrow'. The second line allows that even if you wait patiently and are careful, you can still miss. The tactic then is to continue on, not pull back. Wu and Zang comment here that baguazhang should be sure, accurate, and ruthless 稳，准，狠 wěn, zhǔn, hěn. If your adversary is not outright panicked he is at least 'rending his teeth', which indicates his frustration and the likelihood of his making an error.

48.33.1   Don't attack rashly if you don't (think you can) land a well aimed technique,

法　　不　　准　　兮　　不　　妄　　发，
fǎ　　bù　　zhǔn　　xī　　bù　　wàng　　fā,

All but one source have this line. Wu has 不空发 bù <u>kōng</u> fā: 'don't make an <u>empty</u> attack'.

48.33.2   If you do an inaccurate hit then hit again.

发　　不　　中　　兮　　第　　二　　发。
fā　　bù　　zhōng　　xī　　dì　　èr　　fā.

Most sources have this line. Huan has 发不准兮 fā bù <u>zhǔn</u> xī: 'if you hit <u>inaccurately</u>'.

48.33.3   No matter if your opponent has supernatural skills,

任	他	鬼	神	多	灵	妙，
rèn	tā	guǐ	shén	duō	líng	miào,

Four sources (Li, Lin, Tu, Wang) have this line, using the term 鬼神 guǐ shén: 'ghosts and gods' or 'supernatural beings'. Two have slightly different ways of wording the supernatural. Huan has 神魔 shén mó: 'ghosts and goblins'. Wu and Zang have 神鬼 shén guǐ: 'gods and ghosts', just reversing the characters. Liu Jingru does not have a supernatural reference, instead having 任他手法多灵巧 rèn tā shǒu fǎ duō líng miào: 'no matter if his techniques are ingenious'.

48.33.4   If you don't panic him you will at least make him rend his teeth.

不	勾(钩)	魂	兮	亦	裂	牙。
bù	gòu	hún	xī	yì	liè	yá.

Three sources (Huan, Lin, and Tu) have this line. Li, Liu, and Zang are almost the same, just with 也裂牙 yě liè yá: 'also rend his teeth'. Wang has 不勿魂兮 bù wù hún xī: 'if he doesn't lose his spirit'. Wu has 也龇牙 yě zī yá: 'also bare his teeth'.

Thirty-four: How to Prevent Slipping
防滑法   fáng huá fǎ

冰天雪地步难牢，
前横后直记心梢。
转动须用小开步，
切忌挺身法打高。

It is difficult to keep to your feet in a world of ice and snow,
Pay close attention – turn the front foot across and keep the back foot straight.
When turning you must use small steps,
Avoid being stiff and erect, or hitting high.

This verse reiterates verse 36.35. It adds the detail of keeping the front foot turned and the rear foot aligned. Perhaps people didn't understand that the point of the original verse was to put the feet at angles to each other. It is generally understood that the front foot is a *koubu* placement, which gives more control should you slip, and prevents knee injury. This is the most secure way to turn or stop on skates of skis. Verse 36.35 said 'avoid pivoting'. This verse says 'use small steps to turn'. This is a better coaching method – telling you what to do instead of what not to do.

Line four clears up some confusion that might have occurred in verse 36.35. I took it to mean to avoid hitting high or low. Li Ziming's commentary took it to mean to avoid unevenness – highs and lows – in the ground. Line four of this verse is either giving different advice from what Li Ziming thought, or is saying that the 'don't hit high' was the intended meaning. One begins to wonder if the forty-eight verses were written to clarify some of the points made in the 36.

As a Canadian, I can vouch for this verse. Taking big steps, spinning, going stiff, and lifting the arms are all sure ways to fall on the ice. Turning the front foot in slightly helps to prevent slipping, whether setting to the gathering stance, striking, or stepping. Beijing gets cold enough for ice, and although it doesn't snow often, when it does, it is the light dusting that is the most slippery of snow.

48.34.1 It is difficult to keep to your feet in a world of ice and snow,

冰　　天　　雪　　地　　步　　难　　牢，
bīng　tiān　xuě　dì　bù　nán　láo,

All sources have this line.

48.34.2 Pay close attention – turn the front foot across and keep the back foot straight.

前　　横　　后　　直　　记　　心　　梢。
qián　héng　hòu　zhí　jì　xīn　shāo.

Most sources have this line. Tu and Wu have 记心稍 jì xīn <u>shāo</u>: 'remember <u>a little bit</u>', probably meaning to pay attention to small details, if this is not a miscopy of a very similar character with the same pronunciation.

48.34.3 When turning you must use small steps,

转　　动　　须　　用　　小　　开　　步，
zhuǎn　dòng　xū　yòng　xiǎo　kāi　bù,

Five sources (Li, Liu, Wang, Wu, and Zang) have this line. Three (Huan, Lin, Tu) have a very slight difference with essentially the same meaning 转动须要 zhuǎn dòng xū <u>yào</u>: 'when turning you <u>must have</u>'.

48.34.4 Avoid being stiff and erect, or hitting high.

切　　忌　　挺　　身　　法　　打　　高。
qiè　jì　tǐng　shēn　fǎ　dǎ　gāo.

In the initial phrase, all sources agree but Zang, who has 切记 qiè jì: 'remember', meaning 'bear in mind what you are not supposed to do'.

There are only slight differences in the phrase for not 'hitting high'. Five sources (Huan, Li, Liu, Wang, and Zang) have this phrase. Two sources (Lin, Tu) have 去打高 qù dǎ gāo: 'go to hit high'. Wu has 打法高 dǎ fǎ gāo: 'high techniques', just reversing the characters.

Thirty-five: The Method for Stable Footwork
稳步法　　　wěn bù fǎ

步不稳兮身必摇，
脚踏实地胜千招。
进取足趾退悬踵，
不扣步兮莫回瞧。

If the footwork isn't stable the body will certainly be unstable,
Having firmly grounded feet will win more than knowing a thousand techniques.
Grab with the toes to advance and lift the heel to retreat,
Don't look back or turn around without using a *koubu* step.

This verse returns to the basic principle and the need for the basic training of baguazhang – that of rooted footwork. A *koubu* step, usually translated as a 'hook-in step' does more than just hook in. If you think of some of the meanings of the word 扣 kòu, such as 'to do up a button or buckle', 'to tuck in', 'to place a bowl upside down', even 'to dunk' a basketball and 'to smash' a volleyball, this helps to get the feeling in the body. As circle-walking is the secret to rooting, *koubu* stepping is the secret to responsiveness and balance.

Some interpret the third line to mean press the toes into the ground first as you land forward – in other words, the flat foot stepping. Some interpret it to mean that on advancing we grip with the toes on landing with natural stepping. Another interpretation is to the action of the toes on advancing – press the toes into the ground as you lift the foot – pressing the ball of the foot into the ground sets the supporting leg well into the ground to support a drive forward – this method is used to advance with a strong *baibu* step in the Cheng style. In general, lifting the toes of the front foot to advance and lifting the heel of the rear foot to retreat ensures that the other foot remains firmly on the ground, and grabbing the ground

THE FORTY-EIGHT METHODS VERSES 181

when the toes touch down ensures continued stability. Each school has its own way of stepping and doing the *koubu* stepping, and each works within the construct of the rest of its power and methods.

48.35.1   If the footwork isn't stable the body will certainly be unstable,

步	不	稳	兮	身	必	摇,
bù	bù	wěn	xī	shēn	bì	yáo,

All sources have these exact words.

48.35.2   Having firmly grounded feet will win more than knowing a thousand techniques.

脚	踏	实	地	胜	千	招。
jiǎo	tā	shí	dì	shèng	qiān	zhāo.

Most sources have these exact words. Only Wang has 脚趾实地 jiǎo zhǐ shì dì: 'the whole foot grounded'.

48.35.3   Grab with the toes to advance and lift the heel to retreat,

进	取	足	趾	退	悬	踵,
jìn	qǔ	zú	zhǐ	tuì	xuán	zhǒng,

Four of the sources (Li, Lin, Tu, Wang) have this line. As described in verse 36.12, advancing starts by advancing the front foot, and retreating starts by retreating the rear foot. This line adds some more detail. The initial phrase 进撬足趾 jìn qiào zú zhǐ: 'pry the toes to advance', is also used to describe the advancing action. Three sources (Liu, Wu, and Zang) have 进驱足趾 jìn qū zú zhǐ: 'advance urging with the toes'. The pronunciation of 驱 qū is close to 取 qǔ, but with three sources agreeing, the use of the character 驱 qū is unlikely to be a typo, and does make sense. For the final phrase, Wu has 退悬钟 tuì xuán zhōng: 'lift the Zhong acupoint'. Wu comments that the acupoint on the inside of the heel is the 大钟穴 dà zhōng xué, so the meaning of the phrase is the same, lifting the point at the heel.

Huan has something completely different, 进身须思退身步 jìn shēn xū sī tuì shēn bù: 'when advancing you must consider your retreating footwork'.

48.35.4   Don't look back or turn around without using a *koubu* step.

不	扣	步	兮	莫	回	瞧。
bù	kòu	bù	xī	mò	huí	qiáo.

All sources have these exact words. I realize that *koubu* step repeats the 'step' but it seems to make more sense in English.

Thirty-six: Method of Small Steps
小步法   xiǎo bù fǎ

回身转步必须小，
步大舍身不灵脚。
欲要转身迈半步，
人难擒兮人不晓。

To turn back you must take small turning steps,
If your steps are large then you give up your body and your feet are maladroit.
If you want to turn around then take a half step,
No one will be able to catch you or figure you out.

This is another verse that gives me the impression that the forty-eight methods verses were written to augment the thirty-six. Small steps were already dealt with in verse 36.30, and, in relation to slippery situations, in verses 36.35 and 48.34. This verse clearly states that turning with small steps is the norm in any conditions. This verse is specifically dealing with turning around, changing direction, not evasive stepping or entry. It is not saying to always use small steps, but that the body is much more stable when turning if you use small steps rather than large steps or pivoting.

I have perhaps over-read the details in the translation. The phrase in the first line is 回身 huí shēn: 'turn back', which means specifically 'to turn towards the side of the foot that is forward' (if the left foot is forward you turn left), so it starts with the front foot doing a *baibu* step, then the other foot does a *koubu* step ahead to complete the turn, so I translated it as plural 'turning steps'. The phrase in the third line is 转身 zhuàn shēn: 'turn around', which means specifically 'to turn towards the other side of the foot that is forward' (if the left foot is forward you turn right), so it starts with the front foot doing a *koubu* step, and you are already around, so I translated it as a singular 'step'.

This is a good time, perhaps, to mention that the verses never say to walk in circles around an opponent, as is often shown in the kungfu movies that make bagua look silly. Outsiders see the circle walking as a tactic, and think that is how bagua fighters get behind them, as described in an overview of martial styles, "The use of the circle walking is to practise stepping quickly so you can make a surprise attack behind the enemy, giving him no chance to maneuver."[66] That just shows that the training of baguazhang is indeed misunderstood by many, or as this verse says, no one can figure out what you are doing and how you got behind them.

Baguazhang's real stepping tactics count on *koubu* step, *baibu* step, side step, following step, gathering step, and others. Circle-walking is for training the body, it is not a fighting tactic. Slow, intense, circle-walking is not a basic to be discarded for fast walking.

48.36.1   To turn back you must take small turning steps,

回	身	转	步	必	须	小,
huí	shēn	zhuǎn	bù	bù	xū	xiǎo,

All the sources have this line.

48.36.2   If the steps are large then you give up your body and your feet are maladroit.

步	大	舍(捨)	身	不	灵	脚。
bù	dà	shē	shēn	bù	líng	jiǎo.

Five sources (Li, Lin, Wang, Wu, and Zang) have this line. Two (Huan and Tu) finish the line with 不灵巧 bù líng qiǎo: '*maladroit*' instead of 不灵脚 bù líng jiǎo: 'the feet are maladroit', which still rhymes, and means the same thing, but more overall. Liu has 步大抢身 bù dà qiǎng shēn: '*if you try to rush in* with big steps'.

48.36.3   If you want to turn around then take a half step,

欲	要	转	身	迈	半	步,
yù	yào	zhuǎn	shēn	mài	bàn	bù,

All sources have this line. Note that it just says 迈半步 mài bàn bù: 'take a half step'. *Koubu* and *baibu* stepping for turning around are assumed. The *koubu* step is only referred to by name once, in verse 48.35, and the *baibu* step never.

48.36.4   No one will be able to catch you or figure you out.

人	难	擒	兮	人	不	晓。
rén	nán	qín	xī	rén	bù	xiǎo.

All sources have this line.

Thirty-seven: Methods of the Palms
掌法   zhǎng fǎ

掌法虽有上中下，
上下不过是掌架。
圆转自如惟中盘，
高下全从此变化。

Although our palms have upper, middle and lower,
The upper and lower are just different frames for the palms.
Only the middle basin moves freely when turning on the circle,
The high and low are variations unfolding from it.

This verse refers to the upper, middle, and lower basins explained in verse 36.08 and repeats that the mid height frame is the most practical. The third line gives a good reason for using the middle posture – freedom of movement. This refers to both the posture at mid-height and the power in the middle of the body (waist and hips).

The reference to the palms here is not to palm techniques, but to circle-walking and the palm changes, which in Chinese are referred to simply as the palms. The first palm changes in most schools, for example, called single palm change, double palm change, and smooth palm change in English, are 单换掌，双换掌，顺式掌 dān huàn zhǎng, shuāng huàn zhǎng, shùn shì zhǎng: 'single-changing palm', 'double-changing palm', and 'smooth-type palm'.

When saying the positions and movements are just 'frames', the word 架 jià: 'frame' is taking the common usage in reference to the postures and movements in the martial arts. In Chen's taijiquan, for example, old frame, new frame, and small frame refer to different branches of the style whose postures and movements take certain characteristics. Long fist is often referred to as having a large frame.

Verse 36.08 defined the low stance as the hips level with the knees, but it simply said that the middle stance should not be too high. Here again the verse doesn't say what height the middle posture should be. It seems that baguazhang people aren't really too fussed about this, which is funny because posture height is one of the things that outsiders have picked up on, and often use in 'describing' baguazhang – "It is divided into upper, middle, and lower basins. The upper basin moves with the legs a bit bent, the middle basin moves with the stance a bit lower than the upper, and the low basin moves even lower."[67] This is saying not much at all.

This illustration shows a middle height 'basin' on the left and a low height 'basin' on the right.

Liu Xinghan has an interesting explanation of 三盘掌 sān pán zhǎng: 'the three basins of the palms'. The 上盘掌 shàng pán zhǎng: 'upper basin palm' is the ox tongue palm, the fingers are up at head height, the walking is done in crane stepping, and the skill trained is that of soaring like a crane. The 中盘掌 zhōng pán zhǎng: 'middle basin palm' is the three attributes palm, the tiger's mouth is stretched open, the hands are held upright with the fingers spread, especially the middle and ring finger, and the forward hand is at eyebrow height, and the walking is done in chicken stepping – the front foot reaches out and the rear foot follows tightly. The 下盘掌 xià pán zhǎng: 'low basin palm' is the clenching power palm, the palms are up at shoulder height with eagle claw shapes, the body sits down below the groin level, sinking the *qi*, and the walking is done is ostrich stepping. The three basins were practised only after first mastering firm circle-walking, then mud stepping circle-walking, and then quick connected circle-walking. Liu also comments that the upper basin palm with the crane stepping was called Yin style, the middle basin palm with the chicken stepping was called Cheng style, and the low basin palm with the ostrich stepping was called Song style.

Cai Baozhong has a brilliant interpretation that puts all 'basin' concepts together in a lovely poetic whole, "In the lower basin the legs and feet are like pearls on a jade mortar, turning is a grinding. In the middle basin the torso and waist are like a silver snake coiling around a trunk, flowing, sharp, and agile. In the high basin the hands are like a twisted rope that spins, turns, and twists.... Upper, middle, and lower basins form a connected whole."[68]

48.37.1   Although our palms have upper, middle and lower,

掌	法	虽	有	上	中	下,
zhǎng	fǎ	suí	yǒu	shàng	zhōng	xià,

Six sources (Huan, Lin, Liu, Tu, Wu, and Zang) have this exact line. Two sources (Li, Wang) differ only in 分 <u>fēn</u>: '<u>categorized</u>' instead of 有 yǒu: 'have'.

48.37.2   The upper and lower are just different frames for the palms.

上	下	不	过	是	掌	架。
shàng	xià	bù	guò	shì	zhǎng	jià.

Most main sources have this line. Liu has 是穿架 shì <u>chuān</u> jià: 'the posture <u>for circle walking</u>'. This use of 穿架 chuān jià, often meaning 'spearing palm', here means circle walking in a posture similar to Dragon Stretches it Talons. Sun Lutang also uses *chuanzhang* with this meaning, calling circle walking with the left hand up into the middle of the circle 左穿 zuǒ chuān: 'left spearing', and with the right hand up 右穿 yòu chuān: 'right spearing'.

8.37.3   Only the middle basin moves freely when turning on the circle,

圆	转	自	如	惟	中	盘,
yuán	zhuǎn	zì	rú	wéi	zhōng	pán,

Five (Lin, Liu, Tu, Wang, Zang) have this wording. Three (Huan, Li, and Wu) have 唯中盘 <u>wéi</u> zhōng pán: '<u>only</u> the middle basin'. Both 唯 and 惟 are pronounced wéi and mean 'only'.

48.37.4   The high and low are variations unfolding from it.

高	下	全	从	此	变	化。
gāo	xià	quán	cóng	cǐ	biàn	huà.

Four sources (Huan, Li, Liu, and Wang) have this phrasing. Wu has 高低全从 gāo <u>dī</u> quán cóng: 'high and <u>low</u> from', not changing the meaning. Three sources (Lin, Tu, Zang) differ in grammatical structure, not the meaning, with 高下全凭 gāo xià quán <u>píng</u>: 'high and low <u>depend</u> on'.

Thirty-eight: Avoid Slouching
忌俯法   jì fǔ fǎ

低头如同眼不开，
亦且身易往前栽。
低头猫腰中枢死，
全步全掌使不来。

Hanging your head is the same as closing your eyes,
And moreover, the body then tends to slouch forward.
Hanging your head and hunching your back like a cat deadens the Central Pivot,
None of your footwork or hand techniques will come off.

This verse makes it very clear that hanging the head and drooping forward from the upper back destroys the ability to see and move smoothly, and blocks the flow of the *qi* in the body. This is a common error both in circle-walking and in training movements. If one looks down during training, sooner or later the pivot point of the back will also break, and the whole body will no longer be upright, functional, and smooth.

The verse seems to have been written to correct errors that were creeping in. It adds detail and explanation to verses 36.01, 36.07, and 36.22. The first line of verse 36.01, 'pull up the crown of the head, settle down the waist' means keep the torso straight, but it does not say why or give more detail. Verse 36.07 says, 'draw the crown of the head straight upwards, and the vitality will pass throughout', adds a reason to keep straight but the focus is on the head. Verse 36.22 says 'you should be connected like the mystical dragon is connected from head to tail', again reinforcing the upright torso and head. This verse emphasizes the importance of the upright position for your health, not just martial application. The mind and body communicate integrally. You hang your head in submission – whether to sorrow, shame, defeat, or exhaustion – there are no positive feelings related to hanging the head. If you hang your head in training, your mind sooner or later will go there.

I took line three to refer specifically to the *Zhongshu* point, the Central Pivot, on the *Du* ('Governing') vessel DU7, rather than simply the central pivot area of the spine. Either could work – the point is named Central Pivot for a reason. The place is the middle of the back, at the depression below the tenth thoracic vertebra, a bit below the shoulder blades. If the spine bends here, the body is bent and awkward, the *qi* is blocked, and any rotational movement of the torso causes the upper body to sway instead of rotate. If this area is held straight, the *qi* can flow, the body can move smoothly, and the spirit remains full. A break at the Central Pivot causes another fault – jutting the chin forward – which is just as bad, if not worse, for the health. If the spine is bent you have to lift the head to see straight, so end up with a breaking point where the neck should be connected straight to the rest of the spine.

48.38.1   Hanging your head is the same as closing your eyes,

低	头	如	同	眼	不	开，
dī	tóu	rú	tóng	yǎn	bù	kāi,

All sources have this line.

48.38.2   And moreover, the body then tends to slouch forward.

亦	且	身	易	往	前	栽。
yì	qiě	shēn	yì	wǎng	qián	zāi.

Five sources (Li, Lin, Liu, Tu, Zang) have this exact phrasing. Wu has 亦且身体向前栽 yì qiě shēn tǐ <u>xiàng</u> qián zāi, which means the same thing. Wang has 亦且身为 yì qiě shēn <u>wéi</u>: 'and moreover the body <u>will</u>...'. Huan has 而且身易 <u>ér</u> qiě shēn yì: '<u>and also</u> the body easily...'.

48.38.3   Hanging your head and hunching your back like a cat deadens the Central Pivot,

低	头	猫	腰	中	枢	死，
dī	tóu	māo	yāo	zhōng	shū	sǐ,

Most sources have this exact line. Huan has 低头<u>垂</u>腰中枢<u>孔</u> dī tóu <u>chuí</u> yāo zhōng shū <u>kǒng</u>: 'lowering the head and letting the back <u>droop</u> <u>makes a hole</u> in the Central Pivot'. This is also sometimes called 弯腰 wān yāo: 'flexing the back'. The standard term 猫腰 māo yāo: 'arch the back like a cat', is the most descriptive of the shape of the back.

48.38.4   None of your footwork or hand techniques will come off.

全	步	全	掌	使	不	来。
quán	bù	quán	zhǎng	shǐ	bù	lái.

Five of the sources (Li, Liu, Wang, Wu, and Zang) have the order I chose as standard 全步全掌 quán bù quán zhǎng: 'all the footwork and hand techniques'. Two sources (Lin, Tu) have the reverse order, 全掌全步 quán <u>zhǎng</u> quán <u>bù</u>: 'all the <u>hand</u> techniques and all the <u>footwork</u>'. Huan has 全<u>身</u>全掌 quán <u>shēn</u> quán zhǎng: 'the <u>whole body</u> and all the hand techniques'.

All sources have the exact words 使不来 shǐ bù lái: 'nothing will come off as it should'.

Thirty-nine: Avoid Arching Back
忌仰法   jì yǎng fǎ

紧背空胸静中求，
挺胸坦腹悔难收。
叠肚吸腰来不及，
最怕转身不自由。

Tauten the upper back and empty the chest to seek a still centre,
With a puffed up chest and flattened abdomen, you will regret your difficulty receiving (an attack).
You won't have time to fold your belly and suck in your waist,
What we fear most is not being able to turn around freely.

This verse is reinforcing previous instructions by adding details of what happens if we break the correct body position. It corrects a possible over-correction of students trying to follow the previous verse. Lifting the head back is just as bad as hanging it forward. You can just see the teacher saying, "No, that's not what I meant!" The first line reiterates what was said in verse 36.01, 'leave the chest empty and settle into the waist', and 36.07, 'tauten the upper back'. 'Tauten the upper back' means to spread it open in all directions so that the skin is taut. It remains upright and open, allowing the chest to remain empty, the *qi* to sink to the *dantian*, and both body and mind to remain centered and calm. If you puff up the chest and squeeze the shoulder blades together this is the opposite of the all the requirements given throughout the verses. You puff yourself up to show yourself off, whether in pride, aggression, or display, and this is not the quiet mindset you need in training or fighting. If you tighten the abdomen you will puff up the chest. This is a position that stiffens the body, raises the *qi*, and makes it difficult to move. If you have lost your proper body structure in any way, when you need to move you won't have time to readjust, and you need to readjust if you want to do anything effective. If you have lost the body structure and don't have time to readjust, then you can't move freely. The main tactic of baguazhang, as explained over and over again in the verses, is to move freely, and especially to turn. The means that for all movement to be spontaneous and immediate, the body needs to be in the ideal position at all times.

48.39.1   Tauten the upper back and empty the chest to seek a still centre,
紧   背   空   胸   静   中   求，
jǐn   bèi   kòng xiōng jìng zhōng qiú,
All sources have this line.

48.39.2 With a puffed up chest and flattened abdomen, you will regret your difficulty receiving (an attack).

挺	胸	坦	腹	悔	难	收。
tǐng	xiōng	tǎn	fù	huǐ	nán	shōu.

The sources have various ways of describing what not to do with the abdomen, though all agree on the word for puffing up the chest. I chose the most standard adjective, 坦腹 tǎn fù: 'flatten the belly' (Liu, Tu, Wu). Three sources (Li, Lin and Zang) have 袒腹 tǎn fù: 'strip the belly', as in stripping off your shirt. Huan has 腆腹 tiǎn fù: '<u>protrude</u> the belly' (as does Di Guoyong). These present two errors, one of puffing up the chest, the other of forcing the belly out. Both cause the lower back to arch, though in different ways. Wang has 旦股 dàn gǔ: '<u>dawn thigh</u>', which must be at least partially a typo.

48.39.3 You won't have time to fold your belly and suck in your waist,

迭（叠）	肚	吸	腰	来	不	及，
dié	dù	xī	yāo	lái	bù	jí,

Almost all sources have this line. Zang has 叠腹 dié <u>fù</u>: 'fold the <u>abdomen</u>', just a bit less colloquial than 叠肚 dié dù: 'fold the belly'. As mentioned earlier, some writers use 迭 dié for 叠 dié, even though it is not an official simplification. Wu has 吸腰叠步 xī yāo dié <u>bù</u>: 'suck in your waist and fold your <u>steps</u>'.

48.39.4 What we fear most is not being able to turn around freely.

最	怕	转	身	不	自	由。
zuì	pà	zhuàn	shēn	bù	zì	yóu.

All sources have this line.

Forty: Method of an Upright Body
正身法　　zhèng shēn fǎ

全身力量在中枢，
自身歪斜力不周。
别看步弯身必正，
发手如箭不停留。

The power of the whole body lies in its central axis,
A misaligned body has fragmentary power.
Even when you bend your legs your body must remain upright,
Then you can attack like shooting arrows nonstop.

Verses 48.38, 48.39, and 48.40 are reinforcing the body structure rules by explaining why this structure is necessary. This is another indication that the forty-eight methods verses are written for more advanced students. At first it is enough to tell students what to do. Later, it is better coaching to explain the reasoning behind the rules. Putting these three verses here is almost as if, after a string of verses about tactics and methods, a need was felt to reinforce the basic structure that allows the methods to work. Earlier, in verse 48.38, it seemed more appropriate to translate the 中枢 zhōng shū: 'centre' as the specific point of the Central Pivot. In this verse the word seems better translated as the central area of the body in general.

If the power is not held and used properly in the centre of the body, spine, and neck, movement and power cannot transmit through. Misalignment covers being off in any direction – forward, backward, or sideways. The meaning is clear enough. Whether circle-walking or doing techniques, the body remains upright, no matter what is going on in the legs. Sometimes people lean forward when the legs aren't strong enough to take the work. This is a good reason to not force the low basin stance if the leg strength and hip suppleness are not up to it, but to gradually work towards the ability to descend with an upright body. If the bow is angled, the arrows will not shoot straight. As one of my teachers likes to say, 'If you are upright and comfortable in contacting your opponent, he is likely unbalanced and uncomfortable, and you can take him out. If you are unbalanced and uncomfortable, there is a good chance your opponent will remain upright and comfortable, and he will easily counter your attack'.

Chang Naizhou's work of the late 1700s explains the inner workings of these three verses, "A posture that drops forward lets the *yang qi* enter the channel (to move up the back), but doesn't allow the *yin qi* to rise (up the front) in support. This is too *yang* and you will certainly fall into the disaster of being pulled forward. A posture that leans back allows the *yin qi* enter the channel (to move up the front) but doesn't allow the *yang qi* to rise (up the back) in support. This is too *yin* and you will have the worry of being pushed backwards. Therefore, those who tend to drop forward need to pull back, so that they are not overly *yang*. Those who tend to lean back need to set forward, so that they are not overly *yin*."[69] What is interesting is that a puffed up chest appears very '*yang*', or masculine, but internally is blocking the *yang* energy from rising, and a caved in chest appears very '*yin*' or weak, but internally is blocking the *yin* energy from rising. Also interesting is that this explanation was in an 'external style' book before schools were categorized into external and internal – that is just the way that the body was seen as working.

48.40.1 The power of the whole body lies in its central axis,
全　　身　　力　　量　　在　　中　　枢，
quán　shēn　lì　liàng　zài　zhōng　shū,

All sources have this line.

48.40.2 A misaligned body has fragmentary power.
自　　身　　歪　　斜　　力　　不　　周。
zì　shēn　wāi　xié　lì　bù　zhōu.

Five sources (Li, Lin, Tu, Wu, and Zang) have this exact line. Other sources have a slightly different expression of 'if the body structure is off the power is gone'. Liu reverses 斜歪 xié wāi: still meaning 'misaligned'. For the final phrase, Wang has 力不同 lì bù tóng: 'the power isn't <u>the same</u>', which doesn't rhyme, and Huan has 力不足 lì bù zú: 'the power is <u>insufficient</u>'.

48.40.3 Even when you bend your legs your body must remain upright,
别　　看　　步　　弯　　身　　必　　正，
bié　kàn　bù　wān　shēn　bì　zhèng,

The sources vary slightly in the description of the bent legs. Four (Li, Lin, Tu, and Wang) have what I have chosen as the standard. Huan has 要使步变 yào shǐ bù <u>biàn</u>: '<u>if you change what your legs are doing</u>'. Liu and Zang have 别看步变 bié kàn bù <u>biàn</u>: 'even when you <u>change your footwork</u>'. Wu has 别看步斜 bié kàn bù <u>xié</u>: 'even when your <u>footwork is angled</u>'.

All sources have the exact wording of the final phrase 身必正 shēn bì zhèng: 'the body must remain upright'.

48.40.4 Then you can attack like shooting arrows nonstop.
发　　手　　如　　箭　　不　　停　　留。
fā　shǒu　rú　jiàn　bù　tíng　liú.

Most sources have this exact line, which says 发手 fā shǒu: 'send out the hands'. Only Huan differs slightly, 发身如箭 fā shēn rú jiàn: 'you can send out the body like shooting arrows'.

Forty-one: Method of Supplementing the Body
            辅身法   fǔ shēn fǎ

身如君王腰腿臣，
君正臣强可制人。
进退躲闪凭身法，
若无腰腿不生神。

The body is like the sovereign with the waist and legs as his ministers,
    An upright sovereign with strong ministers can control the people.
Advancing, retreating, dodging and evading all depend on the bodywork,
    But without the waist and legs, the spirit cannot grow.

Movement is the main tactic of baguazhang, and it is the legs that enable this, but not at the expense of or independent of the body posture and power. The purpose of the foundation of the straight body that has been the focus of the last three verses is shown. The title says that the legs supplement the power of the torso – we must not focus entirely on the legs. Again, this verse seems to be making sure that we do not forget some of the basics, perhaps getting carried away with the stepping without keeping the structure and connection that makes the stepping so effective. All sources agree on the meaning that although the torso gives the main impetus, the waist and legs have to work together as a unit with the body.

Many schools of baguazhang refer to the hip joints as 腰腿 yāo tuǐ: meaning 'what is in between the waist and legs'. This would make the references to the hip joints rather than to the 'waist and legs'. I am quite partial to this interpretation.

48.41.1   The body is like the sovereign with the waist and legs as his ministers,

身	如	君	王	腰	腿	臣，
shēn	rú	jūn	wáng	yāo	tuǐ	chén,

There is a split in the versions of this verse, between personification of the body and a mechanical analogy. Five sources (Li, Lin, Liu, Tu and Wang)

have this line, giving the leader and assistants metaphor. Wu has this line, just using 是 shì: '<u>is</u>' instead of 如 rú: 'is like'. Two (Huan and Zang) have 身如主宰腰腿随 shēn rú zhǔ zǎi yāo tuǐ suí: 'the torso is the <u>dominant factor</u> and the waist and legs <u>follow</u>'. The mechanical analogy variation also appears in other sources that I have not used as 'official sources'. Liu Jingru has 身如重轴腰腿从 shēn rú zhòng zhóu yāo tuǐ cóng: 'the body is like the <u>main axle</u> and the waist and legs <u>follow</u>'. The 'king and ministers' is a commonly used metaphor so I have kept it.

48.41.2   An upright sovereign with strong ministers can control the people.

君	正	臣	强	可	制	人。
jūn	zhèng	chén	qiáng	kě	zhì	rén.

The five sources (Li, Lin, Tu, Wang) that started with this metaphor kept with it, as have I in the translation. Liu differs in the wording, with 主正臣强要制人 zhǔ zhèng chén qiáng <u>yào</u> zhì rén: 'an upright <u>leader</u> with strong ministers <u>will</u> control the people'. Wu has 君弱臣强能制人 jūn <u>ruò</u> chén qiáng <u>néng</u> zhì rén: 'a <u>weak</u> leader with strong ministers <u>can</u> control the people', which seems a bit odd.

Huan and Zang also continue to agree, with 主正身强力能催 zhǔ zhèng <u>shēn</u> qiáng <u>lì néng cuī</u>: 'if the <u>dominant factor</u> is upright and the <u>body</u> is strong, then the power <u>can be urged out</u>'. And Liu Jingru has an interesting version, 主弱从强难制人 zhǔ ruò cóng qiáng <u>nán</u> zhì rén: '<u>if the leader is weak</u> even if the <u>follower</u> is strong it is <u>difficult to control the people</u>'.

48.41.3   Advancing, retreating, dodging and evading all depend on the bodywork,

进	退	躲	闪	凭	身	法，
jìn	tuì	duǒ	shǎn	píng	shēn	fǎ,

Six sources (Huan, Li, Lin, Tu, Wang, and Wu) finally agree on this line. Getting to the point, stepping depends on the bodywork. Liu and Zang have reversed word order, without changing the meaning 进退闪躲 jìn tuì shǎn duǒ: advancing, retreating, <u>evading and dodging</u>.

48.41.4   But without the waist and legs, the spirit cannot grow.

若	无	腰	腿	不	生	神。
ruò	wú	yāo	tuǐ	bù	shēng	shén.

Six sources (Li, Lin, Liu, Tu, Wang, and Wu) have this line. For the final phrase, Zang has 力必微 lì bì wēi: 'the <u>power must be weak</u>'. Huan has the result being 力心微 lì xīn wēi: 'the <u>power and heart are weak</u>', which makes me think I miscopied the Huan text. The characters 心 xīn and 必 bì in a messy hand written text look awfully alike, so this is a possible agreement of sources.

Forty-two: Method of Twisting the Body
扭(拗)身法　　niǔ (ǎo) shēn fǎ

人来制我已贴身，
此时手脚不赢人。
左右吸收用扭法，
化险为夷把人擒。

If someone tries to control me and has already gotten in close,
At this point I can't win using my hands and feet.
Suck in and gather left and right, using the twisting method,
Turn danger into safety, grabbing him.

This verse gives us another sticky situation. You are bound up by your opponent so cannot save yourself with your feet or hands by kicking or striking. There is a saying in the martial arts, 'kick when distant, hit when close, throw when connected' 远踢近打贴身摔 yuǎn tī jìn dǎ tiē shēn shuāi. That is why getting in close is a tactic in baguazhang – it puts your adversary in a difficult situation. The first and second lines set up a typical baguazhang attack, but with you the one getting caught. Rather than trying to move away from a close hold, roll and turn to gain control over your opponent. The twisting power is developed through circle-walking in the set turned postures and the techniques training. The waist has become very strong in its ability to twist from side to side, and its ability to apply power while doing this, without hurting itself. The use of the words 'suck in and gather' is key to the technique. Some schools take it to shift and cut back into the hips, that takes the body back without stepping, some take is as a turning of the hips – however it is done, the power of a defensive drag comes from the hips. It looks to me that verses 48.38, 48.39, 48.40, and 48.41 went back to basics so that the student could do the methods in 48.42, 48.44, and 48.45 without hurting themselves.

48.42.1　　If someone tries to control me and has already gotten in close,

人	来	制	我	已	贴	身，
rén	lái	zhì	wǒ	yǐ	tiē	shēn,

Most sources have this exact wording. Tu differs slightly in the final phrase with 已贴心 yǐ tiē xīn: 'already close to the heart', meaning the same thing.

48.42.2   At this point I can't win using my hands and feet.

此	时	手	脚	不	赢	人。
cǐ	shí	shǒu	jiǎo	bù	yíng	rén.

All sources have this exact line.

48.42.3   Suck in and gather left and right, using the twisting method,

左	右	吸	收	用	扭 (拗)	法，
zuǒ	yòu	xī	shōu	yòng	niǔ (ǎo)	fǎ,

Five sources (Huan, Li, Liu, Wang, and Zang) use the phrase 左右吸收 zuǒ yòu xī shōu, while two (Lin, Tu) have 左右吸腰 zuǒ yòu xī yāo: 'suck in the waist to left and right'.

Five sources (Huan, Li, Lin, Tu, and Wang) have 用 yòng: 'use' to describe the use of the technique. Three have slight differences – Wu, with 拗身法 ǎo shēn fǎ: 'twisting body method', Liu and Zang, with 四扭法 sì niǔ fǎ: 'four twisting method'. Di Guoyong, in his unpublished manuscript, also has 四扭法 sì niǔ fǎ, and he comments, "This refers specifically to the single palm change, which contains four directional changes to left and right, front and back. It completely manifests the most foundational applications of baguazhang. In any close quarter fighting, if you use the skill developed in this most foundational training you have defense and offense. This will not only protect you, it can strike, grab, or throw down your opponent."[70]

Sources have either 扭法 niǔ fǎ (Li, Lin, Liu, Tu, Wang, and Zang) or 拗法 ǎo fǎ: 'the twisting method' (Huan, Wu, and Liang Shouyu), and throughout the thirty-six and forty-eight verses these characters are used interchangeably. Interestingly, this split is also seen in the title of this verse, with five sources having 扭 niǔ (Li, Lin, Tu, Wang, and Zang) and four having 拗 ǎo (Huan, Liu, Wu, and Liang Shouyu) – not quite the same as this line.

48.42.4   Turn danger into safety, grabbing him.

化	险	为	夷	把	人	擒。
huà	xiǎn	wéi	yí	bǎ	rén	qín.

Most sources have this exact line. Huan, perhaps remembering the admonition against grabbing in verse 48.46, has 把人折 bǎ rén zhé: 'breaking him'.

Forty-three: The Tactic of Sidestepping and Turning Sideways
跨步侧身法   kuà bù cè shēn fǎ

穿梭直入势难停，
先发制人显他能。
若遇此手接连退，
不如跨步侧身灵。

It is difficult to stop spearing palms coming straight in like a weaver's shuttle,
Your opponent has attacked first to gain control, and shown his ability.
If you meet this opponent, continuously retreat,
But it is more effective to sidestep and turn your body sideways.

This verse gives us a tactic for counter attacking driving spearing palms. From the context of the whole of the verse, you see that it refers to a counter attack, and once again a verse is giving us the counter to a common baguazhang technique. It further describes possible attacks dealt with in verse 48.22. This time, however, it gives a bit more respect to the straight-line attack. As a general principle, 'whoever attacks first has the control'. In this context, it is understood that your attacker has the advantage over you by attacking first with strong spearing palms. This shows that he has some skill. Sometimes you need to just back up, and your opponent here has shown ability and gotten the upper hand. Of course you can't back up forever, but it is a good setup for a throw. The tactic of sidestepping and turning is not only a dragging throw, but also a manner of drawing the opponent forward by backing up, making him chase you. This verse combines two of the thirty-six stratagems, Lead Away a Goat in Passing, and If All Else Fails Retreat. Retreating gives you time to sort out a counter, draws in your adversary, and causes him to overreach himself, thinking he has got you on the run. When you eventually sidestep, you turn and pull someone who you have already taken off balance by making him chase you. Either a *dai shou* or a *ling shou* work, but as Yan Dehua's expressive

drawing of Lead the Sheep Along at Your Ease shows, with a *ling shou* you can add a trip.

48.43.1   It is difficult to stop spearing palms coming straight in like shuttles,

穿	梭	直	入	势	难	停，
chuān	suō	zhí	rù	shì	nán	tíng,

All sources have this exact line.

48.43.2   Your opponent has attacked first to gain control, and shown his ability.

先	发	制	人	显	他	能。
xiān	fā	zhì	rén	xiǎn	tā	néng.

Five sources (Li, Lin, Tu, Wu, and Zang) have this exact line. Huan and Liu have 显彼能 xiǎn bǐ néng. The character 彼 bǐ is a more literary way to write 他 tā: 'he' or 'him'. Both are used throughout the verses. Wang has 先他能 xiān tā néng: '<u>to advance</u> his ability', with the repetition of 先 xiān indicating perhaps another typo.

48.43.3   If you meet this opponent, continuously retreat,

若	遇	此	手	接	连	退，
ruò	yù	cǐ	shǒu	jiē	lián	tuì,

Most sources have this exact line. Only Wang has 若遇<u>对</u>手 ruò yù <u>duì</u> shǒu: 'if you meet this opponent, <u>who is your match</u>'.

48.43.4   But it is more effective to sidestep and turn your body sideways.

不	如	跨	步	侧	身	灵。
bù	rú	kuà	bù	cè	shēn	lǐng.

All sources have this exact line. The step 跨步 kuà bù: 'sidestep', is a sideways, sometimes arcing or advancing, step, and has been described in verses 36.12, 48.20, 48.22, and 48.28. Turning to the side implies using a 带手 dài shǒu: 'pulling drag' along the direction he is already going. You turn so that the opponent goes past. The technique 侧身 cè shēn 'turn sideways' is to turn fully sideways to present only one side to your opponent.

Forty-four: Method of Shaking Off Side to Side
左右甩身法　　zuǒ yòu shuǎi shēn fǎ

闪躲东方西又来，
摇身一变甩身开。
左右连环皆如此，
前推后拀腰安排。

If you evade an attack from the East and there comes another from the West,
Change shape in a single shake, shaking the body free.
Repeat continuously side to side like this,
Push forward and pull back, all set up from the waist.

This verse gives a counter to multiple attacks, either from one or a number of assailants. It can be understood as an attack from one side then the other or, you dodge one assailant and you are hounded by another from the other side.

The forty-eight methods verses are intended for more advanced students, so the arms should by now follow the shoulder girdle and connect through the waist movement. When the body throwing method is applied, one hand is pulling back and the other is pushing forward, without having to do anything at all. The Ma Gui branch practises 涮腰 shuàn yāo as a special drill, called, for want of a good translation, '*shuanyao*'. This skill is trained within the changes, and with specific exercises in baguazhang, so the waist is able to move and turn with power and without injury. Using the waist means using the 甩 shuǎi: 'shake off' technique of the waist, which can direct the power into a push with one arm and/or a pull with the other, as both arms are attached to and move with the waist.

Wu groups 48.41, 48.42, and 48.44 together as three similar but different methods, commenting, "Supplementing the Body is a rubbing turn of the body, with the key in the waist. Twisting the Body is a coordination of the rotation of the waist and upper torso. Shaking the Body is a coordination of the waist and the lower limbs, with the key being the coordination between stepping and the body technique."[71]

48.44.1 If you evade an attack from the East and there comes another from the West,

閃	躲	東	方	西	又	來，
shǎn	duǒ	dōng	fāng	xī	yòu	lái,

Most sources use this wording. Only Huan differs with 避躲西方東又來 bì duǒ xī fāng dōng yòu lái: 'if you close off and dodge to the West and your opponent comes back again at the East'. The technique 閃 shǎn: 'evade' is a stepping evasion to the side. The technique 避 bì: 'close off' or 'jam' is a bit more proactive.

48.44.2 Change shape in a single shake, shaking the body free.

搖	身	一	變	甩	身	開。
yáo	shēn	yī	biàn	shuǎi	shēn	kāi.

Six sources (Li, Lin, Tu, Wang, Wu, and Zang) use this exact wording. The phrase 搖身一變 yáo shēn yī biàn: 'change shape in a single shake', here taken literally, figuratively means 'take on a new lease of life', as in 'give yourself a shake and change into another form or identity'.

For the technique, Huan uses the phrase 抖身開 dǒu shēn kāi: 'to jerk the body free'. Liu and Liang Shouyu uses the word 摔身開 shuāi shēn kāi: 'to throw the body free', instead of 甩 shuǎi: 'to shake'. The character 甩 shuǎi is not the simplified character for 摔 shuāi. The character 摔 shuāi means 'to throw', 'to take down'. The character 甩 shuǎi is a rolling swing, and 甩身 shuǎi shēn is a specific body technique, turning side to side and rolling at the same time, which is used to shake off, throw, or pull. Neither of these really disagrees with the text that the others have. The power used for a short 甩 shuǎi: 'shake' is 抖 dǒu: 'jerk'. The effect of a 甩 shuǎi: 'shake' can indeed be a 摔 shuāi: 'throw'.

48.44.3 Repeat continuously side to side like this,

左	右	連	環	皆	如	此，
zuǒ	yòu	lián	huán	jiē	rú	cǐ,

All the sources have this exact line.

48.44.4 Push forward and pull back, all set up from the waist.

前	推	後	捋	腰	安	排。
qián	tuī	hòu	lǚ	yāo	ān	pái.

All sources have this line.

Forty-five: The Tactic of Hunkering Down
蹲步沉身法　　dūn bù chén shēn fǎ

身高架大路上三，
举手招封势所难。
蹲步沉身使就下，
入我机关使法宽。

If you meet a tall, massive opponent who attacks your upper three (passes),
 You will be in trouble if you raise your hands to block the attack.
 Squat down to lower your body, inducing him to come down,
 Once he enters your space you have a wide range of applications.

  This verse gives a counter for the tactic suggested in verse 48.13 – that of staying above someone. This time you are the shorter one. The three passes of the upper limbs – wrist, elbow, and shoulder – were explained in verse 48.14. You are playing into your attacker's strengths if you react simply to a high attack. You should lower yourself even more, rather than trying to raise yourself to his level. This will cause him to over reach, lean down, or put strain on his legs to try to get you. Once your attacker has been pulled off balance by leaning to get down to your level, or been made uncomfortable getting his longer legs down into the same height as you in order to reach you, you can pick and chose what you do. He is restricted in his choices, especially since you have taken away his relaxed middle stance, and you have everything available to you. You take the initiative, concentrating on attacking his lower passes.

48.45.1　If you meet a tall, massive opponent who attacks your upper three (passes),

身　　高　　架　　大　　路　　上　　三，
shēn　gāo　jià　dà　lù　shàng　sān,

All sources have this line.

48.45.2　You will be in trouble if you raise your hands to block the attack.

举　　手　　招　　封　　势　　所　　难。
jǔ　shǒu　zhāo　fēng　shì　suǒ　nán.

Five sources (Li, Lin, Tu, Wang, and Zang) have this line. Huan and Wu have 封招 fēng zhāo, just reversing the characters 招封 zhāo fēng: 'block the attack'. Liu has 举手招对 jǔ shǒu zhāo duì: 'if you raise your hands to meet his attack'. I wonder if there is some confusion with the traditional character for 对 duì, which is 對, resembling 封 fēng.

48.45.3 Squat down to lower your body, inducing him to come down,
蹲　　步　　沉　　身　　使　　就　　下，
dūn   bù   chén   shēn   shǐ   jiù   xià,

Most sources have this exact line. Only Huan differs from it, and only in one character, 使低下 shǐ dī xià which still means 'to cause him to lower'.

48.45.4 Once he enters your space you have a wide range of applications.
入　　我　　机　　关　　使　　法　　宽。
rù   wǒ   jī   guān   shǐ   fǎ   kuān.

Five sources (Huan, Lin, Tu, Wang, and Wu) have this exact line. Three sources (Li, Liu, and Zang) have 用法宽 yòng fǎ kuān: 'a wide range of applications', with the same meaning.

Forty-six: Avoid Grabbing
忌拿法   jì ná fǎ

八卦之手不讲拿，
我拿人兮我亦差。
设若人多不方便，
直出直入也堪夸。

The techniques of bagua do not stress grabbing,
If I grab someone then I am also at a disadvantage.
I am inconvenienced if there are a lot of attackers,
'Straight out and straight in' also rates praise.

In the verses, grabbing has been referred to specifically in verses 48.20 and 48.42, after stepping around to the side of your opponent. A counter to grabbing has been given in verse 48.16. This verse is reminding us to not count too much on joint lock type of grabbing, especially with two hands. The disadvantage was explained previously as being stuck to the person with your hands occupied and unable to do other things. You are stuck with the person you grabbed. You can take them down, throw them into someone, or use them as a shield, but sooner or later you need to free yourself from hanging onto them. And with multiple assailants, sooner is better than later.

Stepping around has been dealt with frequently throughout the verses, as has the straight-line triple spearing palm. This verse is pointing out that a straight-line attack and withdrawal is sometimes more appropriate than triangulation or the half circle. The verses have explained a variety of techniques, and have given counters to many of them. This verse is not saying 'never grab', but just 'only use this technique when it is appropriate'. In multiple attack situations, particularly, it is better to stay clear and use the 'threading through blossoms' method explained in verse 48.23 rather than grab and control methods.

This is the only time in the verses that baguazhang is referred to as 八卦之手 bā guà zhī shǒu: 'the hands of the eight trigrams'. It is referred to once as 转掌 zhuàn zhǎng: 'turning palms' (36.22), and that is generally accepted as one of its original names. The title of the book written by Zeng is given as 八卦转掌汇览 bā guà zhuàn zhǎng huì lǎn: '*Notes Collected on Eight Trigrams Turning Palms*', and my handwritten copy of the verses is 八卦转掌 bā guà zhuàn zhǎng: 'eight trigrams turning palms', which is also generally accepted as another of its names. It is also often referred to as 八卦门 bā guà mén '*eight trigrams school*', though not in these verses. Throughout the verses it is called 'our style' using various phrases such as 此掌 cǐ zhǎng: 'this palm' (36.12, 36.13, 36.14, 36.15), 我之掌法 wǒ zhī zhǎng fǎ: 'my/our palm method' (48.32), 我家 wǒ jiā: 'our family' (48.47), or just 我 wǒ: 'me', or 'we', meaning 'those of us who do this style'. The verses were oral transmissions for baguazhang practitioners, so it is quite natural to call the style 'us'. Using a name even once in the verses indicates that that name was in use at the time of the verses, whether or not as the main name of the style. No style name was written on the first stele erected by the disciples of Dong Haichuan – not *zhuanzhang, bagua zhuanzhang* or *baguazhang* – but all were probably used in common speech.

So why did baguazhang come to be called baguazhang?

Many books say it is so named because the *bagua*, eight trigrams, can be used extensively in naming the body. The body is defined in eight parts in the Book of Changes: *Qian* as head, *Kun* as belly, *Zhen* as feet, *Xun* as thighs, *Kan* as ears, *Li* as eyes, *Gen* as hands, and *Dui* as mouth. Another way of correlating the trigrams with the body is: Since *Qian* is three connected lines it is the hands, elbows and shoulders. *Kan* is full in the centre, so is the qi settled in the *dantian*. *Gen* is the upturned bowl, so it the brain. *Zhen* is face up bowl, so is the mouth. *Xun* is broken at the bottom, so is the legs. *Li* is insubstantial in the centre, so is the empty chest. *Kun* is six broken lines, so is the shoulders, hips, and knees. *Dui* is broken on top so is the neck. This body labeling is used in other styles, and is just a cultural understanding, not at all specific to baguazhang. It seems pointless to give a name to your style based on an inconsistent system that everyone else uses. Yin Yuzhang (1880-1950) listed these labels in his 1932 book, but wrote that there is no evidence that it is how baguazhang got its name, and that this far fetched theory shouldn't even be narrated in this modern day and age.[72] Sun Xikun

(1889-1952) also listed these labels in his 1934 book, simply saying they make 8x8, and thus 64, without turning that information into anything useful. His book then goes on to describe in detail the movements of the changes without using any trigrams at all.

Renowned martial researcher Tang Hao (1897-1959), in his 1930 book on Taijiquan and Neijiaquan, also became frustrated with this constant need to call things by empty names. After a long section explaining the body's correspondences with the seven stars, eight trigrams, and three attributes he wrote " 'The three attributes are the head, hands, and feet, that is, upper, middle, and lower'. This just saying the head is above, the hands are in the middle, and the feet are below. The author is just claiming to be profound. This is called 'using abstruse language to write what could be said in simple language', and is just trying to make people think you are clever."[73]

It has been suggested that the name Baguazhang comes from the *bagua* cult, called 八卦教 bā guà jiaò, that appeared during the Qing period. At first the cult was not anti-Qing, but gradually became so after governmental oppression of folk cults. From the late 1700s through the early 1800s many leaders of the sect were imprisoned, and the sect led uprisings from time to time. The growth of the *bagua* cult coincided with the peak of popularity of baguazhang in Beijing – the years 1866-1894. "Analysing historical materials, the appearance of baguazhang during the Qing dynasty coincided with and was inextricably linked to the folk cult called the *bagua* cult... And moreover, practically all baguazhang practitioners were members of the *bagua* cult." [74] This would be an interesting avenue to explore, though if I were a member of an illegal cult I would not to lend its name to something I taught every day in a public park.

Another suggestion is that since Dong Haichuan, Yang Luchan, and Guo Yunshen were great friends in Beijing, they just decided to give names to their styles that fit together – one Taijiquan with the *yin/yang*, one Xingyiquan with the five elements, and one Baguazhang with the eight trigrams. Baguazhang certainly does use the circle and use the eight directions more than the other styles, and the size of a comfortable circle with *tangnibu* is about eight steps. In baguazhang it is vital to know your eight directions and where you are within them at all times, not more or less, but exactly. So if you were looking for a set of names that expresses that the three are 'the same but different' or 'different but the same', *taiji*, *bagua*, and *xingyi* are pretty good.

In his book, Yin Yuzhang uses the trigrams as directions for stepping and facing. He says in the introduction, "Baguazhang is all about walking in circles, circling, and turning, so it is harder than in other styles to explain the directions and placements. So when describing the positions, we say the foot is at the *xun* direction and the face is towards the *qian* direction, this is to set the beginning and end points, it is just a standard for beginners. You don't want to stick with these directions forever."[75]

As an example of the directional use, this illustration from Yin Yuzhang's book, is captioned, "Drawings 1 and 2, the right leg takes a step to the *qian* direction and the left foot turns the toes pointing to the *kan* direction – this is accomplished at the same time. The drawings separate the steps for teaching purposes. Drawing 3, the right foot lifts and turns to the *kan* direction while the left foot steps around to the *gen* direction."

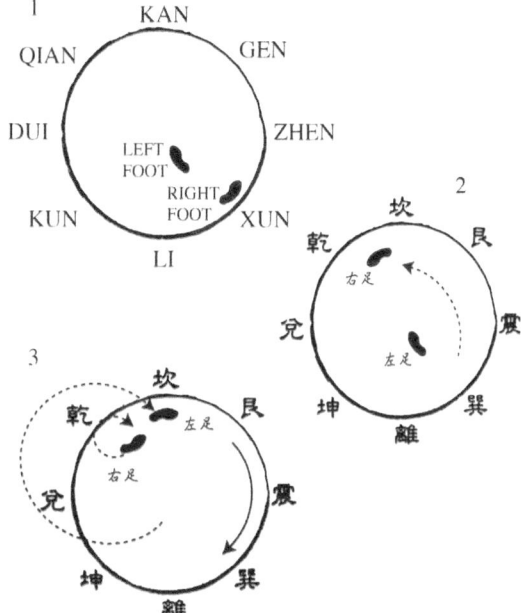

Some traditionally use the trigrams as exact compass points, such as *kan* at the north and *li* at the south, but this is inconsistent – some have *kun* as north and *qian* as south. The trigrams are better used as a simple way of finding or explaining your directions relative to your body, not absolute compass directions. You need to know where you are in your placement at all times, but you do not have to correspond this to specific trigrams – it is the other way around, they are used for convenience.

This seems the most likely to me – a style named 'after' the trigrams, though not really 'of' the trigrams. Similarly, there is a battle array called *bagua* that sets up like the patterns on a tortoise's back, which happen to look like trigrams. The array entices the enemy into the pattern of enveloping shapes and lines then changes the lines to entrap, confuse, and destroy them. Baguazhang could well be named after the trigrams because of a general feeling – one-to-one correspondence is not required – and then the style further developed to fit that name. For instance, the use of the number eight since the beginning. As Liu Jingru pointed out, "The Cheng branch has eight great palms, the Yin branch has eight great postures, the Shi banch has eight great palms. No schools have seven or nine great palms. Clearly the ordering by eights comes from the name of baguazhang."[76]

48.46.1　　The techniques of bagua do not stress grabbing,

八　　卦　　之　　手　　不　　讲　　拿，
bā　　guà　　zhī　　shǒu　　bù　　jiǎng　　ná,

All sources have this line. The word 讲 jiǎng: 'speak' in this case I have taken with its frequent meaning of 讲究 jiǎng jiǔ: 'emphasize'.

48.46.2　　If I grab someone then I am also at a disadvantage.

我　　拿　　人　　兮　　我　　亦　　差。
wǒ　　ná　　rén　　xī　　wǒ　　yì　　chà.

Six sources (Li, Lin, Liu, Tu, Wu, and Zang) have this exact line. Wang has 我也差 wǒ yě chà: 'I am also at a disadvantage'. Huan has 我不擦 wǒ bù cā: 'I am not applying my rubbing technique', which I suspect is a mis-copy.

48.46.3　　I am inconvenienced if there are a lot of attackers,

设　　若　　人　　多　　不　　方　　便，
shè　　ruò　　rén　　duō　　bù　　fāng　　biàn,

Most sources have this line, which literally says 'supposing there are many people, it is inconvenient'. Wang has the same meaning with slightly different grammar, 假若人多 jiǎ ruò rén duō: 'supposing there are many'.

48.46.4　　'Straight out and straight in' also rates praise.

直　　出　　直　　入　　也　　堪　　夸（誇）。
zhí　　chū　　zhí　　rù　　yě　　kān　　kuā.

All sources have the phrase 'straight out and straight in', referring to direct attack and direct withdrawal. They differ only in the exact wording for saying that it is a good thing. We have already seen in the verses that both 夸 kuā and 誇 kuā are used for 'praise' or 'boasting'. Four (Li, Lin, Tu, and Zang) have 也堪夸 yě kān kuā: 'also rates praise'. Huan and Liu have 已堪誇 yǐ shén kuā, which means the same thing. Wang has 也湛垮 yě zhàn kuā: 'also deeply praised'. Wu has 也侃夸 yě kǎn kuā: 'also praised'.

The Forty-eight Methods Verses

Forty-seven: Avoid Standing Still
忌站法　　jì zhàn fǎ

混元一气走无涯，
八卦真理是我家。
招招不离脚变化，
站住即为落地花。

When your original *qi* is full then you can walk without boundaries,
The truth of the eight trigrams is in our school.
Every single technique comes from the changes of the feet,
If you stand still you are like fallen blossoms.

There is a lot in this verse. It is not a simple admonition against standing still in a fight, although it is certainly that. This verse sums up some overall principles. First, the ideas of Daoist *hunyuan qigong* training have influenced baguazhang. The *qi* resulting from this training is robust, the mind is clear, and the body is in repose. Second, baguazhang achieves original *qi* through circle-walking rather than separate *qigong* exercises. Walking in the pressing down posture, with the hands down, connects the Ren and Du vessels (see note 22), completing the small circulation 小周天 xiǎo zhōu tiān: 'small heavenly circuit'. The different postures then connect different meridians, and the final result of circle-walking in all the postures is the full and continuous flow of *qi* throughout the body. You can move freely when you have developed the full original *qi* in your training, and the *qigong* training is the circle-walking itself.

Third, when you have trained enough to combine the two, you are free to apply all the tactics and methods explained in the verses. Circle-walking is not a basic exercise that can be discarded once you feel you have 'mastered' it. All footwork, all methods, and all tactics come from all that is involved in circle-walking.

The use of the feet for movement has been emphasized over and over in the verses. The image is of trampling on blossoms that have fallen off the trees in spring, or trampling through a border of flowers that have dropped their petals. Chen's style Taijiquan free step push hands calls this smooth flowing walking 踏花 tà huā: 'trampling on flowers'. Pausing quietly to take in the situation before reacting has been encouraged as a tactic quite a few times throughout the verses. Verse 48.11 says 'watch out and keep centered, and do not issue any empty attacks'. So 'fallen blossoms' is meant as just plain stupidly stopping – stopping the mind, not just the feet.

The style was referred to as 八卦之手 bā guà zhī shǒu: 'eight trigram hands' in verse 48.46 but this is the first time that the eight trigrams themselves are referred to. What does 'the truth of the eight trigrams is in our school' mean?

As a Chinese martial art, you would think that baguazhang naturally incorporated the traditional Chinese worldview of the *yin/yang*, five phases and eight trigrams and the Book of Changes. But was this originally in the style, or a later addition? In verse 48.05 I discussed how we can identify the first generation of bagua masters more as *jianghu* brothers than scholar-gentlemen. Very specific correspondences between the eight trigrams and baguazhang is generally credited to to the next generation. Sun Lutang (1861-1932) was concerned with examining and combining Taijiquan, Xingyiquan, and Baguazhang into his own system, so turned to the distinguishing features of *yin/yang*, five elements, and eight trigrams for his theoretical foundation, and places value on these correspondences. Sun was well educated, and a strong proponent of integrating Chinese medicine and philosophy into the martial arts. He taught at the *Guoshuguan*, and his books, published in 1926 and 1928, were the first published on baguazhang, so naturally he was influential in certain circles. Gao Yisheng (1866-1951) was also working out his system of baguazhang based on the trigrams, but apparently was not pleased that it was published by one of his students in 1936.[77]

It is a big step from saying that the style 'has correspondences with' the trigrams to the style 'is based on' the trigrams. Authors of the next generation did not use the trigrams. Yan Dehua did not refer to the trigrams at all. Sun Xikun only gave them passing recognition. Yin Yuzhang, as discussed earlier, used the trigrams for directional indications. Cao Zhongsheng said, "As to the names of styles such as *taiji, bagua, wuxing* (referring to Xingyi), *liuhe*, etc., these are just names taken to distinguish between themselves. If you draw the conclusion that these names form the basis of the theory of the style, and then use that to explain the skills, you are causing people see them indistinctly and dimly – as if they are unfathomable."[78] Jiang Rongqiao clearly stated in an unpublished manuscript, "Baguazhang was created by Dong Haichuan, but Dong Haichuan never used the trigrams, and never spoke of a certain move being such and such a trigram. His ten main disciples Cheng Tinghua, Yin Fu, and the others, never used the trigrams. This shows that baguazhang at its root did not use the trigrams. Later, some people put the trigrams into baguazhang routines, which not only served no purpose, but on the contrary, served just to pull people training baguazhang into a big vat of paste – the more they struggled the more muddled they became."[79]

In the same manuscript, Jiang reported that his teacher Zhang Zhankui said, "My teacher said that thirty years ago (c. 1930) bagua masters Wu Junshan and Fu Jianqiu tried very hard to put the trigrams into baguazhang, but try as they might they couldn't do it. They asked my teacher, 'how can we make the first palm change into eight palms?' My teacher simply said, 'you will never succeed'.... Baguazhang has absolutely nothing to do with the trigrams. Using the trigrams is a doctrine without foundation, it is devoid of content and absurd. If, for example, you say such and such a palm change is *qian*, and the sky, someone else can say it is *kun* and the earth. This type of empty naming isn't even as good as trying to connect metaphorical theory to reality."[80]

You can force correspondences and labeling to make sense, but what is the point? As Liu Jingru said in an article called 'Baguazhang is not *bagua*', although some say that the trigrams is where Baguazhang got its name, "they are as much alike as matching a phoenix, a horse, and an ox",[81] and that the masters of yesteryear did not use the trigrams. The question of when the verses were written comes up here. They do not mention the trigrams until the final verses. Is it possible that most of the verses were the words of Dong Haichuan, but by the time the writing was finished – in the last verses – the author felt a need to recognize a predilection for the trigrams amongst some of his fellow second generation masters?

The one to one correspondence of the eight trigrams and sixty-four hexagrams to specific methods is held by some lineages. Gao Yisheng is probably the most successful at developing a way of basing the methods on the trigrams, to better organize training. For example, the pre-heaven organization applying to the foundational training methods, and the post-heaven organization applying to the practical applications. Does this organization make the training more effective? Some lineages base their training on eight animals, with just as much justification and effectiveness. Over intellectualization of the art takes away from the internal feeling, and baguazhang is about training until you get the feeling. We can study animals and emulate their spirit without getting bogged down in theories. If someone uses the trigrams to help organize his training and teaching, then that is useful. If they are used to confuse people and distract them from training, than that is counter productive. The most basic connotation of the trigrams is that they grow from *yin* and *yang*, and spread to encompass all possibilities. Isn't that enough? Does re-naming things help? Baguazhang's unfettered mind and movements, natural reactions, and use of opportunities are a result of the training, not a result of a fixation on names and theories.

48.47.1　　When your original *qi* is full then you can walk without boundaries,

混 (浑)	元	一	气	走	无	涯,
hùn (hún)	yuán	yī	qì	zǒu	wú	yá,

All sources have this meaning. Throughout the verses 混元 hùn yuán (Huan, Li, Lin, Liu, Tu, Wu, and Zang) and 浑元 hún yuán (Wang) are used for the qigong method of clearing the turbid *qi* and bringing out the original clean *qi*. The sources say 'walk without boundaries' in two different ways. Six sources (Huan, Lin, Liu, Tu, Wang, and Wu) have 走无涯 zǒu wú yá: 'walk without boundaries', and two (Li and Zang) have 走天涯 zǒu tiān yá: 'walk to the end of the world'. Both phrases mean the same thing.

48.47.2　　The truth of the eight trigrams is in our school.

八	卦	真	理	是	我	家。
bā	guà	zhēn	lǐ	shì	wǒ	jiā.

Two sources (Li, Wang) have this exact line. Four (Huan, Lin, Tu, and Wu) use 吾 wú instead of 我 wǒ, which is the more literary way of saying 'I'. Liu and Zang have 是法家 shì fǎ jiā: 'is the Legalist school of thought', which is obviously not the intended meaning.

48.47.3　　Every single technique comes from the changes of the feet,

招	招	不	离	脚	变	化,
zhāo	zhāo	bù	lí	jiǎo	biàn	huà,

Five sources (Huan, Li, Wang, Wu, and Zang) have this exact wording. Two sources (Lin, Tu) have 步步不离 bù bù lí: 'every single step doesn't leave'.

48.47.4　　If you stand still you are like fallen blossoms.

站	住	即	为	落	地	花。
zhàn	zhù	jí	wéi	luò	dì	huā.

All sources have this line. This line could be the motto for baguazhang, which is why I incorporated it into the title of this book.

The Forty-eight Methods Verses

Forty-eight:　　The Supreme Method
太上法　　　tài shàng fǎ

力要足活招要准，
即或使空三不紊。
招套招兮无穷极，
精神法术在乎纯。

> Power must be full and lively and moves must be accurate,
> Even if you miss, 'the three' must not get confused.
> Inexhaustible moves within moves,
> Your spirit and technique depend on your mastery of them.

Even when you are forceful and accurate, you can still make mistakes, but you cannot let them throw you off. Some commentaries say 'the three' are the mind, the hands, and the feet. Some say they are the waist, legs, and hands. This has been explained in verse 48.33. The ability to flow effortlessly and inexhaustibly from one move to another is what makes baguazhang the 'supreme skill'. And all that is needed is complete mastery of yourself.

48.48.1　Power must be full and lively and moves must be well aimed,
力　　要　　足　　活　　招　　要　　准，
lì　　yào　　zú　　huó　　zhāo　　yào　　zhǔn,

Five sources (Li, Lin, Liu, Tu, and Wu) have this line. Zang says this slightly differently with 力若足活 lì ruò zú huó: 'if power is full and lively', which makes the line mean 'if power is full and lively then the moves will be well aimed'. Wang has a slightly different interpretation (or a typo), with 力要足法招要准 lì yào zú fǎ zhāo yào zhǔn: 'power must be full, techniques must be well aimed'. Huan has 力要活合招不准 lì yào huó hé zhāo bù zhǔn: 'power must be free and connected or the techniques won't be accurate'.

48.48.2　Even if you miss, 'the three' must not get confused.
即　　或　　使　　空　　三　　不　　紊。
jí　　huò　　shǐ　　kōng　　sān　　bù　　wěn.

Most sources have this line. Huan has 法不紊 fǎ bù wěn: 'my techniques don't get confused'.

48.48.3　Inexhaustible moves within moves,
招　　套　　招　　兮　　无　　穷　　极，
zhāo　　tào　　zhāo　　xī　　wú　　qióng　　jí,

Five sources (Li, Lin, Liu, Tu, and Zang) have this line. Huan and Wu have 无穷尽 wú qióng jìn, which also means 'inexhaustible'. Wang has another typo, with 无穿极 wú chuān jí: 'with no limit to spearing', unless he really likes the spearing palm.

48.48.4　　Your spirit and technique depend on your mastery of them.

精　　　神　　　法　　　术　　　在　　　乎　　　纯。
jīng　　shén　　fǎ　　shù　　zài　　hū　　chún.

Six sources (Li, Lin, Liu, Tu, Wu, and Zang) have this line. Huan and Wang have 精神法求 jīng shén fǎ qiú: 'in your spirit and technique, seek'. The word 纯 chún: 'proficient' or 'well versed', also means 'pure', so this line can also be taken to mean that you must remain pure in intent if you hope to achieve all that is contained in the thirty-six and forty-eight verses.

In Praise of the Forty-eight Methods Verses

歌赞　　　　gē zàn

四十八法意真切，
练练说说不为神。
要得所传纯功到，
几人三年试验深。

The meaning of the forty-eight methods verses is clear,
If you just train and train, discuss and discuss, you will not achieve their essence.
If you want to achieve what they transmit and gain pure skills,
You need to train three years with others and gain much experience.

This verse 'In Praise of the Forty-eight Methods Verses', said to be from Dong Haichuan himself, is quoted only by Huan, Li, and Wu. Although Li Ziming originally published the above 'verse of praise', two of his students (Di Guoyong and Zhang Quanliang) and Zang have a different version that serves to praise both the 36 and 48 verses.

line 1　　　The meaning of the forty-eight methods verses is clear,

四　　　十　　　八　　　法　　　意　　　真　　　切，
sì　　shí　　bā　　fǎ　　yì　　zhēn　　qiè,

The Forty-eight Methods Verses

The three sources with this verse agree on this line. The three with the different version have this same line, but referring to 三十六歌 sān shí liù gē: 'the thirty-six verses' instead of the forty-eight methods.

line 2   If you just train and train, discuss and discuss, you will not achieve their essence.

练	练	说	说	不	为	神,
liàn	liàn	shuō	shuō	bù	wéi	shén,

Most sources have 说说练练 shuō shuō liàn liàn: 'talk, talk, train, train'. Li has 练练说说 liàn liàn shuō shuō: 'train, train, talk, talk'. I like having training coming before talking.

line 3   If you want to achieve what they transmit and gain pure skills,

要	得	所	传	纯	功	到,
yào	dé	suǒ	chuán	chún	gōng	dào,

Most sources have this line, whether referring to the 36 or the 48 methods. Li and Huan have 神功到 shén gōng dào: 'gain magical skills'.

line 4   You need to train three years with others and gain much experience.

几	人	三	年	试	验	深。
jǐ	rén	sān	nián	shì	yàn	shēn,

All sources have this line, whether referring to the 36 or the 48 methods.

The three sources that refer the preceeding verse of praise to the 36 verse have this verse for the 48 methods.

四十八法甚难求，
见招使招不自由。
十年纯功研究到，
单人凭艺傲五洲。

The forty-eight methods are deeply difficult to seek,
If you just see techniques and copy you won't become natural.
After ten years pure training you can research their meaning,
And you can stroll the world alone confident of your skill.

line 1   The forty-eight methods are deeply difficult to seek,

四   十   八   法   甚   难   求,
sì   shí   bā   fǎ   shèn nán   qiú,

The three sources with this verse have this line.

line 2   If you just see techniques and copy you won't become natural.

见   招   使   招   不   自   由。
jiàn zhāo shǐ   zhāo bù   zì   yóu.

Another version of the first phrase is 克招使时 <u>kè</u> zhāo shǐ shí: 'when you <u>use</u> the techniques'.

line 3   After ten years pure training you can research their meaning,

十   年   纯   功   研   究   到,
shí   nián chún gōng yán   jiū   dào,

The three sources with this verse have this line.

line 4   And you can stroll the world alone confident of your skill.

单   人   凭   艺   傲   五   洲。
dān   rén   píng yì   ào   wǔ   zhōu.

The three sources with this verse have this line.

Part Three

Notes
References
Illustrations
Glossary
Pronunciation Guide

NOTES

Acknowledgments

1 I should mention that I do not mix-and-match the styles that I train. Each one has its own way of doing things, and its own reasons. The hand shapes, circle-walking methods, ways of developing and applying power, all the techniques and the rest are integrally part of each style. I believe that each school develops me in some way that it cannot if mixed with another. My lineage style is Jiang Rongqiao's. I did Ma Gui's style almost exclusively for about ten years. For the others, some I have learned and trained quite a lot, while others I have just begun or just practise certain things. I am naturally an all-rounder, so do Chen Taijiquan, Taiji Changquan, and Xingyiquan as well as Baguazhang. I practise all to some extent, mostly Baguazhang, and change my emphasis from time to time. I would also like to thank my Aikido sensei, Mike Chin, for some great years when I was in Victoria.

Preface

2 The Shi lineage has a different version of the verses. They apply specifically to the Shi lineage, so I do not include them here. They were published by Di Zhaolong 狄兆龙 in Wulin magazine, September 1983. I was told the Shi verses were written in response to the publication of Li Ziming's verses. I did not find Li Ziming's original publication, but it was around that time. There need not be a time lag between publications, as Di and Li were in contact and most likely shared information. There are quite a few verses that are almost the same as the verses published by Li Ziming, but I do not know if this is because of working together, copying or similar transmission. The Fan lineage does not use the 36 and 48 verses, but has a series of verses for each technique. I cannot include those here, as I have them only as a personal favour. The Gao lineage has 64 eight line verses plus 12 four line verses, which are almost all specific to techniques, and which are in the Du book.

3 "Copied three times, 鸟 and 焉 become 马" is complete nonsense when translated, but the point is still made – 'birds and participles become horses'. The saying points out how easy it is to copy wrongly, especially when copying hand written texts. Just think of the whispering game, where we try to repeat a sentence and pass it on down the line.

Introduction

4 Zeng Zengqi was a '清代皇室的族亲': 'a clansman to the Qing imperial house'. The 'imperial household' was the bureaucracy within the imperial palace. The members would be bannermen or bondservants, not necessarily relatives.

They would have contact with the imperial family, since they managed personal affairs as well as business. This reference does say 'clansman', so he may have been a relation.

5 A website that reported Kang Gewu's research said, "Ts'eng's written work was never made public, however, K'ang Ko-Wu has Ts'eng' original manuscript." Lawrence C. Toliver Arts Institute Web Site, 2000. But if Kang Gewu has the original manuscript, why has absolutely no one mentioned it, either in publication or in personal conversations? Everyone who does Baguazhang knows him and knows of his work. He most likely has a copy like everyone else. I know from experience trying to track down original manuscripts, that they tend to disappear – lost while moving house, borrowed and not returned, burned during the Cultural Revolution, or thrown away by unknowing relatives after death.

6 Chinese Wushu Encyclopedia Editorial Committee, page 469 and 483. The name of the book written by Zeng is given as 八卦转掌汇览 *Notes Collected on Bagua Turning Palms.*

7 That the 1880s Baguazhang masters were members of the *bagua* cult is general knowledge in Baguazhang circles. I discuss this further with verse 48.46. It is also stated in Qiu Pixiang, *A History of China's Martial Arts*, pp. 134-135.

8 In the 101 volume *Compendium of Classic Writings of Chinese Wushu*, of over 240 books or writings on the martial arts, the editors picked about 8 from pre-Ming dynasty, about 30 from the Ming dynasty, about 32 from the Qing dynasty, none from 1900-1910, about 15 from 1910-1919, about 30 from 1920-1929, about 120 from 1930-1939, and about 20 from 1940-1949. Only eight were about Baguazhang. I went through the entire set, it seemed that they tried to include as much as they could find, and that in periods when there were more or less materials it was because that is what was there. This compendium even included some unpublished materials, so I believe it was quite thorough. Shi Yongxin, editor 释永信主编，中国武术大典 (*Compendium of Classic Writings of Chinese Wushu*)，中国书店, 2012.

9 There were also a few books in that period that sounded like they may be about baguazhang, but are not. Ren Zhicheng's *Yinyang Bapanzhang*, 1937, has an odd lineage claim in the preface, which involves a Dong, but not Dong Haichuan. There is still argument about whether Bapanzhang and Baguazhang are branches from the same origin. The Origins of Pa Kua Chang, *Pa Kua Chang Journal*, volume 3, number 1, Nov/Dec 1992 says that Kang Gewu's research indicates that the author of this book had actually learned Liu Baozhen's Baguazhang. The stances all look very particular to a coiling type stance to me, not the stances of Baguazhang, and the section on basic training does not look much like Baguazhang. The sabre is a big one, though.

Jiang Rongqiao's *Depiction of Bagua Invisible Spear*, 1930, is not about baguazhang, but a traditional spear routine.

Yuan Chucai's *Wudang Baguazhang*, 1942, is not about baguazhang.

10 Xu Zhen's *A Brief Discussion of the National Sport*, 1929, Bian Renjie's *Introduction to the National Sport*, 1936, Chu Mingxuan's *Origin of the National Art*, 1936, Li Yingzhu's *A History of Chinese Martial Arts*, 1936, and Wu Tunan's *Introduction to the National Sport*, 1937.

NOTES

11 "練習此功不限年歲。凡能動作者均可學習。一則無曲腿之苦。再則無跳躍之勞。動作均如走路。不拘窄袖短衣。如着長服亦可練習。" Huang Bonian, Introductory remarks, p. 1.

Part One: The Thirty-Six Verses

12 Nine sources for the text of the 36 verses: Huan Dahai 宦大海 (Zhang lineage, Zhang Zhankui 张占魁: Jiang Rongqiao 姜容樵). This copy of Dong Haichuan's words was noted as coming from Pei Xirong 裴锡榮, as copied from Liang Zhenpu 梁振蒲. I refer to this source as Huan or 'my copy of Huan' in the discussions. Li Ziming (Liang lineage from Liang Zhenpu). First open publication of the verses, and one of the few books to include extensive commentary. Refer to as Li. Lin Sui (Wu Lingshan 吳岭山: Liu Menqiang 刘门墙. The book says Wu Lingshan was 2nd generation, but other sources put him in the 3rd generation). Refer to as Lin. Liu Xinghan (Cheng lineage, Cheng Tinghua 程廷华: Liu Zhenzong 刘振宗). Refer to as Liu. Luo Hongxuan 罗洪宣 (Shi lineage, Shi Jidong 施继栋: Wu Lingshan 吴峻山) Refer to as Luo. Tu Xingjian 涂行健 (Yin/Ma Gui lineage, Dong Haichuan 董海川 and Yin Fu 尹福: Ma Gui 马贵: Liu Wanchuan 刘万川: Yu Zhiming 于志明). Refer to as Tu. Wang Shangzhi 王尚智 (Yin lineage, Yin Fu 尹福: He Zhongqi 何忠祺). There were quite a number of typographical errors. Refer to as Wang. Wu Yue (Guo lineage, Liu Dekuan 刘德宽 and Liang Zhenpu 梁振蒲: Guo Gumin 郭古民). Refer to as Wu. Zang Xuefan (Guo lineage). Refer to as Zang.

Secondarily also used commentaries for occasional clarification. Di Guoyong (Li Ziming's student) unpublished manuscript and personal communication. Gao Jiwu (Gao lineage, Yin Fu and Liu Dekuan 刘德宽: Gao Wencheng 高文成. Liang Zhenpu and Liu Dekuan: Guo Gumin. Gao Wenchang and Guo Gumin: Gao Ziying 高子英). Refer to 2007 as Gao and 2010 as Gao2. Li Gongcheng (Li Ziming's student). Li Xiuren (Li Ziming's daughter). Refer to as re-edited Li. Liang Shou-Yu and Yang Jwing-Ming (text from Pei Xirong 裴锡榮, in the Yin lineage (Yin Fu: Yin Yuzhang: Pei Xirong). Liu Jialin (Liang lineage). Liu Jingru (Cheng lineage, Cheng Tinghua: Li Wenbiao 李文彪: Luo Xingwu 骆兴武). Liu Yongchun (Yin lineage, Yin Fu 尹福: Men Baozhen 门宝珍: Wang Jingshan 王景山). This book did not have the complete poems but commented on the meaning of some lines. Shi Naijian (Shi lineage, Shi Jidong 史计栋: Shi Fuwen 史富文). This book had different Shi clan verses, but some of those clarified these verses. Xiang Yuncai (Cheng lineage, Liu Xinghan's student). Zhang Quanliang (Li Ziming's student).

Choice of which sources to use involved differences and similarities of text, plus practical concerns such as copyright and permissions. Since the secondary sources were also referenced for clarity, sometimes my sources add up to more than nine. See References for details.

13 In verse 36.01. "转身叠步时，则须先动足次掰膝再拗胯。" Li Ziming, p. 16.

14 Liu Xinghan learned from many 'uncles' in the Cheng lineage. His book that included the 36 verses involved quite a large editorial committee, with no indication of where they had input and where it was Liu's own writing. His book that included the 48 verses was published posthumously, so again I am not sure the input was all his.

15 切胯 qiē kuà: 'cut at the hip joint' means to tuck the thigh in at the hip joint, to settle inward slightly to give a feeling of ease of movement and power transference. You can 'cut' into the crease with your palm edge. Also called 吸胯 xī kuà: 'breathe into or suck in, the hip joint'.

16 "扭步掰膝抓地牢" Gao (2), page 38, "扭步合膝抓地牢" Gao (2), p. 39.

17 In verse 36.02. "足踏巽方，面向離方立正；右掌停於乾方，肘微屈，掌與眉齊，目向食指第一線注視，左掌停於右肘下，肘對心口，兩腿稍彎，挺頸，含胸，弜背，溜臀，下頜收回，對右肩窩，閉口，用鼻呼吸，氣沈丹田。" Yin Yuzhang, Techniques section, p.1 "圈點之處特別重要，是關鍵點，因為人只要一走動，肘，掌，下頜的位置很容易跑掉。這是立勢的標準，標準一失，就不必練了。" Notes section, p. 2.

18 In verse 36.03. "足有伸翅。足尖伸而下入者。氣下降而沈栽也。足尖翅而上勾者。氣上升而浮漂也。" Chang Naizhou, roll 2, p. 27.

19 This is one of those throw away lines that I didn't note down, but of course remembered. I can't find the reference again, but it is too good a quote to not include.

20 In verse 36.04. "我單鞭壓他變馬…" Wang Minghe, Shi's *Compendium* volume 1, page 488. "他大門單鞭坐腳直滾入殺…" p. 499.

21 In verse 36.07. "方腰駢肋" Dong Haichuan's third stele, erected in 1930.

22 任脉 rèn mài: 'Conception vessel' and 督脉 dū mài: 'Governing vessel' are not meridians, but 'extraordinary vessels' that start from the lower part of the torso, the prenatal source. They flow up the front and back of the torso respectively. The *Ren* (Conception) vessel in front links the *Yin* channels, and the *Du* (Governing) vessel in back links the *Yang* channels. When they are connected, the qi flows up and down in the torso like water in a paddlewheel.

23 In verse 36.10. Interestingly, a 'willow leaf' shape also refers to the arched eyebrows of a woman. I have also heard the palm shape called 兰花掌 lán huā zhǎng 'orchid palm', which normally refers to a shape with the tips of the thumb and index finger touching and the other fingers separated. This is a graceful hand gesture made on the Chinese opera stage, and also a hand shape used in Buddhist art. I like that a style that was recognized as devastating was also somehow seen as graceful.

24 In verse 36.15. "八卦門是个黑道門派"，"八卦門所至之處，其他門派均讓三分"，"八卦門不擇手段，武林望之却步" Xiaoyi 萧逸, 金弓女杰, (c. 1862-1951) in Xie Yanci 谢燕辞, 完全武林門派手册, p. 103.

25 "響而後進進而後響分別明白可以語技矣。" Wang Minghe, Shi's *Compendium* volume 1, p. 521.

26 In verse 36.16. "進身於敵來臂之裏門則打其胸，於其外門則可雙手或單手推打敵背或腋下。" Cao Zhongsheng, Shi's *Compendium* volume 75, p. 289.

27 In verse 36.18. "陰來陽逆。陽來陰逆。… 高者還之以低。低者還之以高。側者還之以正。正者還之以側。以及斜歪紐縹。旋轉來往。無不皆然。" Chang Naizhou, roll 1, p. 4.

28 "斜身：身之正門斜向敵人。" Cao Zhongsheng, Shi's *Compendium* volume 75, p. 294.

NOTES 221

29 In verse 36.19. "郭老名济元，山东人，与董先师同时，从未下山，董先师尝与门人道及，郭老曾言：凡习此掌高深者，皆知柔刚之理，故刚柔两相调济之，方臻佳境。" Zang Xuefan, p. 33.

30 "八卦掌之始祖董海川太夫子。與形意專家。郭雲深太夫子。一處研習若干日。遂覺愈趨愈近。息息相通。動作雖異。理法無殊。乃合而為一。" Jiang Rongqiao, *Teaching Materials for Taijiquan*, p. 10.

31 In verse 36.23. "山東河南各處教師相傳楊家鎗法其中陰陽虛實之理與我相同其最妙是左右二門拏他鎗手法其不妙是撒手殺去而腳步不進。" Wang Minghe, Shi's *Compendium* volume 1, p. 521.

32 In verse 36.25. Takuan Soho, *The Unfettered Mind: Writings from a Zen Master to a Master Swordsman*, trans. William Scott Wilson (New York: Kodansha, 2002), p. 38.

33 In verse 36.26. "剛柔相濟輪。勢無三點不落。氣無三儘不盡。此陰轉陰中間一陽。陽轉陽中間一陰之謂也。蓋落處盡處是氣聚血凝止歸之所。宜用剛法。而間陽間陰。是氣血流利。宜用柔法。不達乎此。絕用剛法。則氣鋪滿身。牽拉不利。落點必不勇猛。絕用柔法。則氣散不聚。無有歸着。落點亦不堅硬。應剛而柔。則氣聚不聚。應柔而剛。則氣散不散。皆不得相濟之妙。故善用剛柔者。如青蜓點水。一沾即起。過氣如風輪。旋轉滾走不停。必如是。則剛柔得宜。方能無氣歉不實。澀滯不利之患。" Chang Naizhou, roll 2, p. 16.

34 In verse 36.28. "兩人大門對打他弱我用強他強我弱。" Wang Minghe, Shi's *Compendium* volume 1, p. 484.

35 In verse 36.31. The names of Heng and Ha are also the origin of the *Jing gang* used in movement names such as Buddha's Attendant Pounds the Mortar of Chen's taijiquan. Heng, or Narayana, is 纳罗廷金刚 nà luó tíng jīn gāng. Ha, or Guhyapada, is 密跡金刚 mì jì jīn gāng.

36 In verse 36.36. Miyamoto Musashi, *A Book of Five Rings: A Guide to Strategy*, trans. Victor Harris (New York: The Overlook Press, 1974), p.54.

Part Two: The Forty-eight Methods Verses

37 Eight Sources for the 48 verses: Huan Dahai, Li Ziming, Lin Sui, Liu Xinghan (2010), Tu Xingjian, Wang Shangzhi, Wu Yue, Zang Xuefan. Choice of which sources to use involved differences and similarities, plus practical concerns such as copyright and permissions.

38 In verse 48.03. "兩人大門對打不進前腳不折後腳不能勝。" Wang Minghe, Shi's *Compendium* volume 1, p. 482.

39 "郭古民先生在世时曾言：步大者三尺，步小者三寸。要使身形的挪动，移至对我有利，对敌不利的位置上，方能有制手壁招的功效。" Wu, p. 162.

40 In verse 48.05. "[A]ll these heroes [in Chinese 16th century novels and plays] were positioned as capable martial artists, so there was a direct connection to people who identified themselves as having mastered a style of martial arts. ... [Shelley Hsueh-lun] Chang listed these traits as the following: 1. Unusual physical strength and incomparable martial arts. ... 2. Fearlessness. A dauntless, fearless spirit, which is heedlessness of consequences. ... 3. Power of endurance. Enduring a great physical pain and corporal punishment without flinching or uttering one cry. ... 4. Selflessness. Always being ready to lay down their own lives for friends. An impulsive generosity, and loyalty to their lords

(or leaders) and their country, with a dedication to reciprocating favors to friends and taking revenge on enemies. 5. Asceticism and other behavioral attributes. Showing little interest in women or men, and never hesitating to fight against the rich or the powerful in order to correct injustice. Showing filial piety to parents, especially widowed mothers. 6. As well as some eccentric traits, such as outspoken bluntness, volcanic temper, and eating and drinking to excess." Joern, pp. 109-110. You can see that these traits continue to define the hero in kungfu, or for that matter Harry Potter, films.

41 "急陽鎮上把武賣。遇仁義宋公明。穆橫穆春行霸道。潯陽江上拜弟兄。" 英雄拳譜 *Tales of Heroes*, 1862 edition of old stories. From Shi's *Compendium* volume 17, p. 626.

42 In verse 48.07. "腰力為上後手力次之前手力又次之。" Wang Minghe, Shi's *Compendium* volume 1, p. 489.

43 "说到两腿平均用力，有人疑为进退不变，这也是错觉的观念，如果力量集中，意识集中，全体一致，发出去的力是整劲。既是一个整劲，全身上下四肢百骸四隅八方也必相因相乘共争一个中心力，这样无论进退杀敌，也必然敏捷有活力，可以从心所欲，否则专用单重御敌，神气意力不合一，那倒是滞而不化了。" Jiang Rongqiao, c. 1960, chapter twelve.

44 "敵當撐步進身卸我右掌而速抽左掌再出右掌擊我左肋我速吸身再將左臂往下由敵之右臂裏黏棚其臂。" Yan Dehua, 7th application.

45 "敵以右掌擊我胸我速吸胸而卸之同時扭身形用右手順敵臂外往下插。" Yan Dehua, 31st application.

46 In verse 48.08. "内三合指视神经，中枢神经，末梢神经。外三合指手与腰合，腰与步合，步与手合。合是配合，合一，协调一致，使上下，左右，内外形成一个整体。" Shi Naijian, p. 24.

47 In verse 48.11. "善戰必定藝精。古云，藝高人膽大。信不誣矣。" Shaolin temple editorial board, 1856.

48 "劍術不精勇力不稱也。" Wang Minghe, Shi's *Compendium* volume 1, p. 470.

49 In verse 48.12. "俱是順人之勢借人之力只要快便又要似進實退而後進則大勝矣。" Qi Jiguang, Shi's *Compendium* volume 6, p. 32.

50 In verse 48.15. "他打來亂時必須忍略退回坐足下中平待少頃他來即用磋手法進自勝絕是以靜待動以逸待勞道理…" Wang Minghe, Shi's *Compendium* volume 1, p. 516.

51 In verse 48.17. "進步楊臂閉住敵伸出之臂， 使其不得近我， 而便我手之打出也。" Cao Zhongsheng, Shi's *Compendium*, volume 75, p. 289.

52 長兵短用說, Wang Minghe, Shi's *Compendium* volume 1, pp. 531-532.

53 In verse 48.18. "所謂不招不架只是一下。" Shaolin temple editorial board, 1856.

54 "不挡不架：敌势勇猛你别怕，他打你时你打他。转移还击途经近，不挡不架只一下。" Shi Naijian, verse 48.29

55 In verse 48.19. "用法 設敵用右手迎面擊我應抽身閃至敵後方用左掌擊敵右耳門 是為抽身換影。" Yin Yuzhang, chapter on moving techniques, p. 3.

56 In verse 48.21. "行氣輪。此交手認路法也。手一出。氣着一面。不能四面俱着。力直出者無橫力。我截其橫。橫出者無直力。我截其直。上出者無下力。

我挑其下。下劈者無上力。我打其上。斜正屈伸。無不皆然。此搗虛之法。攻其無備也。" Chang Naizhou, roll 2, p. 20.

57 In verse 48.22. "將棍堅把住用身勢（棍頭高）慢慢浸入他大門來我大門接一下只離一寸他小門來我小門接一下只離一寸待他何門處我盡身入。" Wang Minghe, Shi's *Compendium* volume 1, p. 505.

58 In verse 48.24. "心似元师，眼似峰，手似兵刃，脚似战马。" Liu Jialin, p. 27.

59 In verse 48.28. "制人：制人须向眼上刺，双目受损敌难傲。轻者受伤重失明，眼上一戳胜千招。" Shi Naijian, p. 58.

60 "艮卦第一式穿手掌歌。行步穿掌着法靈。左右穿掌似龍形。下穿撥草巡蛇式。上穿二龍取珠睛。外穿上步山入海。裏穿單撞打前胸。穿掌着法打不盡。倒步穿掌回本營。" Du Zhaotang, p.85.

61 In verse 48.29. "伏回之鎗俱是哄我殺去他即起彈殺我也記之記之。" Qi Jiguang, Shi's *Compendium* volume 6, p. 414.

62 "兩棍相交他抽回伏地開小門我直捧慢慢指去待他發殺然後揭牽或剪進殺他。" Wang Minghe, Shi's *Compendium* volume 1, p. 495.

63 In verse 48.30. "彼不動兮我不動，彼欲動兮我先動。" Chang Naizhou, roll 3, p. 55.

64 "險行者，我先居之，必居高陽以待敵。" Sun Zi, p.74.

65 In verse 48.31. "得門而入輪。手之門有三。手腕一也。此大門也。肘心二也。進一層外二門也。膀根三也。此更進一層三門也。進此三門。已近內院。可以升堂入室矣。" Chang Naizhou, roll 2, p. 23.

66 In verse 48.36. "凡圓行之用，所以習行步凱捷，襲敵之背，使敵不及迴旋。" Xu Zhen, Shi's *Compendium* volume 52, p. 67.

67 In verse 48.37. "有上中下盤之別，上盤行時腿微屈，中盤行時較上盤取勢較低，下盤行時則取勢更低矣。" Xu Zhen, Shi's *Compendium* volume 52, p. 67.

68 "下盘腿脚如珠走玉盘，转如磨磨；中盘腰身如银蛇缠柱，游刃灵活；上盘手如拧绳，翻转旋拧." "上中下三盘形成一个整体。" Cai Baozhong, p. 123.

69 In verse 48.40. "以俯勢入陽氣。不將陰氣扶起。則偏於陽必有領拉前患。仰勢入陰氣。不將陽氣扶起。則偏於陰。必有掀推後倒之憂。故俯勢出者。落點疾邊之以仰勢。使無偏於陽也。仰勢出者。落點疾邊之以俯勢。使無偏於陰也。" Chang Naizhou, roll 1, p. 4.

70 In verse 48.42. "四拗法就是单换掌的前后左右的四种变化，它完全显示了八卦掌的最基础的用法。如果对方用贴身法来制我时，我就用这最基础的技法来防守和打击，它不但能很好的防守，而且还可以发放和摔 拿。" Di Guoyong, p. 72.

71 In verse 48.44. "辅身法，拗身法，甩身法，三法相似而不同。辅身法是腰身的磨转，关键在于腰；拗身法是腰与上身转动的配合；甩身法是腰与下肢的配合，在于身法与步法的配合。" Wu, p.170.

72 In verse 48.46. "處此科學時代，似不應述此穿鑿之語。" Yin Yuzhang, chapter on theory, p.2.

73 "三才者，頭手足，即上中下也。此不過說明頭在上，手在中，足在下之部位而已。著者自稱為奧義。昔人云：'以艱深之詞，文淺易之說'是亦欺世感人之妙技也。" Tang Hao, Shi's *Compendium* volume 59 p. 631.

74 "拘史料分析，清代八卦掌的出現應該与当时民间教门中的八卦教有着密不可分的联系．"，"并且习练者基本上都为八卦教徒。" Qiu Pixiang, p. 134.

75 "八卦掌原本走圈，循環迴轉，其方向地位，較編他拳尤為難定，特於走掌姿勢中，說明足踏巽方，面向乾方，為起訖之點，此不過作初學者之標準，並非一定不移之限制。" Yin Yuzhang, pp. 1-2.

76 "董先生的著名弟子史计栋的墓碑…'号其曰八卦掌'．再说程式八卦掌中有八大掌，尹氏有八大式，史先生门中有八大掌，而不是七掌或九掌，显见这是根据八卦掌这一名程中的八字而来。" Liu Jingru, p. 30.

77 In verse 48.47. "傳聞此書版本原為高義盛所有，但高氏並無公開本拳譜之意，而是杜召棠自其師處取得草本之後，膳自加以整理出版。後高氏得知，對此行徑大為不滿，遷怒之餘…" Du Zhaotang, preface to 2000 reprint, p.1.

78 "如太極八卦五行（即形意拳門）猊六合等等，均不過各派之所自命以別其餘耳；喝可牽強附會以之為拳法所本之理，而用以解說着術，令人視之渺茫，恍惚，無從捉摸耶。" Cao Zhongsheng, Shi's *Compendium* volume 75, p. 255.

79 "八卦掌是董海川老先生所传的，可是海川先生从来没有用过纳卦，也没有谈那一卦是乾卦，那一掌是坤卦。他的十大弟子，程廷华，尹德安等也没有用过什么纳卦。由此可以证明八卦掌根本不用纳卦。后来有人把乾坤坎艮离巽兑震八卦加进八卦掌套路里去，不但没有起一点作用，相反把练八卦掌的人拉近酱糊缸，越闹越糊涂了。" Jiang Rongqiao, c. 1960, chapter eight.

80 "以前吴峻山，傅剑秋他俩都是八卦掌专家。吾师说他俩在三十年前就想把纳卦拉近八卦掌里去，左搞右搞也拉不进去。他俩问吾师；第一掌怎样能变八掌？吾师很简单地回答说：你们永远也变不成功的！… 纳卦是与八卦掌毫不相干的。用纳卦是无根据的学说，也是空词无稽的。列如你说这一掌是乾为天别人也可以说是坤为地。这种空洞的名词，不如象形的理论可以结合实际。" Jiang Rongqiao, c. 1960, chapter eight.

81 "凤马牛不相及" Liu Jingru, article 八卦掌不是八卦 in Wuhun magazine, 1987.

REFERENCES

Bisio, Tom. *Beyond the Battleground: Classic Strategies from the Yijing and Baguazhang for Managing Crisis Situations*. California: Blue Snake Books, 2016.

Cai Baozhong 蔡宝忠。武术与文化 (*Wushu and Culture*). Taiyuan: 山西科学技术出版社, 2015.

Cao Zhongsheng, Xu Jinggui 曹鐘昇，虛景貴。曹氏八卦掌譜 (*A Record of Cao Clan Baguazhang*). 1942. In Shi's *Compendium of Selected Classic Martial Writings*, volume 75, pp. 249-374.

Chang Naizhou 萇乃周。萇氏武技書 (*Book of the Chang Clan Martial Skills*), Hebei，c. 1770. Reprinted by Xu Zhen 徐震. Shanghai: 上海书店出版，1990.

Chinese Wushu Encyclopedia Editorial Committee 中国武术大辞典编辑委员会。中国武术大辞典 (*Encyclopedia of Chinese Wushu*). Beijing: 人民体育出版社，1990.

Di Guoyong 邸国勇。八卦掌三十六歌和四十八法 (*Baguazhang's Thirty-six Verses and Forty-eight Methods*). Beijing: unpublished manuscript, 2012. Personal communication, 2016.

Di Zhaolong 狄兆龙。八卦掌锻炼要领三十六歌诀 (*Baguazhang: Thirty-six Verses Training Requirements*). Guangzhou: Wulin magazine, September 1983, pp. 19-20.

Du Zhaotang 杜召棠。游身連環八卦掌 (*Swimming Body Linking Baguazhang*). 1936. Reprint Taibei: Lion Books 逸文出版有限公司, 2000.

Gao Jiwu 高继武 with Tom Bisio. *The Essentials of Ba Gua Zhang*. New York: Trip Tych Enterprises, 2007.

Gao Jiwu 高继武 with Tom Bisio. *The Attacking Hands of Ba Gua Zhang*. New York: Trip Tych Enterprises, New York Internal Arts, 2010.

Gao Yuan. *Lure The Tiger Out of the Mountains: How to Apply the 36 Stratagems of Ancient China to the Modern World*. London: Judy Piatkus Publishers, 1991.

Huan Dahai 宦大海。八卦掌纲要董海川传 (*The Essentials of Baguazhang, Transmissions of Dong Haichuan*). Shanghai: unpublished handwritten copy, 1980.

Huang Bonian 黄柏年。龍形八卦掌 (*Dragon Baguazhang*). 1928. Reprint Taiyuan: 山西科学技术出版社, 2000.

Joern, Albert Travis. *The Repositioning of Traditional Martial Arts in Republican China*. Montreal: Masters Thesis, McGill University, 2012.

Jiang Rongqiao 姜容樵。八卦掌 (*Baguazhang*). Shanghai: unpublished hand written manuscript, c. 1960.

Jiang Rongqiao 姜容樵。太極拳講義 (*Teaching Materials for Taijiquan*). Shanghai: 上海武學書局出版, 1930.

Jin Sizhong 金思忠。國術名人錄 [附錄:國術叢談]. (*Records of Famous Martial Artists [Appendix: Collected Writings on the Martial Arts]*). 1931. Reprint Taiyuan: 山西科学技术出版社, 2000.

Li Gongcheng 李功成。董海川八卦转掌技击术 (*Dong Haichuan's Bagua Turning Palms Applications*). Beijing: 北京体育大学出版社, 1994.

Li Ziming 李子鳴。董海川八卦掌 (*Dong Haichuan's Baguazhang*). Jilin: 吉林科技出版社, 1985.

Li Ziming translated by Huang Guo Qi. *Liang Zhen Pu Eight Diagram Palm*. Pulaksi, Vermont: High View Publications, 1993.

Li Xiuren 李秀人。八卦掌汇宗 (*Baguazhang Gathered from the Ancestor*). Beijing: 人民体育出版社, 2015.

Liang Shou-Yu and Yang Jwing-Ming. *Baguazhang (Emei Baguazhang) Theory and Applications*. Boston: Yang's Martial Arts Association, 1994.

Lin Sui 林燧。正宗八卦掌 (*Genuine Baguazhang*). Fujian: 福建科学技术出版社, 1987.

Liu Jialin 刘佳霖。八卦转掌密功 (*Secrets of Bagua Turning Palms*). Beijing: 北京体育大学出版社, 2015.

Liu Jingru 刘敬儒。八卦掌 (*Baguazhang*). Beijing: 北京体育大学出版社, 1999.

Liu Xinghan 刘兴汉。八卦掌秘传诀谱 (*The Secret Transmissions of Baguazhang*). Beijing: 北京体育大学出版社, 2010.

Liu Xinghan 刘兴汉。游身八卦连环掌：健身篇 (*Swimming Body Bagua Connecting Palm: Health Training Volume*). Beijing: 北京体育科学研究所八卦掌研究组, 1986.

Liu Yongchun 刘永椿。尹式八挂掌释秘 (*Secrets of Yin School Baguazhang Explained*). Beijing: 北京人民出版社, 1998.

Luo Hongxuan 罗洪宣。八卦掌和八卦掌对打 (*Baguazhang and Baguazhang's Sparring*). Yunnan: 云南人民出版社, 1982.

Qi Jiguang 戚繼光。紀效新書 (*New Book on Effective Discipline*). 1560. In the *Compendium of Selected Classic Martial Writings*, volume 6.

Qiu Pixiang 邱丕相。中国武术史 (*A History of China's Martial Arts*). Beijing: 高等教育出版社，2008.

Ren Zhizhu 任致著。阴阳八盘掌 (*Yinyang Bapanzhang*). Tianjin: 百城书局印行, 1937. Reprint Taiyuan: 山西科学技术出版社, 2001.

Shaolin temple editorial board 少林寺传。少林寺拳棍刀枪谱, (*Shaolin Temple Fist, Staff, sabre, and Spear*). Henan: Shaolin temple, 1856. In Shi's *Compendium of Selected Classic Martial Writings*, volume 15, pp. 499-end.

Shi Naijian 史乃健。史式八卦掌 (*Shi School Baguazhang*). Beijing: 人民体育出版社，2012.

Shi Yongxin, editor 释永信主编。中国武术大典 (*Compendium of Selected Classic Martial Writings*). Beijing: 中国书店, 2012.

Sun Fuquan (Sun Lutang) 孫福全。八卦劍學 (*Study of Bagua Sword*). 1927. Reprint Macau: 新聯出版社, undated.

Sun Fuquan (Sun Lutang) 孫福全。八卦拳學 (*Study of Bagua Style*). 1928. Reprint Macau: 新聯出版社, undated.

Sun Xikun 孫錫堃. 八卦掌真傳 (*Real Transmissions of Baguazhang*). 1934. In Shi's *Compendium of Selected Classic Martial Writings*, volume 75, pp. 1-182.

Sun Zi 孙子，Sun Bin 孙膑。兵法 (*The Art of War*) Chinese-English edition. Beijing: Foreign Languages Press. 1999.

Tang Hao 唐豪。太极拳与内家拳 (*Taijiquan and Neijiaquan*). 1930. In Shi's *Compendium of Selected Classic Martial Writings*, volume 59, pp. 583-end.

Tu Xingjian 涂行健。马派八卦掌:上册 (*Ma School Baguazhang: volume one*). Hong Kong: Language House Publishing Company, 2008.

Wang Minghe 王鳴鶴。登墙必究 (*Essential Studies to Ascend the Arena*). 1599. In Shi's *Compendium of Selected Classic Martial Writings*, volume 1, pp. 454-562.

Wang Shangzhi 王尚智。董海川八卦掌 72 擒拿法 (*72 Capture Methods of Dong Haichuan's Baguazhang*). Beijing: 北京体育大学出版社，1995.

Wu Yue 吴岳。九宫八卦连环掌 (*Nine Palaces Bagua Connecting Palms*). Beijing, 北京体育大学出版社，1997.

Xiang Yuncai 向运彩。程氏八卦掌 (*Cheng Clan Baguazhang*). Wuhan: 长江出版社，2014.

Xie Yanci 谢燕辞。完全武林门派手册 (*Complete Handbook of Martial Arts Schools*). Beijing: 新世界出版社，2004.

Xu Zhen 徐震。国技论略 (*Brief Discussion of the National Skill*). 1929. In Shi's *Compendium of Selected Classic Martial Writings*, volume 52, pp. 1-96.

Yan Dehua 阎德华。少林破墙 (*Shaolin Wall Destroying Insights*). Hebei: 1936. Reprinted as 八卦掌使用法 (*Baguazhang Applications*). Hong Kong: Unicorn Press. Also the translation, *Yan Dehua's Bagua Applications*. Victoria: tgl books, 2000.

Yin Yuzhang, Wang Qintang 尹玉章，王芹塘。八卦掌简编 (*Concise Edition of Baguazhang*). Qingdao: 青岛市国术馆, 1932. Reprint Taipei: Lion Books, 2002.

Zang Xuefan 藏学范。八卦掌术集成 (*Integrated Baguazhang Skills*). Jilin: 吉林科学技术出版社, 2000.

Zhang Quanliang 张全亮。八卦掌精要 (*Essentials of Baguazhang*). Beijing: 人民体育大学出版社, 1999.

ILLUSTRATIONS

Dedication	Huan Dahai, photo by Andrea Falk, Shanghai, 1996.
Preface	From right to left, Zou Shuxian, Jiang Xiaoying, Andrea Falk, photo by Hans Järling, Shanghai, 2016.
Introduction.	Timeline by Andrea Falk.
Part One	Beijing Temple of Heaven training ground, photo by Andrea Falk, 2016.
36.01	Zhang Zhaodong.
36.02	Cai Yuhua, photo by Andrea Falk, Shanghai, 1990.
36.03	Drawing © Graham Elliott Falk, 2016.
36.04	Single whips from: Qi Jiguang, 1560, from Shi's *Compendium*, volume 6. He Rubin 何汝賓 兵錄大全 (Complete Records of Arms)，1628, from Shi's *Compendium*, volume 11, p. 217. 英雄拳譜 (*Tales of Heroes*), 1862 edition of old stories, from Shi's *Compendium*, volume 17, p.491. Chen Xin 陈氏太极拳图解 (*Illustrated Chen's Taijiquan*), 1986 reprint, p.170. Cheng Jiefeng, Shanghai, photo by Andrea Falk.
36.05	Cheng Zongxian 程宗猷，程氏心法三種 (*Three Methods of the Cheng Clan*), 1621. Shi's *Compendium*, volume 16, pp. 500, 502.
36.08	Cheng school long mud stepping Lu Yan. Short stepping Andrea Falk.
36.10	Hands of Di Guoyong (photo Byron Jacobs), Cai Yuhua, Andrea Falk, Philip Morrell, Zou Shuxian (photo Hans Järling), Lu Yan.
36.14	Andrea Falk, 2009.
36.16	Yan Dehua's Bagua Applications, 29th application, 'Drift Along in a Boat with the Current'.
36.17	Cai Yuhua, photo by Andrea Falk, Shanghai, 1990.
36.22	Image © chi-pod, photoshopped by Andrea Falk.
36.24	Andrea Falk, 2011.
36.31	Photo by Andrea Falk, Kojima, Japan, 2008.
Part Two	Beijing Temple of Heaven training ground, photo by Andrea Falk, 2016.
48.05	英雄拳譜 (*Tales of Heroes*), 1862 edition of old stories. From Shi's *Compendium*, volume 17, p. 625.
48.07	Jiang Rongqiao, *Depiction of Bagua Invisible Spear*, 1930, photo #7, Reverse Stance. Yin Yuzhang, Sixth Palm Change.

48.16	Yan Dehua's Bagua Applications, 2nd application, Thrust in the Palm.
48.19	Andrea Falk and Neil Bates, Basingstoke, 2012.
48.21	Yan Dehua's Bagua Applications, 14th application, Lift and Pour the Golden Brazier.
48.24	赤壁之战，绘画 徐正平，凌淘. Red Cliff, illustrators Xu Zhengping, Ling Tao. Shanghai: 上海人民美术出版社，2016. Illustration 83.
48.28	Yan Dehua's Bagua Applications, 10th application, Cleverly Carry the Flower Basket over your Arm.
48.32	Circle from Yin Yuzhang, pointers page 2, photoshpped by Andrea Falk.
48.37	Middle basin Xia Bohua, low basin Andrea Falk.
48.43	Yan Dehua's Bagua Applications, 32nd application, Lead the Sheep Along at your Ease.
48.46	Yin Yuzhang, chapter on commentary, page 4.
Part Three	Willow tree, photo by Andrea Falk.

GLOSSARY

Terms in Chinese within English text.

Aobu 拗步 aò bù   Reverse stance, twisted stance, different hand and foot forward.

Bagua 八卦 bā guà   Eight trigrams. *Qian* is the trigram of three solid *yang* lines, called 'three connected'. *Kan* is the trigram of one solid *yang* line within two broken *yin* lines, called 'middle full'. *Gen* is the trigram of one solid *yang* line over two broken *yin* lines, called 'overturned bowl'. *Zhen* is two broken *yin* lines over one solid *yang* line, called 'upturned cup'. *Xun* is two solid *yang* lines over one broken *yin* line, called 'lower broken'. *Li* is one broken *yin* line within two solid *yang* lines, called 'middle empty'. *Kun* is the trigram of three broken *yin* lines, called 'three broken'. *Dui* is one broken *yin* line over two solid *yang* lines, called 'upper missing'.

Baibu 摆步 bǎi bù   A turned out step, hook-out step, ranging from about 90° to 135°, can be close to the other foot or quite extended. In English I have called it *baibu* step. The other *baibu* 掰步 bāi bù is a type of setting power used in stepping, not usually a step per se, though some schools do use this terms for the opening out step.

Chuanzhang 穿掌 chuān zhǎng   Spearing palm, piercing palm, penetrating palm. A straight strike with the fingers or lower edge of the palm/forearm.

Dai shou 带手 dài shǒu   Drag: pulling drag, on the smooth side.

Dantian 丹田 dān tián   In martial arts, usually refers to the lower *dantian*, the body core within the lower belly and pelvic girdle. Specifically three finger widths below the navel and a third of the thickness of the torso into the body, but usually refers to a fuller area.

Gongfu 功夫 gōng fǔ   Deep skill, skill developed over a long period of work, mastery, workmanship, effort devoted to a task. In English, kungfu is colloquially used for traditional wushu.

Guoshuguan 国术馆 guó shù guàn   The National Martial Arts College, 1928-1937. A centralized college that used indigenous physical training to strengthen the people, instead of adopting Western sports. It did not develop standardized styles, but invited masters of many styles to teach what they knew. It wanted the teacher to be literate and understand the traditional medicine and philosophical concepts, and the students to become strong and healthy. It also funded research and publication. The styles were divided into Shaolin and Wudang, with Taijiquan, Baguazhang, and Xingyiquan in the Wudang department and mostly everything else in the Shaolin department. Later this was changed, but the catagories seem to have made a lasting impact. Baguazhang masters Sun Lutang and Fu Zhensong taught there, and Jiang Rongqiao was in the writing department.

Jianghu 江湖 jiāng hú The society of 'rivers and lakes', refers to the brotherhood of martial artists who live in the margins of society.

Koubu 扣步 kòu bù A hook-in step, either to a T step, a box step, an open V step, or a passing step. Usually fairly close to the other foot. In English I have called it *koubu* step.

Ling 领 lǐng Draw: a drawing pull, on the reverse side.

Heng Ha 哼哈 hēng hā Strong exhalations to assist power. See verse 36.31 for details.

Huiyin 会阴 huì yīn Acupoint Huiyin: 'meeting of *yin*'. On men, between the anus and the scrotum. On women, between the anus and pelvic diaphragm.

Qi 气 qì Vital energy, breath, both energy and the matter that carries vital energy.

Qian Kun 乾坤 qián kūn Heaven and earth, the cosmos. The *qian kun* hands get their name from the most *yang* and most *yin* of the trigrams. The hands are one high, forward, and turned up, one low, back, and turned down, a defensive posture able to turn to attack in an instant.

Santi 三体 sān tǐ Short for the 'three bodies' stance, a 70/30 back-weighted stance.

Shuanyao 涮腰 shuàn yāo A waist training exercise, turning and rolling with power.

Shunbu 顺步 shùn bù Smooth stance, same hand and foot forward.

Tangnibu 蹚泥步 tāng nī bù Mud stepping: baguazhang walking adding a forward pushing step. Originally referred to a shuffling type of walking where soldiers would keep their feet on the ground to sweep aside sharp objects thrown down to injure their feet.

Glossary

Yin and *Yang* 阴阳 yīn yáng *Yang* corresponds to male, heaven, heavenly formation, the attribute of strength. It expresses the generative power of the sun. *Yin* corresponds to female, earth, earthly formation, the attribute of yielding. It expresses the reflective forces of the moon.

Chinese for the Stratagems and Tactics within the text.

The stratagems used from the 36 stratagems

The second stratagem, Besiege Wei to Rescue Zhao. 圍魏救趙 wèi Wèi jiù Zhào.

The fourth stratagem, Wait Leisurely and Tire the Enemy, Substitute Leisure for Labour. 以逸待劳 yǐ yì dài láo.

The sixth stratagem, Make Noise in the East and Attack the West, Threaten the East and Strike to the West. 声东击西 shēng dōng jī xī.

The twelfth stratagem, Lead Away a Goat in Passing, Take the Opportunity to Pilfer a Goat, Lead a Sheep Along. 顺手牵羊 shùn shǒu qiān yáng.

The eighteenth stratagem, In Order to Catch the Bandits Catch the Leader, Capture the Chief to Defeat the Thieves. 擒賊擒王 qín zéi qín wáng.

The thirtieth stratagem, Turn the Guest into the Host, Turn from Guest into Host. 反客為主 fǎn kè wéi zhǔ.

The thirty-sixth stratagem, If All Else Fails Retreat, Of all the Stratagems Fleeing is Best. 走为上 zǒu wéi shàng.

Tactics

Lead Along with a Light Touch. 四两牵 sì liǎng qiān.

Point at the Mountain to Get the Millstone. 指山打磨法 zhǐ shān dǎ mò.

Shed the Body and Trade it for a Shadow. 脱身化影 tuō shēn huà yǐng.

Use a Single to Remedy a Double. 接单补双 jiē dān bǔ shuāng.

Pronunciation Guide for Chinese in Pinyin

CONSONANTS

p	like p̲et with a considerable puff of air.
b	similar to the *pinyin* "p" but without the puff of air (unvoiced, neither p̲et nor b̲et).
t	like t̲ag with a considerable puff of air.
d	similar to the *pinyin* "t" but with no puff of air (unvoiced, not d̲og).
k	like k̲ill with a considerable puff of air.
g	similar to the *pinyin* "k" but with no puff of air (unvoiced, not get).
c	like exaggerating cat̲s̲.
z	like the *pinyin* "c" but without the puff of air (unvoiced).
ch	somewhat similar to ch̲at with a puff of air, but with the tip of the tongue rolled back.
zh	like the *pinyin* "ch" but with no puff of air (unvoiced).
q	somewhat similar to ch̲at with a puff of air, but with the front of the tongue raised and the tip on the lower teeth.
j	like the *pinyin* "q" but without the puff of air (unvoiced).
m	like m̲et.
n	like n̲et.
ng	like sin̲g̲.
f	similar to t̲at, but with the teeth just touching lightly behind the lower lip.
s	similar to s̲et.
sh	somewhat similar to sh̲ow, but with the same tongue placement as the *pinyin* "ch" and "zh."
x	somewhat similar to sh̲ine but with the same tongue placement as the *pinyin* "q" and "j."
h	raise the back of the tongue and let the breath come through the obstructed passage without vibrating the vocal cords.
l	like l̲et.
r	like the *pinyin* "sh" but with voicing.

VOWELS

a	usually close to f<u>a</u>r (not p<u>a</u>t). Like <u>ye</u>t when written "-ian" or "yan."
e	usually similar to p<u>e</u>t.
i	usually similar to b<u>ee</u>. Similar to <u>we</u>t when written "ui." After c, z, s, ch, zh, sh, and r it is similar to s<u>ir</u>.
o	usually close to r<u>o</u>ll. Similar to c<u>ow</u> when written "ao," and <u>owe</u> when in "ou."
u	usually similar to b<u>oo</u>t. After the *pinyin* "x", "q", and "j" and in the vowel groups starting with these consonants, it is pronounced "ü."
ü	pronounced <u>ü</u>. It is written after "n" or "l," because these are the only positions where both "u" and "ü" are possible.

When written as groups, the vowels are more a combination of 'w' or 'y' with a clean vowel. For example, 'die' is pronounced 'd^{y}e', not like the English word die, and 'dui' is pronounced 'd^{w}e' a bit more towards a Canadian 'eh' sound than a pure 'e' sound.

TONES

#	*pinyin*	name	range
1	v̄	high level	55
2	v́	high rising	35
3	v̌	dipping	214
4	v̀	high falling	51

In a normal vocal range, 5 is high and 1 is low.

ABOUT THE AUTHOR

Andrea Falk has practised external and internal Chinese martial arts since 1972. She has studied Chinese art, geography, history, language, linguistics, literature, philosophy, politics, religion, and sociology since then, as well. Andrea received a Bachelor of Arts majoring in Chinese (1978), a Bachelor of Physical Education (1980) and a Master of Physical Education with an emphasis on coaching science (1990) from the  University of British Columbia. She trained in wushu full time on scholarship from 1980 to 1983 at the Beijing Physical Culture Institute (Beiti), earning an Advanced Studies Diploma in Wushu under the tutelage of Professor Xia Bohua and instruction from Men Huifeng and others. There she learned the basics of Yang and Chen style Taijiquan, Baguazhang, Xingyiquan, Chaquan, Tongbeiquan, and modern Longfist (Longfist included barehand and four standard weapons forms). Andrea spent two further extended summers at Beiti in 1984 and 1986.

Starting in 1984, Andrea gradually changed over to learning traditionally, visiting China on extended trips as often as possible to learn in parks, parking lots, and courtyards. She has trained and/or is training Chen style Taijiquan, Baguazhang, and Taiji Changquan as an inside apprentice of the late Huan Dahai (1924-2015) and elder martial brothers in Shanghai, Xingyiquan and Baguazhang as a close student and friend of Di Guoyong in Beijing, and Baguazhang from friends Li Baohua and Lu Yan. When not in China or travelling to teach, she is usually in Québec City, or at a cabin in the Laurentian hills.

Andrea has taught and translated books about Chinese martial arts since 1983. She founded *the wushu centre* in Montreal in 1984, in Victoria in 1992, and in Québec City in 2007. Andrea has taught Chen Taijiquan, Baguazhang, and Xingyiquan around the world, but mostly in Canada and England.

trois   gros   lapins   traversent le   chemin

www.ingramcontent.com/pod-product-compliance
Lightning Source LLC
Chambersburg PA
CBHW020944230426
43666CB00005B/167